PARADISE DIVIDED

Paradise Divided
A Portrait of Lebanon

Alex Klaushofer

Signal Books
Oxford

First published in 2007 by
Signal Books Limited
36 Minster Road
Oxford
OX4 1LY
www.signalbooks.co.uk

A catalogue record for this book is available from the British Library

ISBN 978-1-904955-35-1 Paper

Cover Design: Baseline Arts
Cover Images: TNT Magazine/Alamy;
Pabis Studio/istockphoto;
Olga Kolos/istockphoto;
Raimond Siebesma/istockphoto
Author Photograph: Guiseppina D'Oro
Printed in India

CONTENTS

v

ACKNOWLEDGEMENTS

Many people in both Lebanon and Britain helped with the writing of this book, offering counsel, contacts, education, and practical and emotional support. Off the page, my thanks go to the many people who cannot be named, but here I would like to mention in particular: Helen Bailey, Donna Baillie, Nicholas Blanford, Eyad Abu Chakra, Colin Chapman, James Ferguson at Signal Books, Giuseppina D'Oro, Diana Bou Ghanem, Sylvia Haddad and the Joint Christian Committee for Social Service, Sister Clemence Helou and Sister Mona at Qannoubin monastery, Alison Hird, David Hirst, Ali Hweidi and the Palestinian Return Centre, Mona Khauli and staff at the Young Women's Christian Association, Otto and Rosemary Klaushofer, Christian Henderson, Tim Llewellyn, Ramse Mahmoud and family, David McDowall, Najwa Nasr, Elfi Pallis, Richard Phillips, Will Phillips, Liz Porter, everyone at the Regis Hotel, Ali Saad and the Lebanese Red Cross, Hadia Saad, Assem Salam, Rana Salam, the Reverend Abu Zaid Shafik, Nadim Shehadi, Maddalena Taras, Rosemary Thomas, Nuhad Tomeh and the Middle East Council of Churches, Barnaby Rogerson, Brian Whitaker and Mona Ziade.

CHRONOLOGY

From 1516 until the end of the First World War Lebanon was part of the Ottoman Empire. Nonetheless, the Ottoman rulers allowed the leaders of the Maronite Christian, Muslim and Druze communities to rule their fiefdoms without much interference.

1860 Mounting tensions between the Druze and the Maronites in the Chouf mountains lead to the death of over 10,000 Christians. French troops arrive to protect the Maronite community.

1861 Although still part of the Ottoman Empire, Mount Lebanon is declared an autonomous province.

1920 The State of Greater Lebanon is formed, taking in Mount Lebanon, the provinces of north Lebanon, south Lebanon and the Bekka Valley. France is given the mandate for both Lebanon and Syria.

1926 Lebanon is declared a republic with a constitution enshrining the principles of democracy and human rights.

1943 The foundations of Lebanon's status as an independent republic are set out in an unwritten National Pact. The Christians are expected to recognize Lebanon's 'Arab face' and not look to the French for protection, while the Muslims are to seek independence from Syria. The agreement formalizes a power-sharing arrangement between the country's Christians and Muslims: the president is to be a Maronite Christian, the prime minister a

Sunni Muslim and the Speaker of the Chamber of Deputies a Shia Muslim.

1948 The state of Israel is created and around 100 000 Palestinian refugees flee north into Lebanon.

1964 The Palestine Liberation Organization is formed and, in the years that follow, its guerrillas use south Lebanon as a base for raids into Israel.

1975 Following clashes between Phalangist and Palestinian militia, the civil war begins. For the next fifteen years, Christians (based in Beirut and parts of Mount Lebanon) fight Muslim and PLO militia across the Green Line (west Beirut and south Lebanon). The conflict is characterized by shifting alliances between the country's different sects and factions and brings both Israeli and Syrian troops onto Lebanese soil.

1976 In response to a request from the Lebanese president to the Arab League for a peacekeeping force, Syrian troops enter Lebanon to protect the Christians.

1978 Israel launches a major invasion of Lebanon and succeeds in pushing the PLO guerrillas north of the Litani river. It forms a proxy Lebanese militia, the South Lebanese Army (SLA), to protect the security zone it has carved out on Lebanese territory along the border and, following UN resolution 425, withdraws from Lebanon. The United Nations Interim Force in Lebanon (UNIFIL) is created to keep the peace.

1982 Israel launches a full-scale invasion of Lebanon, 'Operation Peace for Galilee', with the aim of curbing PLO activities. Israeli forces invade west Beirut and, in revenge for the assassination of their leader, the president-elect Bashir Gemayel, the Phalangist Maronite militia enter the Sabra and Shatila refugee camps. With the co-operation of the Israeli forces guarding the camps, they kill hundreds of Palestinian civilians.

1982 Shia militants begin to form Hezbollah, the 'Party of God', with Iranian backing, as a political and military organization whose goal is the destruction of Israel.

1986 Western hostages, including John McCarthy and Brian Keenan, are kidnapped by Islamic militants in Beirut, remaining in captivity for up to five years. The following year, the Archbishop of Canterbury's envoy Terry Waite is also kidnapped while attempting to negotiate their release.

1989 The National Assembly, meeting in Taif, Saudi Arabia, endorses a National Reconciliation Charter which marks the beginning of the end of the fighting. The Taif Accord transfers some power away from the Maronites to the Sunnis, reflecting Lebanon's changing demographics and assuaging Muslim resentment.

1991 All the militias taking part in the fighting except Hezbollah are dissolved, bringing the civil war to an end. It has claimed the lives of more than 100,000 civilians, injured another 100,000 and left much of Beirut in ruins.

1996 Israeli forces launch 'Operation Grapes of Wrath', bombing Hezbollah bases in south Beirut, southern Lebanon and the Bekka. An Israeli attack on a UN base at Qana results in the death of over a hundred Lebanese civilians sheltering there.

2000 After the collapse of the SLA and the rapid advance of Hezbollah forces, Israel withdraws its troops from southern Lebanon. The end of the Israeli occupation is widely seen as a victory for Hezbollah.

2005 On 14 February, former prime minister Rafik Hariri is killed by a car bomb in Beirut, along with twenty-two other people. The culprits are widely believed to be the Syrians, and the following month the UN sets up a special inquiry to investigate the killing. Following the assassination, calls for Syria to withdraw from Lebanon intensify. Hezbollah organizes a pro-Syria demonstration in Beirut on 8 March and, on 14 March, a million people gather in Martyrs' Square calling for an independent, democratic Lebanon free from Syrian control.

2005 In April, following increasing pressure from the UN and the West, Syrian forces leave Lebanon.

2005 June sees the killing of two prominent anti-Syrians in car bombs: the journalist Samir Qasir and George Hawi, former leader of the Lebanese Communist Party. The next month Deputy Prime Minister Elias Murr survives a car bomb. In an explosion in September, the well-known Lebanese journalist May Chidiac loses her left arm and leg; in December, anti-Syrian MP and journalist Gibran Tueni loses his life in a car bomb.

2005 In October the UN inquiry into the Hariri assassination publishes its first report as part of an ongoing investigation. It points to Syrian involvement, with co-operation from the Lebanese security forces, but does not name any of the individuals responsible.

2006 On 12 July, following a raid into Israeli territory in which Hezbollah captures two Israeli soldiers, Israel launches air and sea attacks on targets in Lebanon. Ground troops enter the south of the country in August. During the course of the month-long war, much of Lebanon's infrastructure is destroyed and over a million people are displaced. Almost 1,200 mostly civilian Lebanese and over a hundred and fifty Israelis die.

2006 A ceasefire between Israel and Hezbollah comes into effect on 14 August, and Hezbollah claim a 'divine victory'. A UN peacekeeping force of 15,000 foreign troops begins to deploy along the Lebanese-Israeli border.

2006 In November the assassination of Maronite government minister Pierre Gemayel, grandson of Bashir Gemayel, plunges the country into a new political crisis.

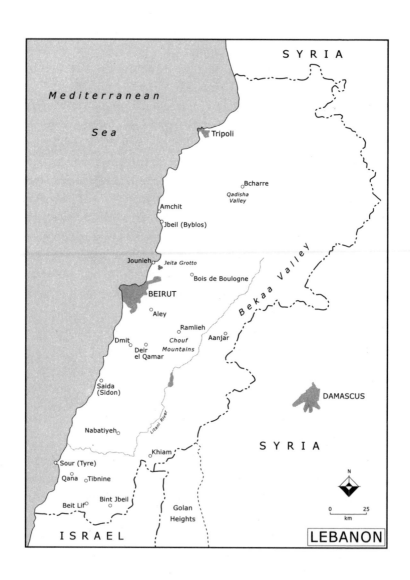

SYRIA

Mediterranean

Sea

Tripoli

Bcharre

*Qadisha
Valley*

Amchit

Jbeil (Byblos)

Jounieh   *Jeita Grotto*

Bois de Boulogne

BEIRUT

Aley

Ramlieh

Dmit   *Chouf   Aanjar
            Mountains*

Deir
el Qamar

Saida
(Sidon)

Litani River

Nabatiyeh

Khiam

Sour (Tyre)

Qana   Tibnine

Beit Lif   Bint Jbeil

Golan
Heights

Bekaa Valley

DAMASCUS

SYRIA

N

0   25
    km

ISRAEL

LEBANON

INTRODUCTION

WHEN I set out for Lebanon for the first time in the spring of 2004, it was the stuff of conventional travel writing that drew me more than anything else. The Lebanon of my imagination was a place of mountains, cedars and sea, an exotic Levantine land bearing traces of old Arabia and the local, nature-based faiths which preceded the Abrahamic religions. Then there was its liberalism and *joie de vivre*, the cultured modernity that had won Beirut the title of 'Paris of the East'. To be sure, as I concocted the rationale for my travel project, some grander ideas went into the mix. Having spent some time tramping around the highways and byways of the Palestinians' plight in the West Bank and Gaza, I was weary of the impasse of the Israeli/Palestinian conflict, at a loss as to what more I could learn or contribute. If, as I suspected, I was an Arabist at heart, I wanted to get to know a more varied, colourful Middle East that was about more than just conflict. Lebanon, on a long, slow path to recovery after the end of its civil war fifteen years before, seemed the ideal place. And, as a unique, multi-confessional society where Muslims, Christians and Druze lived side by side, it was almost a living exploration of the themes that, post-September 11th, were fast becoming the questions of our age: the intertwinement of faith, identity and politics, the possibility of tolerance and sectarianism in multi-cultural societies of the twenty-first century.

1

So while I was fascinated by these questions, a more primitive curiosity about the people and the place was the stronger motivation. The fact that to Westerners Lebanon, still weighed down by the image of its hostage-taking days, had become one of the lesser-known countries in the Middle East was a bonus. Plus, its relative peace and reconstruction meant that nothing much happened. For a travel writer, that made it a territory less-charted, a place which bore a lighter imprint of the region's big politics than some of its more newsworthy neighbours.

I wasn't disappointed. I found a place of richness and diversity which confounded my perceptions of the Arab world, where religious communities rubbed along together in a way unimaginable in a secular society and vulnerable minorities lived out their unique identities. It was like walking into a huge, colourful tapestry full of different pictures and stories. Sometimes the stories clashed, and it was easy to see how they could give rise to the tensions that characterize Lebanese politics and which could, if cleverly exploited, lead to conflict. But overall, I found a huge commitment to the experiment that makes Lebanon unique among Middle Eastern states and a country particularly receptive to engagement with the West.

My approach was partly that of the travel writer, part journalistic. I aimed to get a sense of life as it is lived for ordinary people rather than try to unpick its political intricacies. I wanted to understand how the religious communities saw the world and each other, and how their perspectives wove into the country's social fabric. So, almost no politicians or members of Lebanon's wealthy social elite feature in this book. Instead, it proceeds through a mixture of chance encounters and interviews with religious and community leaders, or others who seemed likely to shed light on the Lebanese scene. This, it turned out, was far easier than I had imagined at the outset: as well as the natural warmth of the Lebanese, I benefited from the code of hospi-

2

tality which leads them to treat foreigners with a special graciousness. With few exceptions, I found people willing to talk, whether about contentious sectarian issues or the personal things that affected their lives. On a couple of occasions, I was on the receiving end of the kind of refusal that an expatriate resident had warned me about, a peculiarly abrupt, aggressive shutting-down that seemed disproportionate to the request. But on the whole people were very open. Many were hugely generous with their time and contacts, making calls and appointments for me, providing lifts and, of course, Lebanese food. This national characteristic—provided you don't want to investigate the security set-up—makes Lebanon a journalist's dream. It also makes it a great place for the tourist, although it may spoil you for future trips to other, less welcoming, countries.

But in a society which is both conservative and highly politicized, there are some things that people cannot afford to be too open about. For this reason, while formal interviews are generally on the record, the names of some ordinary people have been changed. Sometimes this is because their lifestyle breaks accepted social mores and would, if made public, ostracise them from their families and society. In the chapter on Syria, it was to protect them from harassment by the secret police, although a couple of leading dissidents insisted on being named. In a few cases, like the Americans whose meeting with Hezbollah was re-written by their horrified institution, I decided to change names myself, for fear of damaging their career prospects.

Initially, this book was finished in the spring of 2006. Despite signs of increasing turbulence generated by the assassination of Hariri and the departure of Syrian forces, I was able to conclude on a lyrical up-note, optimistic about Lebanon's chances for peace and prosperity. Then came 12 July, and the war between Israel and Hezbollah. It propelled Lebanon back into the headlines and the international political arena, destroying much of the infrastructure and the economic confidence that it had gradually built up. So I went back to record the aftermath, adding the last two chapters of the present volume. As well as the physical impact, the conflict shook up the tribal divisions, creating a new source of disagreement which cuts across Lebanese society about how it should run its affairs and relationships with the wider world. The new Lebanese politics is less purely sectarian and more deeply political than before, and accentuates the long-standing tendency of external forces to interfere in the country's business. At the time of going to print, the assassination of yet another anti-Syrian public figure has sharpened these tensions yet further and deepened the sense of a country in crisis.

This, then, is a book about post-war Lebanon in two senses: that created by the civil war and the sudden, recent conflict. Its evolution, in following the country's fortunes over two and half years, mirrors the way Lebanon has been pulled out of a period of relative peace and back into power struggles, both internal and external. Readers who are so minded will draw their own conclusions about the part the West should, or could, play in its future stability. But in spirit and style, the book remains primarily a record of one Westerner's attempt to get to know a corner of potential paradise in the Middle East.

London, November 2006   A.K.

1
A TALE OF TWO CITIES

'WHAT religion do you think I am?'

I look closely at his long, oval face, with its smooth brown skin and grey-green eyes, and say the first thing that pops into my head.

'Greek Orthodox.'

'Yes!'

His name, Alexander, had given me a clue, too. It was my first day in Beirut and I was already grappling with its sectarian realities—the fact that names, faces, clothes, everything said something crucial about who a person was and where they stood in society. It was part of the complexity of Lebanon, a mosaic of religious communities as divided by tribal rivalries as it was united by a sense of its specialness. Fifteen years after the civil war, the jury was still out as to how well the Lebanese experiment in coexistence was working.

My new companion had evidently already made up his mind about his countrymen. 'These are bad people, bad people,' he kept repeating in his sing-song voice. 'It is difficult to live among them.' Having grown up abroad during the civil war years, he had the young returnee's ambivalence towards his homeland, a confusing mixture of alienation and belonging. 'I have only two Lebanese friends,' he went on earnestly. 'It is better for me to stay alone.' But just as the words were out of his mouth, a car pulled up, full of young men smiling and shouting. 'They really just want to know about you,' he said, as we pass yet more of his acquaintance on the pavement. 'Are you married?'

Telling him I'm engaged, I excused myself and headed off down the Corniche. The pavement that curled along the city's eastern Mediterranean shore was full of Lebanon's other contradictions, its cheek-by-jowl poverty and wealth, brash modernity and tattered antiquity. Joggers pounded the pavement, their faces set in grim concentration, patches of sweat spreading over their outsized T-shirts. On the other side of the road, fast-food restaurants mingled with chic new apartment blocks and the odd Ottoman townhouse, pockmarked with bullet holes. The women on the esplanade were heavily made up, and some had the static, stretched look that comes from the plastic surgery so popular in Lebanon. Syrian immigrants wove gloomily between them, wheeling carts bearing little rounds of seeded bread, or half-heartedly offering garlands of flowers to the drivers of the BMWs and Mercedes that were crammed, beeping furiously, across several lanes.

That evening, I strolled along the seafront with Abir, a young Druze woman living across the corridor from the room I had rented at the YWCA. The wide pavement coursed with Beirutis taking the night air. Whole families strolled together arm in arm, and a few had set up for the evening with chairs, urns of coffee and *nargileh* filling the side-walk. Bored young men loitered along the railings, and some sent Abir looks charged with sexual intent as we pass. From the far end of the promenade, the light of the Manara lighthouse winked periodically.

Abir had moved to Beirut only a few weeks before. At twenty-one, she was brimming with energy and determination, her pretty, childlike features framed by a shock of glossy black curls. She was quick-witted and fluent in American English but, despite her apparent resourcefulness, this was her first taste of adult life. She had left the family home in the Chouf mountains against her parents'

6

wishes—a brave move for a young Lebanese woman in this conservative society, tantamount to losing respectability. 'Don't tell anyone, or they'll make me leave the Y,' she confided, as we bit into rolls of *schwarma* from one of the fast-food joints.

She had been struggling against her parents' restrictions since her late teens. 'I couldn't do anything without permission—I couldn't go out, even to a friend's house,' she explained. 'They wouldn't permit me to go to a party, unless it was a friend's wedding.' Finally her father's controlling behaviour had got too much and she had taken a room in Beirut. Finding the money to support herself, even for the room she shared with another girl, wouldn't be easy in Lebanon's low-wage economy. 'But I want to try,' she declared cheerfully, staring into the darkness.

She was fascinated by my project, and eager to volunteer her own perspective. 'I'm not religious,' she said. 'I am Druze, but I'm not related to any religion in the way people understand religion here. I believe that all the religions are the same, and I think that now, in 2004, we must realize that. And not believe that we have to put on certain things to pray, or go to mosques. Just be good and believe in God.'

The ringing of her mobile interrupted our talk. After a long, formal conversation, she dropped the phone back into her bag with a sigh. The call was from a suitor, she said, a dull, older man whose attentions were unwelcome, at least to her. Her parents adored him.

'Have you been under pressure to marry?'

'Yes. Mother and Father sometimes say, "What about this guy? What about that guy?" I would like to get married and have children, but I think it's important to have my own life sorted out first. I want to get my career established.'

Then she broke off, pointing to one of the luxury apartment blocks on the other side of the road. It was an aggressively modern construction, its white stone frontage segmented by huge windows of single, costly sheets of glass. Inside, brightly lit chandeliers hung from pristine white ceilings.

'From these flats, it's possible to get to the sea without going out!' she exclaimed excitedly. 'I'd have one, if I had money!' She gestured to the stretch of road under which an underground passage connected the apartment block to the beach. It seemed a rather optimistic architectural decision, given that only fisherman and the lonely hung about on the rocks below the esplanade. But Abir's enthusiasm was undimmed. 'Can you imagine?' she repeated. 'Without *going out?*'

In the days that followed, I settled in well at my accommodation at the Y in Ain el Mreisse, a couple of streets above the Corniche. The Beirut branch of the Young Women's Christian Association was home to around seventy young women, and acted as a staging post between the parental home and marriage. Unlike Abir, most residents were there with their parents' blessing while studying at one of the universities or starting their first jobs, returning to the family home at weekends. Residence at the Y ensured respectability, as its director Mona Khauli explained to me from her office on the seventh floor. 'If you're a single woman, you're much more respected here than if you're living in a furnished apartment on your own,' she said. 'People would question that, and you could be receiving men. Here you have respect, and are socially credible.'

The hostel had a clutch of rules to enforce this respectability, including a one o'clock curfew—to my relief, recently raised from eleven pm—and a ban on alcohol. Visitors to residents' rooms were strictly forbidden, and round-the-clock staff made sure that no one slipped past the reception desk. Madame Victoria was the manager, a wide-faced, middle-aged woman whose expression alternated between anxiety and a big, soppy smile. She was delighted to discover that her resident *ajnabiya* spoke French, one of the three main languages spoken in Lebanon, along with Arabic and English. What unexpected gentility! From then on, our encounters were punctuated with a sing-song, reciprocal ritual. *Bonjour, Madame! Comment allez-vous?*

Despite its institutional feel, the Y was the ideal place for a visiting writer. It was quiet, safe and cheap. My room, although sparsely furnished with 1970s Formica, looked onto the sea, and blazing Mediterranean light flooded through the French window that took up an entire wall. The view was only improved, to my mind, by the icons of war and poverty that stood out against it in sharp relief—a derelict high-rise, riddled with bullet holes, an apartment block with balconies overflowing with the washing of poor families. Inside the hostel, every surface was kept spotlessly clean by two tireless Muslim women who could be seen sluicing water over its long, white corridors six days a week. When they came to the end of their mammoth cleaning task, they simply started again.

The place buzzed with Lebanese girl-life. Some seemed little more than children, shuffling about in over-sized animal slippers, rabbity ears skimming the floor. Through their half-open doors, you could see soft toys piled shamelessly up on their beds. Others had already acquired the hyper-glamour expected of Lebanese womanhood. They ran in and out of the shared kitchens, a blur of brown flesh in tight vest tops, eyeliner and shiny dark hair, propelled along by gossip and shrieks of laughter. Some had fiancés and boyfriends; a few, it was said, even took advantage of living in central Beirut to go dancing. As this was something only done by 'bitches'—the Lebanese term for women of loose morals—it paid to be careful. It was rumoured that one young woman had so loved her clubbing that she often broke curfew to return, visibly the worse for wear, in the morning. She had been asked to leave.

The Y was also home to a smaller, less ebullient population, a handful of older, unmarried women exempt from the three-year limit normally placed on residency. One had been there over thirty years. 'They're like YWCA children,' Khauli told me with protective fondness. 'They have nowhere to go, and no family.' These women generally kept to themselves, but when they heard I came from England, their faces took on wistful expressions, as they called up the picturebook image they held in their minds. 'Ah, London, very foggy!' said one knowingly, adding that she knew all about it from her reading of Agatha Christie. 'England used to be very pretty,' another told me sympathetically. 'But now it has been spoilt by foreigners.'

One afternoon, I fall into conversation with a group in the TV room. One of them, far from her parents in Saudi Arabia and studying at the prestigious American University of Beirut, radiates assurance. Everything about her is as smooth and glossy as the Gulf state where she grew up, from her flawless skin to her regular, rather bland features. She is concerned that I get a good impression of Lebanon. 'Lebanon is not like other Arab countries. Lebanon is different. It is open. You'—she jabs her finger emphatically at me, apparently not seeing any contradiction—'will write that.'

But her friend Aisha is a different creature altogether, a *jolie-laide* Arabian beauty, with an angular, sculpted face and one eye-brow arched, in permanent irony, high up her brow. She is possibly one of the most poised people I have ever met. 'Lebanon is complicated,' she tells me in her deep, sonorous voice.

'Everything is politics here.'

'What, for example?'

'If you know a politician, you can get a job. Even if you don't have a degree, you can have a job, a salary. Someone will call and say, "Hire this girl".' She takes a movie-star like drag on her cigarette from the corner of her mouth. Personally, she goes on, she isn't worried about Lebanon's endemic corruption because she plans to emigrate, to Canada or to the Gulf, with her fiancé.

10

'Won't that be hard?'

'I'm in love with him,' she says simply, as a smoke ring floats slowly up past her face. 'If I'm in the Gulf, I'll work, and I'll come home. I'll have children—we'll have a family life. In Canada, the same. I've known him a long time; we're like friends. It would only be hard if I was getting to know someone and I couldn't go out.'

Her elegant eyebrow arches even higher as she considers what she'll be leaving behind. 'You have everything here, if you have money. You have education, entertainment. You can be in the mountains in an hour. But for jobs, people are very disappointed. That's why they emigrate.'

One morning, Abir and I are having breakfast in the kitchen. She had recently cooked her first meal, having watched me admiringly as I chopped some onions and garlic and then added tomatoes and chickpeas. She had copied the process and been amazed at the result. 'I'm a cooker!' she declared triumphantly. Now we are eating a strange dish which combines eggs with her mother's homemade tomato paste.

'What would your parents say if you were to marry someone from another religion?' I ask suddenly.

She replies without hesitation: 'First they would think about killing me, then they would'—her hands push the air in front of her—'put me away from them.'

'Why?'

'Society.' In a single word she sums up the weight of history, custom, tribe, religion and social respectability.

'They are society,' I point out.

'They don't think like this.' She puts another forkful of pinkie-red egg into her mouth.

The discussion slides into religion, the allegiances it demands, and its tentacle-like reach into every area of life. In Britain, I tell her, most people don't believe in God any more. Abir stops eating, visibly astonished.

'What, most? Like more than twenty per cent?' She liked to quantify any kind of general assertion statistically.

Something like that, I say. There's a pause, while she digests this information. Then:

'Do they have proof?'

'That's what they ask people who believe in God.'

'But it's not something you can prove. It's the power.' She waves her fork vaguely around the Formica kitchen, to the sweep of azure outside. 'It's what makes everything.'

In the weeks that followed, I gradually got to grips with the practicalities of life in Lebanon. Using the shared taxis that formed the city's transport system was a challenge at first. You had to stand in the road and solicit a passing *servis*, stating your destination. More often than not, the driver wasn't going that way, and would tut an Arab 'no' in your face or, even more humiliatingly, pull away fast with the passengers he already had. Even when your destination and the driver's did coincide, an awkward negotiation might ensue, in which he tried to persuade you to pay for a private taxi, or asked for two thousand Lebanese lira—double the usual fare. Knowing if this was the going rate for a longer journey, or whether he was simply trying it on with a foreigner, required a good knowledge of the city's myriad areas. It was all a bit much for my delicate English sensibilities, and for the first few days I found myself walking miles in the heat rather than engage in such lowly dealings. Abir scolded me when she learnt of my reticence. 'Live with it!' she said. 'Negotiating with the taxi drivers won't kill you!'

12

She was amused by my reluctance to adopt the Beiruti approach to crossing the road, an optimistic process which involved stepping out in front of several lanes of traffic and hoping that the car heading towards you would stop. Despite repeated evidence that it generally did, I tended to hover about at the road's edges until Abir, screaming with laughter, grabbed my hand and dragged me across.

Even getting around on foot had its difficulties. Beirut is a city without formal addresses, and places are located through their proximity to nearby landmarks, a system which relies heavily on the individual's local knowledge. It took me weeks to realize that 'It's near here,' was the euphemism for 'I can't tell you.' Even maps didn't help, as people often didn't know how to read them. One morning, setting out for a nearby appointment, I knocked on Abir's door for directions. She was still in bed, but convinced she could help. 'Oh, it's near here,' she repeated, turning the map round and round, 'Very near.' Then she fell back on her pillow exhausted with the mental effort, my shiny street plan covering her face. Fifteen minutes later, having watched her expression grow even more perplexed as she tried to read the map upside down, I left, none the wiser.

Fortunately for my low blood sugar, getting food was easier. The Lebanese pizza *mannoush* was plentiful and cheap, sold straight from the oven in little bakeries, with toppings of thyme, cheese, or lightly cooked meat. Then there were *fatayer*, pastry triangles filled with spinach or meat, kebabs or *schwarma* and, in the more commercial areas, a glut of places selling burgers, chips, giant sandwiches, crepes and ice cream. I liked this hybrid Arab-American food less, but it was obviously popular with the Lebanese. The fast food restaurants were crammed with fleshy customers consuming super-sized portions of this fat-laden fare and doubtless many attempted to exorcise their gluttony on the Corniche later. Simpler, more traditional Lebanese food such as *fuul*, beans cooked in olive oil, was harder to find.

13

The street in which the Y sat served many immediate needs. It had a bakery which baked the thinnest, crispest *mannoush* in town. The shopkeepers obligingly went along with me when I insisted on conducting my purchases in my very minimal Arabic, patiently correcting my confusion of *khamsein* and *khamsea*. The greengrocer, operating out of a shack of corrugated iron and breeze blocks, provided a regular source of bananas. He also had a kitten, whom I visited regularly. After weeks of friendly small talk in a mixture of English and French, an important question suddenly occurred to him. *Tu es de Londres*, he said, by way of confirmation. 'Is London in England or in France?'

I tramped around Beirut, getting to know its various areas. In Bliss Street, gaggles of good-looking young Arab students clustered outside the honey-coloured walls of the prestigious American University of Beirut, holding high-tempo conversations in English and Arabic. It was easy, as a Western woman, to slip unchallenged into the university grounds, a spacious, terraced park full of aromatic trees overlooking the deep blue sea. Students strolled along its wide paths and lovers sat interlaced on its shady benches. Best of all, was its enormous population of cats, a legacy of the civil war and its aftermath when thousands of Beirutis emigrated, leaving their abandoned pets behind. The campus had become a kind of unofficial outdoor animal home, where cats of every colour prowled, snoozed and scavenged for food. Not everyone approved of their presence, but a committee had been established to look after their welfare and a daily meal of sorts was distributed. I loved to see them whenever I sought sanctuary there, and often acquired a few new friends, particularly if I had a chicken sandwich.

Behind AUB rose the gently bustling streets of Hamra, with its network of streets crammed with shops, internet cafés and coffee houses. My favourite was Café Younis, a tiny place serving a myriad

14

of different kinds of coffee which you could drink at the rickety breakfast bars which were put out on the pavement every morning. All in all, Beirut had an oddly familiar air, both like-the-West and distinctively Eastern. In Christian areas such as Gemayezeh, you could almost believe you were walking through the quieter streets of Paris, between apartment blocks of elegant grey stone and patisseries displaying the finest confectionary. But other areas were definitively, exclusively Muslim. The decaying Ottoman houses of Bachoura were full of poor Shia families, their crumbling balconies crammed with washing, household objects and children's toys. Turbaned, bearded sheikhs looked out from pictures on the walls, asking for votes or just good conduct. Ignored in other areas, here I got curious glances and would instinctively cover any bare flesh with a jacket.

And, of course, there was Downtown. The centre of the city, having been razed to the ground by the militias during the war, was now is immaculate as an architect's model, with crisp-cornered buildings in fresh tawny stone. Place de l'Etoile and its surrounding streets were lined with the tables and chairs of European café life. Glamorous evening wear and expensive watches filled the shop windows. Many of the new buildings were empty, but slowly life was returning to the heart of Beirut.

The massive reconstruction, I soon realized, masked a battle for the soul of the city by other means. Solidere, the company leading the development, had some vocal critics. It had been founded by Prime Minister Rafik Hariri, a businessman who had made his fortune in Saudi Arabia and who still held shares in the company. His opponents felt he was using the development to impose a crass, Gulf-style opulence on Beirut which was wiping out its Ottoman heritage. Instead of re-creating the mixed Christian-Muslim communities who had populated it before the war, they argued, Downtown was now

15

a playground for wealthy tourists and businessmen, while the poor were pushed to its derelict fringes.

It was as if the city was enacting, in architectural terms, some of the main tensions of modern Lebanon. It was barely a week before someone told me a joke satirizing the particular brand of competitive materialism that characterized this mercantile culture. Abu Abed and Abu Stef were a duo who made regular appearances in the oral tradition of Lebanese humour: friends, but also jealous rivals. One day, they found a magic lamp and agreed to share it. Abu Abed rubbed it, and out popped the genie.

'What is your wish?' he asked.

'I would like a BMW,' said Abu Abed firmly.

When Abu Stef saw the shiny new car, he was green with envy. He summoned the genie, and ordered two BMWs. Sighing, the genie obeyed.

A few days later, Abu Abed used the lamp to get himself a big, elegant house. Furious, Abu Stef wished for an enormous, many-turreted castle, which duly appeared on the horizon.

A few weeks went past, and the two did not see each other. Then Abu Stef heard that his friend had been very ill with testicular cancer but, thanks to an operation removing part of his manhood in one of Beirut's best private hospitals, was now on the mend.

Immediately, he rubbed the lamp. 'I want two of those!' he demanded. [1]

But the biggest tensions arose from the many religious groups that made up Lebanon's distinctiveness, a rich diversity that went far back into its history and set it apart from other Arab countries. Once Beirut had even had a flourishing Jewish quarter, although it

---

[1]   Readers wishing to extend their repertoire of Abu Abed jokes can consult a website devoted to the subject at: abuabed.net

was said that these days the few Jews who remained were too fright-ened to admit their true identity. When Lebanon became a modern nation state in the mid-twentieth century, its religious pluralism gained constitutional form, and the state recognized eighteen differ-ent faiths. The spectrum embraced Sunni and Shia Muslims, Druze, and a rainbow of Christians from Maronite Catholics to evangelical Protestants and Copts. The dark side of this multi-confessionalism erupted during the fifteen-year civil war when, in a series of shifting hostilities and alliances, its various sects battled for power. While Christians and Muslims fought over the green line which divided Beirut, the conflict was more complex than a straightforward strug-gle between two opposing faiths; there were regional interests at play too. The Palestine Liberation Organization, routed from Jordan, was using Lebanon as a base for anti-Israeli activity. Israel occupied the country in retaliation and Syria, fearing the rise of Islamic militancy, jumped in to help the Christians. Finally, in 1989, the peace plan called the Taif Accord brought the fighting to a close. As well as addressing some of the Muslims' grievances about the power-sharing arrangement, it made key commitments for the future: the disarming of militias such as Hezbollah in the south, and a move to abolish political sectarianism at some point in the future.

Meanwhile the Syrian forces stayed on, becoming a permanent presence on Lebanese soil. As well as stationing up to 14,000 troops there, the Damascus regime kept a grip on its neighbour's affairs with a network of intelligence agents who effectively ran the country. Around a million Syrian workers took advantage of Lebanon's higher wages and the relaxed borders between the two countries, working in lowly jobs or as street-sellers. They were widely looked down on by the Lebanese and for many, gratitude for Syria's role in the war mu-tated into resentment. The Christians, in particular, called on them to leave, denouncing their president Emile Lahoud as a Syrian pup-

17

pet. The Shia, on the other hand, welcomed their continued presence as a protective, pan-Arab force. For many people, the Syrians were simply a fact of Lebanese life and, after nearly thirty years, the ties between the two countries seemed unbreakable. Abir explained the relationship with her customary acuity. 'Lebanon is our *Mother*,' she said, adding with even greater irony: 'Syria is our *Sister*.'

The tribal divisions that had emerged during the war had left the Lebanese with a deep awareness of their country's sectarian nature. But it also engendered a determination that differences between the sects would not disrupt the country's peace and prosperity, a determination which formed the basis of the new national identity that was slowly emerging. According to the accompanying orthodoxy, what mattered was being Lebanese, rather than classification as Sunni, Shia, Christian or Druze. Politicians and community leaders made full use of the new rhetoric about common values while the young, the first generation to grow up since the war, embraced this vision of the new Lebanon with fervent sincerity. 'We are all Lebanese now,' was a repeated refrain from everyone I met in their teens or twenties. 'The differences between us don't matter.'

Yet, in reality, many of the differences remained deeply entrenched, with each group retaining its own allegiances and ideas about what kind of country Lebanon should be. Wrangles about power and representation continued, and each group, with the possible exception of the wealthy Sunna, seemed to hold onto a deep-rooted sense that it was particularly hard-done by, deprived of the support it deserved from the government. Post-war Lebanon, I was realizing, had a kaleidoscopic quality about it: look now, and it was a modern, tolerant country, determined to build a future based on consensus and co-operation. A moment later, it was a deeply conservative society, riven by sectarian tribalism, its traditions formed by the landscape and hardwired into the soul.

18

⊗

Georges swings open the door of his BMW as he picks me up in Ain el Mreisse. With his slicked back hair and sharp suit, he is a typical secular, well-to-do Maronite, a thirty-something professional with international connections. He is visibly disappointed that I am not more like Sylvia, the mutual friend who put us touch. Sylvia is blond and statuesque. Moreover, she works in marketing. 'I like her profile,' grins Georges toothily.

As we head towards Downtown, we chat about the state of Lebanon. 'You won't find many people here like me who speak frankly, directly,' he says, his dark eyes earnest behind their rimless designer frames. 'The Lebanese will say that everything is fine, but they are lying. We have peace here, but it is a forced peace. This is a—' he struggles to find the right expression—'*conflictive* place.'

'You have everything here,' he goes on, as we emerge from the underground car park into Martyr's Square. 'The weather, nature—all the touristic elements. But people in Lebanon don't have the maturity to recognize that it's possible to live together with other communities or, after the conflict, to build something new.'

A few hundred yards away, the restaurants and cafés around Place de l'Etoile glitter, their lights beckoning. The gloomy wasteland of Martyr's Square stretches out around us, weeds poking up through the expanse of concrete.

Georges gestures to the huge mosque which is rising, half-formed, under a network of scaffolding. In previous visits to the area, I have already noticed how quickly it was growing, cranes swinging late into the evening and tiny figures scaling the minarets. Begun six months before with money from Hariri, its site next to Lebanon's largest Maronite church, St. George's, was causing disquiet among the Christian communities who felt that, with several other mosques

19

nearby, it was being built simply to out-do them. 'You will see,' says Georges indignantly. 'When the people start praying in the church, next door they will start the call to prayer louder. It's an expression of hate.'

He pauses as we come to rest before five lanes of fast-moving Beiruti traffic. 'Are you understanding me?' he asks anxiously. 'Is my English clear enough?' I hazard a summary of what he has said. 'Sectarianism expressed through architecture?'

'Exactly,' says Georges, and departs across the road, fast and alone.

A few minutes later, we hunt for a restaurant that can satisfy the various demands of his friends, a young European-Lebanese business elite. It's a fine evening, and the tables lining the streets are packed with tourists from elsewhere in the Middle East. Headscarves and *nargileh* are everywhere. 'I don't want to sit with Arabs,' says Georges, steering us firmly inside an empty Italian restaurant.

One afternoon I venture into the Muslim world that so aroused Georges' distaste. The Omari mosque had been the city's oldest until its proximity to the Green Line that marked the border between the Christian and Muslim territories during the civil war had led to its destruction. Following a $3.5-million investment from Kuwaiti businesswoman Suad al-Humaydi and four years of renovation, it had finally re-opened its doors the previous week.

A long latticed panel of rich brown wood and white marble runs the length of the mosque's outer wall, shielding the sanctum from busy Rue Weygand, which is noisy with rush-hour traffic. Already veiled, I step across the threshold and take off my shoes. Inside, a space of light and air opens up. The courtyard's white marble floor gleams in the late afternoon sunlight. Elegant white columns rise at

20

its edges, including two Byzantium originals, decorated with time-eaten friezes.

The mosque guide approaches me. He is very young, possibly the age of the sixth formers I once taught.

'This is a mosque,' he says, explanatorily.

'I know.'

'You have to put something else on.' He motions to my flimsy veil, and leads me to a pile of material in the corner of the courtyard. He unfolds an enveloping piece of fabric with what appears to be a tiny hole for part of the face. I must look alarmed because, pointing out the garment's elasticity, he pulls it over his own head. With only his pointed nose and close-set eyes exposed, he looks rather like an animal character in a children's book, dressed up for humans' amusement. My first attempt at donning the poncho is rejected: there's too much hair showing. But my second, which hardly allows me to breathe or see, wins approval. 'That's good,' he nods. We begin our tour.

'This'—he points to a panelled wall at one end of the courtyard—'is the women's section.' Then, seeing an opportunity, he asks, 'You know why there is a separation between men and women?'

While I'm wondering how to respond, he answers himself.

'It is out of respect for women.' His enthusiasm for his subject is palpable, the sentences tumbling one after the other. 'And you know why women wear the veil? It's for the protection of the woman. It's because she's the one who educates the children. When she goes out, into the street, into society, to work, she is protected from being looked at'—he pauses just slightly—'in a sexual way.' I feel the elastic tight around my chin; it is a hot day and this unexpected addition to my clothing adds to the feeling of suffocation. 'You know when there is an advert for Pepsi or a car, and the woman is naked?' he continues. 'Then she becomes an object. When she wears the veil, she is protected. You understand me?'

Various Western responses swim, half-formed, in my mind. It might be nice to have some intercultural dialogue. But there seems to be no way of stopping the flow. 'A woman must be happy in the home,' he concludes, finally pausing for breath.

Seeing my chance, I fast-bowl in a question. 'How old are you?'

'I'm eighteen. I'm not married.' He smirks at the idea, before continuing: 'If a wife is not happy at home, the family is destroyed. And I would like to tell you another thing. We cannot force the woman to wear the veil. That's because she must want to wear the veil herself, from the inside,' he points to his heart. 'It is obligatory, but it's from God, not from us, the men. That's what people don't understand about Islam. They don't know that the veil is about respect for women. If we could explain it to them, they would understand. So that's it, it's about respect.' He nods to himself with a pleased smile.

I steal a few moments alone inside the mosque. Colonnades of blond stone border a central nave, and there are rich red carpets underfoot. High, arched windows suck in the light and cool air flows in from the open doors at each end. There's a shelf of Korans in one corner, a water cooler and little boxes of tissues have been placed thoughtfully about. In a shadowy alcove, two men are reclining sleepily on floor cushions.

The adjoining prayer room for women is a smaller, plainer, affair. In one corner, a man hunches over a desk. 'Are men allowed in here?' I ask the guide, who is now at my elbow again. 'Oh yes, it's not about rules,' he answers. 'He is studying. He has exams.'

He leads me down some stairs into a cavernous basement which is clearly in the final phase of refurbishment. 'We don't normally show people this part,' he says. 'When it is finished, it will be for young people. There will be computers here'—he waves to the left. 'And here'—his arm sweeps to the right—'there will be ping pong tables.'

Back upstairs in the sunlit courtyard, a car draws up outside the main door, its occupants shouting and waving. Something awkward is attached to the roof. 'The ping pong tables have arrived!' exclaims the guide, excitedly. 'You need anything else? No?' He races off to help unload.

By all accounts, interfaith relations were taken very seriously by those at the top of Lebanese society. Through a contact, I had the opportunity to talk to one of its leading figures, who was also at the heart of the political establishment. Mohammed Sammak, adviser to Hariri and the Mufti of Lebanon, was a prolific journalist and active on several of the country's interfaith committees.

We meet in his office at the newspaper *Al Mustaqbal*; he is a large, unsmiling man with considerable physical presence. His wife Nabila, a pretty woman in a lilac top and matching eye-shadow, sits silently beside his desk as we talk. Hariri looks down on us from his picture on the wall above.

The Taif Accord that ended the civil war, explains Sammak, put an end to a long-running grievance of the Sunnis about the dominance the Maronites had acquired under French colonial rule. It re-structured the political system, moving power away from the president, traditionally a Maronite, to a cabinet divided equally between Christians and Muslims. The change meant that the Sunnis no longer had cause to resent the modern state of Lebanon, with its hybrid Muslim-Christian nature, as a pretext for Christian supremacy. 'Now things have changed; Lebanon is Christian and Muslim, Muslim as much as Christian now,' he concludes.

'Why the change in attitude?' I ask.

'Being Lebanese doesn't mean that you are not Arab anymore. Taif established the identity of Lebanese as an Arab country—as "a final homeland for all Lebanese Christians and Muslims". The question of identity and the question of religion are separate. You have a different religion and the same ethnicity, which is unique for Christians in the Middle East. In Europe it's thought that Arabs are Muslims—such a simple idea.'

'Is Lebanon's special nature threatened by rising Islamicism?'

'Fundamentalism is very weak and limited here,' he replies. 'It gains strength from outside. I think it will be overcome with the increasing liberalism in the Middle East. These people have no future, I'm sure of it.'

'What about attitudes to other faiths?'

'The Jews left Lebanon of their own will. We don't have any problems in living with Jews from a religious point of view—believing in Judaism is part of Islamic doctrine.'

'These are all people of the book, whose religions have common roots,' I persist. 'But do radically different faiths, like Buddhism or Hinduism which are not officially recognized by the Lebanese state, receive the same degree of tolerance?'

'Why not? What's wrong with them?' he responds comfortably. 'According to Islamic law and doctrine, I do not have the right to force people to join my religion. That is none of my business. Who knows if Buddhism, Confucianism or Hinduism is not originally a message from God? Islam says that all people should know God and the only way is by sending messengers. Maybe Buddha is a prophet—I don't know. Whether they are people of the book, or not, I don't have to judge. Maybe they have their own book, thousands of years before Islam, Judaism or Christianity.'

The interview drawing to a close, he gestures to his wife. 'Ask her a question.'

I turn to her. 'What's the nature of your faith?'

She smiles sweetly. 'Actually, I don't practise. I have many friends from different religions in this country. I share their sickness, their happiness; I feel they are my second family. I believe in Christianity, and I believe in other religions.'

Sammak, his saturnine countenance now relieved by a faint smile, offers me a sweet from a fluted glass bowl and presents me with a thick, colourful booklet. Published by the Lebanese government and the UN, it lays out 'The Youth Charter on Combating Corruption' for 15-24 year-olds. A series of pledges translated into Arabic, French and English enjoin the young to avoid corruption in politics and public life, their work and social relations, resisting temptations such as bribery and cheating in exams. 'The confrontation of corruption is a joint responsibility that requires the combined efforts of the State, with its various administrative, judicial and security agencies, and of civil society and the people in general,' declares an opening paragraph. 'Combating corruption is a continuing process, related to multifaceted moral, educational and national issues.'

The booklet was hardly a page-turner likely to be devoured by its target audience of adolescents. But as I leafed through its red and green pages afterwards, I realized that it was an attempt to remedy one of Lebanon's greatest problems—a pervasive cynicism which saw everything, from politicians to wider society, with a jaundiced despair. One day, as I popped out of the Y to recharge my phone at the local shop, I unwittingly ran into its personification.

He was lolling against the counter, an unshaven man in his late thirties with a world weary air, talking intermittently to his friend the sales assistant.

They were immediately sympathetic to my moans about Lebanese telecommunications, an extortionate system run by a private duopoly producing considerable revenues for the government. Having a mobile phone was essential in Lebanon's communication-oriented soci-

25

ety, but running one was so expensive that people often ran out of the money to maintain credit. A culture of 'missed-calling' had evolved: if you wanted to tell someone you were on your way, or to ring you back, you simply rang their number and then rapidly cancelled the call. It could be mystifying to the foreigner: one expatriate I knew answered his phone at midnight, to be told: 'Oh, I didn't mean you to answer. I just miss-called you to say goodnight!' My gripe was that I had signed up to a deal that involved buying a new compatible phone, sim card and phone units where a minute had forty seconds without being told there were other, cheaper options.

'People here have become like that,' said World Weary, his eyelids heavy with disenchantment. 'After fifteen years of civil war, the culture has changed. They always try to get more. Especially when they see a foreigner—they think you don't know anything about how things work here.'

People seemed nice, I ventured, thinking of the many examples of Lebanese hospitality I had already experienced.

'On the surface,' he responded slowly, his words slouching out of his mouth. 'If I get run over in the street, people will let me lie there. No one will call an ambulance—they'd be afraid someone would blame them. All that's needed here is a scapegoat.'

The young man behind the counter, his innocent face framed by a dark beard, agreed. 'Lebanon breaks you,' he said. 'We try to change the system, but we end up going along with it.' His hand traced a vertical line in illustration. 'You can't go against the current.'

'Poverty is growing,' continued the other. 'Many people live below the poverty line, while others are very rich. They have billions—twelve cars, some of them! They made money with our blood during the war, by trading drugs and guns. Everything is corrupt. The politicians—the prime minister, the president—all corrupt. Lebanon is finished.'

He was working on his escape plan, he went on: emigration to the ordered calmness of Europe. 'I want to go to Switzerland. I like order, tranquillity, a peaceful life. Here it's disorganized, chaos.'

'But people come back here.' He sounded as if he despaired of his countrymen. 'If they were born here, they're stuck. They want to come back to their roots; they want to be buried here.'

I stepped back out into the sun-soaked street, where a pair of BMWs were jostling for space, and the greengrocer sat in his shack, patiently waiting for customers. The encounter had illustrated many of the frustrations that had created the Lebanese diaspora, an exodus of—although no exact figures exist—between five and fifteen million people who live abroad, vastly outnumbering the three and a half million who stayed. Yet, as he said, the country also drew them magnetically back. What was the nature of these roots, I wondered, that people returned when they had worked hard to build prosperous lives elsewhere? It was time to explore how the country's largest and most powerful Christian sect saw things.

2

THE WORLD OF THE MARONITES

IT'S a curious face, both reassuring and disturbing, framed by a black hood surrounded by a halo of light. You never see the eyes, which are veiled by lowered lids. The impression is of both humility and great power, and it's easy to see how the image has achieved iconic status, adorning posters and totems in Christian parts of the country.

The face is St. Charbel's, the first of Lebanon's three saints and a central, beloved figure for the Maronites. His story began in 1851 when the young Joseph Makhlouf became a monk, taking the novice's name of Charbel. Later, he left the comforts of his monastery at Annaya to become a hermit, spending the remaining twenty-three years of his life in solitude. A few months after his death, bright lights suddenly danced on his grave, and when his body was exhumed, it was found to be intact and oozing blood. The same thing happened on two subsequent disinterments. Then the miracles began. In one three-week period in 1950, three hundred and fifty healings took place at the monastery, enabling the lame to walk and the blind to see. St. Charbel's reputation was assured, and he was canonized in 1965.

His monastery, high in the mountains above Byblos, had become a place of pilgrimage for devout Christians. 'You really feel something there,' a British expatriate told me. 'I don't usually feel these things, but I did there. You ought to go.'

So here I am, deposited in the car park by one of the few buses that make the journey up the mountainside. The place is not easy to get to without a car, and I have relied on a kind of travel-floating, setting off with only a vague idea of how to get somewhere, and trusting in the locals' willingness to help. Thanks to the Lebanese code of hospitality, it was an approach that worked well, and it had paid off again today. I had been effortlessly directed through the different stages of the journey, with one man even driving me to the bus stop and hailing the right bus. As the bus disappears back down the road, I wonder how I'll get back to civilization, and then decide to worry about it later.

The monastery's wide façade stretches out in front of me. A few other white buildings are dotted around the plateau: there is a retreat for visitors requiring a longer stay and a large, modern church for full-blown services. Wooden signs placed around the site dispense spiritual *bons mots*. 'If you do not understand my silence, you will not understand my words,' says one. Despite various ambient noises—music blaring from a nearby coach, the chipping and banging of the maintenance men, leaves rustling busily in the breeze—the place does have an underlying silence about it.

I wander into the circular church. Inside, rows of light wood pews fan out around the central altar; the hooded, heavy-lidded face of St. Charbel on a giant canvas hangs above it. Modernist stained glass windows feature the saint engaged in various activities: teaching his disciples, healing the sick, working the land. Often he holds an oil lamp, a reference to the time when his fellow monks played a trick on him, swapping its oil with water. Unawares, the saint tried to light the wick and—to the amazement of the mischief-makers—the flame leapt up all the same.

I sit down in one of the pews. An afternoon stillness has settled on the church. A black-cassocked priest walks in, sinks into a pew

29

and bows his head in prayer. A young couple follows, a tiny baby collapsed against the father's chest. The man holds the child up to see the saint's giant canvas face, whispering in his ear. Whether it's to this vision of holiness or to his father's encouragement, it's impossible to tell, but the baby responds happily, gurgling and waving its tiny socked feet.

Back in the bright sunshine, I start as a black-robed figure with a pointed hood glides silently across the main concourse. He looks uncannily like the images of St. Charbel that have been flooding my consciousness. Then I realize that he's just one of the modern monks going about his business. The figure disappears into the gift shop.

A sudden rush of visitors breaks the quiet. Cars drive up and park in the forecourt; young men and women in tight T-shirts and trainers jump out, chatting and smoking. A group of middle-aged women tumble out of a minibus and make a beeline for their favourite spots. Two prostrate themselves in front of the imposing statue of St. Charbel outside the main entrance. In a corner of the lobby, another woman is having a private moment with a smaller version. She takes its outspread hands in her own, caressing them, and gazes up into the saint's face, her face suffused with adoration. Then she runs her fingers up and down the folds of his metal robes.

I tour the three tombs that mark the saint's various exhumations, sit in the tiny chapel and stare at the relics in the mini-museum, mainly the saint's robes splattered with blood. A man behind a grille is selling pieces of the fabric, doused in oil. A small queue of people is lining up to buy.

In the car park, I look around for possible transport. But there are no buses and the one dozing taxi driver is unwilling to leave without more passengers, and I fall into conversation with two of the women from the minibus. A band of Maronites and Greek Catholics, they are on a day out with a priest, away from husbands and children, touring the main shrines of their faith.

'Do you feel something special here?' I ask curiously.

'I do' says the dark one. 'I don't know whether it's me,' she pats her chest diffidently, 'but I feel there's something here. They say that if you believe, you really believe, St. Charbel will cure you. But if you don't, it doesn't work.'

'Have you had any experience of miracles yourselves?'

'Yes', says the other, a woman of about thirty with neat, pretty features and a blond ponytail. 'When I was twelve, he appeared to me in my sleep. I was lying in my bed, and I looked up and saw him standing there. He blessed me'—she makes the sign of the cross—'he was very pleased with me!' She smiles happily at the memory. 'Then I woke up, and I found that I was kneeling by my bed, like this.' She folds her hands in prayer. 'I have no idea how I got there.'

'And as an adult?'

'Yes. I have two daughters, and I dreamed that St. Charbel was in front of one of them, and he sent a ball of fire into her body. I think that when she is older, she will become a sister.' I wonder whether the prospect of her young daughter disappearing into a convent would please her. 'Oh yes,' she nods categorically.

The group offer me a lift back to Beirut. The dark woman, Joumana, exudes practicality and a quiet goodwill, and I feel instantly comfortable with her. She pats the front seat of the bus beside her. 'I will not leave you alone now,' she says, adding with an ironic snort of laughter: 'The Lebanese are very nice to foreigners, but they are not nice with each other.'

There is one more stop to make before the women's day is complete. The hermitage where St. Charbel spent his years of solitude is lodged on a yet higher peak, and the larger women heave themselves out of the bus and up the steep steps, puffing heavily, their enthusiasm apparently undiminished. Joumana and I exchange amused glances and plod up after them. Inside the low stone building, a narrow corridor gives onto a series of tiny rooms, including a miniature chapel and study. We peer through the grill to his bedroom, where a strip of hessian lies along one wall. 'Underneath,' whispers Joumana reverently, 'it is just wood, with a pillow of wood. He slept just on that.'

In the saint's kitchen next door, pots and pans of grey metal have been carefully laid out on the floor. Joumana points to a woven circular tray. 'It's bamboo,' she whispers. 'It's what Lebanese women used to present the food to their husband. In the past.'

'Now, they just throw it at him.' I quip. We double up in the narrow passageway.

Back on the bus, she talks of the importance of St. Charbel and monastic life to Lebanese Christians, her tone shifting between reverence and matter-of-factness. Day trips to religious sites are very common, she says, but most of the visitors are women. 'Some people say that it's because they're weak. Other people say it's because they're more sensitive, more receptive to the holy.' She waves her hand airily, conveying that she herself is not taking a position on the matter. Monastic life and its virtues are highly prized, she goes on. 'The most important is poverty, at least here, in Lebanon. But the orders have money. You can see that they have big cars, mobile phones, good quality clothing. And they travel, they travel a lot.' She pauses for a moment. 'Some really are poor, though'

Her own situation is little better, struggling on wages that barely meet the cost of living. Since becoming a widow in her mid-twenties, she has brought up her four children single-handed by doing lace-work at home.

'Is it hard?'

32

She gives me a straight look. 'Very hard. I make big tablecloths'—
she opens her arms wide—'and it can take me two or three months
to finish one. I chose this work because it allows me to stay at home
with the children. I didn't want to leave them alone. A friend taught
me how to do it.'

There has been no help from anyone, not even her in-laws. But
her eldest daughter, at twenty-one, now contributes to the household. 'She is only fourteen years older than I am', she says. With a
shock I realize that she's younger than I am.

'What age were you married?'

'Thirteen.'

'Did you want to?'

She shakes her head ever so slightly. Then she says significantly, 'I
had a stepmother.'

'And she wanted to get rid of you?' I'm amazed at this real-life
Cinderella story that is emerging. She nods, silently. For a few minutes, we stare at the road unfurling in front of us.

'I've made a lot of sacrifices, a lot,' she adds matter-of-factly. 'But
I have good children—intelligent and kind.'

'Have you ever been abroad?'

She shakes her head, adding with a glow of pride: 'But I have a
friend who lives in Belgium. She is eighty, and we write to each other
regularly. I've never met her. I had a friend who went to Belgium and
showed her my picture. She has no children, and she started to write
to me. I got to know her through her words, and I liked her. I feel
she is my mother.'

'But you must go and meet her.'

'How? There is no money for that.'

As the bus rattles along the coastal road to Beirut, the priest suggests that his large, middle-aged companions go skinny-dipping in
the sea. The women scream in scandalized delight.

⌘

The Maronite community was born of St. Maron, a fourth-century hermit who lived in the Syrian mountains and impressed his followers with his extreme asceticism and ability to heal the sick. But the new Christian sect was persecuted for its unorthodox beliefs about the nature of Christ and, branded as heretics by the Byzantine Church, finally fled to the relative sanctuary of Mount Lebanon in the tenth century. Later, they retreated even further from Ottoman persecution into the Qadisha Valley, an inaccessible gorge which had long sheltered spiritual dissidents.

Wider political forces improved the Maronites' fortunes. Their status as Christians in the Muslim-dominated Middle East, together with their strong ties with the Roman Catholic Church, won them friends in the West. Backed by their allies, the Maronites saw the opportunity to play a unique role as a break against the pan-Arabism that was sweeping the region. They developed a Francophile culture and French-speaking education system, and some went as far as to disassociate themselves from the Arab world, claiming that their roots lay with ancient Phoenicia. After the fall of the Ottoman Empire in 1920, Lebanon fell under French rule, and when it became an independent republic in 1943, France assured the survival of its Christian character. The new constitution guaranteed the Maronites the presidency, leaving the posts of prime minister and speaker of parliament to the Sunnis and Shia. Better educated, connected and more moneyed than many of their Muslim counterparts, the Maronites prospered socially too.

But the civil war cost them their sense of privilege. By the time the fighting stopped in 1990, the Islamic militia had gained control over the south of the country and Christian homes lay empty. In the Chouf, where the Maronites and the Druze fought 'the war of the mountains', entire Christian villages fled, leaving the Druze the victors. During the fifteen-year war, 850 000 Christians left the country. It was Lebanon's particular version of the story of emigration that was rapidly reducing the numbers of Christians all over the region.

These experiences had left the Maronite community depressed by its declining fortunes, but more convinced than ever of the special role it had to play, as a strong Christian community, in today's Middle East.

Bcharre Rai, bishop of Byblos, was one of their leading prelates. An authority on interfaith relations in Lebanon and the situation of Christians in the Middle East, he would, I had been told, be well placed to provide an insight into how the Maronites now saw their position. Securing an interview with him hadn't been easy—numerous calls to his office had been met with requests to ring back another time. On the several occasions when I had spoken to the bishop himself, his low, almost bored tones strongly suggested that this was not a man who suffered fools.

But finally I am here for a nine o'clock appointment, sitting in the entrance hall of the bishop's seat at Amsheet near Byblos. It is a dazzling Lebanese morning, and light floods through the flung-open wooden doors, bouncing off the marble floor and highly polished furniture. I see the bishop as he arrives, striding almost processionally up the stairs and along the hall, reading a document as he walks.

Vous allez bien? He is holding out his hand, a square-jawed, solidly built man who, despite his black vestments and large silver cross, retains an air of worldliness. He ushers me into his office. It is packed with Maronite icons: St. Charbel looks out serenely from a silver plaque on one wall; a colourful Cubist painting hangs on another, in which Christ dances in a circle of disciples, angular limbs flaying with movement. The bishop helps me worry about my dictaphone, and we begin the interview.

'Have things got worse or better for the Maronite community?' I ask.

'Things have got worse for all the communities in Lebanon,' he replies in measured, formal French and I recognize the unhurried manner I encountered on the phone. 'In this sense, it has got weaker. The war was called a civil war, but it wasn't: it was linked to the regional situation, to the Arab-Israeli and Israeli-Palestinian conflicts. It was also linked to international politics in the region: the Lebanese civil war was part of that chain in events which continues with the war in Iraq.'

As I listen, I realize that trying to understand the Maronite perspective without reference to the myriad factors that shape the geo-politics of the Middle East is impossible. The bishop talks on, describing Lebanon's unique, multi-confessional nature, its sharing of power between Christians and Muslims. But this same religious plurality makes it vulnerable to outside interference, he goes on, with the Christians pulled towards Western secularism and the Muslims towards pan-Arab theocracy.

'That's why, through Lebanon, the "big plan" can be launched because—I'm going to be frank, you're going to write interesting things'—he nods benevolently at me—'Israel needs to survive in a Muslim world. The big conflict that exists between Israel and the Palestinians is a conflict about land, first of all. But the wider Arab-Israeli conflict is a theocratic conflict—a war between two religions, two Gods, le Yahweh and Islam. Israel cannot exist in an Arab world which is strong and united. The plan, if I speak frankly, is to weaken the Arab world, divide it between communities and confessions, and to weaken it economically and militarily. One can start that in Lebanon, because it's the easiest.'

36

Behind him, a pearl and bead cross hanging over a large icon of Christ sways gently in the breeze and birdsong floats in through the open window. The high politics he is evoking seem improbable in this calm, light-soaked morning.

'Syria has collaborated in these Middle East stakes, playing both a positive and a negative role,' he goes on. 'The positive role is that Syria, with the international community, has safeguarded all the Lebanese communities. But it has also weakened everyone. I cannot say that the situation of the Maronites has got worse or better—everyone's situation is weak. The Muslims have strengthened their position, due to the Muslim world which surrounds us and to the Syrian presence on our soil. There is a certain Islamicization in terms of jobs, public posts and the buying of land. The Muslims are expanding, profiting from poverty and buying up as much as much land as they can.'

'What can you do to combat this?'

'All Lebanese, both Christians and Muslims, need to take responsibility for the reconstruction of the country,' he replies grandly. 'All of us Lebanese need to become aware of our country's values, and understand that no one can survive without the other—the Christian cannot live without the Muslim, the Muslim cannot live without the Christian, because Lebanon was formed by Christians and Muslims in all their varieties and they have created a state entirely different from all the countries in the world. The other Arab countries have totalitarian systems, where freedom doesn't exist, so Lebanon has a message to convey. Neither a Christian nor a Muslim Lebanon can play the role, but an Islamic-Christian Lebanon can. So the Lebanese have to take up their responsibility, re-open a national dialogue, re-establish mutual trust and begin to rebuild the country together.'

Palpable conviction now animates his formal delivery. 'Second point,' he continues emphatically. 'We have to sort out the relation between Lebanon and Syria. Things cannot go on like this. It should be one of mutual respect and collaboration and not as it is today, where Lebanon is under Syria's thumb. That's not in Syria's interest, or in Lebanon's. In spite of all the good it has done Lebanon, Syria has also done a lot of harm. I'm not casting blame on anyone, but one of the solutions, in addition to the responsibility of the Lebanese themselves, is to sort out the relation with Syria.'

The big picture now laid out, I wonder whether the bishop's plain speaking will extend to issues closer to home. 'Is the Hariri mosque being built in Beirut a sign of coexistence or sectarianism?' I ask, slightly mischievously.

Gentle, ironic laughter issues from the episcopal throat. 'You know that in the Middle East, we always need to build churches and mosques. We say that they have the right to build a mosque. But why an enorrrrrrmous mosque?' He rolls the 'r' theatrically around his tongue. 'It's a question of sensitivity and mutual respect. But our brothers, unfortunately, do not respect.'

The same thing had happened with the construction of a mosque next to the monastery in Byblos. He had counselled against it in vain; then he had boycotted meetings with the parties concerned. 'I have tried to tell them a lot—you shouldn't build this mosque. It doesn't help conviviality—it separates us. So I cannot attend. One shouldn't be duped—that doesn't help conviviality.'

But his gravitas gives way to expansiveness as he returns to his favourite theme. 'To conclude, it's not uniformity we seek, it's diversity!' He opens his arms as if to illustrate the vastness of the space available for difference. 'Lebanon has its role to play—we will try to maintain that! *Voilà.*'

'I am sorry it took so long to arrange to meet,' he smiles, offering me a sweet from a large glass bowl on his desk. Then he begs me a lift back to Byblos from a departing visitor and returns me to the sunshine.

38

⊗

'*Yalla*, Alex! Let's go!' It's late on a Saturday night, and I'm lying on my bed when Abir bursts into my room, black curls streaming out in all directions. Above her lemon-yellow nightdress, her face is sallow. She has just woken from a brief nap after thirty-six hours without sleep. But, driven by the youthful fear that life might pass her by, she is desperate to go clubbing.

As soon as we step over the threshold into Acid, a night club south-east of the city centre, I'm on familiar territory. Bodies sway to the pounding music in the semi-darkness of the dance floor. A long bar, rows of bottles gleaming seductively, curves around the back wall below a stone relief of Indian gods and goddesses. We could be in a club anywhere in the West.

A gay club. Amid the largely male crowd, the subtle gestures and signs are unmistakeable. A delicate net T-shirt sets off a sculpted torso; some carefully applied make-up enhances the curve of an eyebrow. Homosexuality is illegal in Lebanon, and I haven't seen anything approaching this display on the streets; Beirut's gays are obviously making the most of a night out in a safe environment. The knowledge, with its promise of a night out free from heterosexual predators, puts me even more at ease.

But Abir, the girl from the mountains, is lost. She clings to a male friend, one of the few unambiguously heterosexuals in the place. Although she has no designs on him, she keeps his attention with intimate, suggestive movements, dancing in a style at odds with the inclusive, open groups of the clubbers around us. She seems unaware of the signals she's giving off, and equally unable to read the codes used by everyone around her. Every now and then, she tries to at-tract the attention of one of our party, the one man she is interested in. But he's immune to her charms and continues his flamboyant bisexual dancing. Later, I see him kissing his boyfriend at the bar.

As I survey the dance floor, I slowly become aware of another cultural fault line. Despite its apparent sophistication, the crowd doesn't know how to respond to the Western dance beats. When the breaks in the techno come, people stop abruptly, puzzled and bored. But the moment that Arab fusion starts, the crowd springs to life. As the arabesque sounds rise and fall, people dance as one, heads thrown back in abandon, faces lit with pleasure. The dancers on the podia are suddenly Eastern, hips thrusting asymmetrically, arms snaking above their heads. The DJ stops the music to let the dancers fill in the lyric, and everyone shouts the lines in joyous unison.

And beneath the Indian deities, the bar staff stand idle, their bottles of spirits untouched. Although unlimited free alcohol is included in the price of the entrance fee, in a sobriety unthinkable in Britain, no one is bothering to drink.

Watching Abir in these first months of life as an independent adult, it was becoming obvious how dramatically, under the surface, her situation differed from that of a Western woman of the same age. Her life was like a game of snakes and ladders: everything, from getting a toehold in a career to finding the rent, was a step-by-step struggle. Once she had climbed a few rungs, it only took one false move or a piece of misfortune to have her sliding right back down again to powerlessness. She had no safety net or source of advice, as her parents offered no money to help fund her studies, and she often had to lie about her circumstances just to keep on speaking terms with them. Yet there were plenty of voices—generally male ones—to warn her darkly of social disgrace if she was seen in the wrong company, or otherwise stepped out of line. And, beneath her apparent resourcefulness, she was monumentally ill-prepared for the challenges of her new life.

At first, she appeared to be flourishing. Experimenting with hairstyles and make-up, she revelled in her burgeoning good looks, self-consciously adopting the dress of the professional woman. At the hotel where she worked as a receptionist, her responsibilities were soon widened to include book-keeping. Further promotion was promised. 'I'm having a really good time at work,' she told me happily. 'We're like a family.'

She listened uncomprehendingly to my worries about a friend's legal case in Britain. 'Can't you do something?' she said. 'That's how it works here. Lebanon is easy.' I mumbled something about protocols and probity, presenting them as better options than the *wasta*, the currency of contacts on which Lebanese society turns. 'Maybe', she said with a bright smile, plainly thinking Western ways a trifle pedantic, 'we value friendship here!'

Meanwhile, a weekend visit to the mountains suggested that her family were accepting her new way of life. Her father told her how proud he was to have such a strong, independent daughter, while her mother and sisters showered her with gifts. Item after item tumbled onto her bed at the Y—clothing, make-up, perfume. 'I don't know why they're giving me all these things,' she said delightedly. The haul also included some much-loved possessions from her wardrobe at home. 'My sea-dress! I have my sea-dress!' she exulted, pulling a denim bikini out of the depths of her bag.

But within weeks, the delicate framework of her new life collapsed. Her boss, a married man, propositioned her, making it clear that, if she declined, she should leave. Indignant, she left the next day. Her only other source of income was an NGO research project contracted to her by one of her university professors. But payment was overdue, and the parties responsible seemed reluctant to cough up. Mean-

41

while, her father had resumed his patriarchal stance and rang her often, questioning her movements and exhorting her to return home. He was particularly angry if he found her going to the shop or eating a café meal in the evening, as the code of conduct that governed life in the mountains decreed that it was improper for a young woman to be 'outside' after dark.

There was no shortage of men seeking to rein her in. Her leaving home had prompted her to finish with her boyfriend, a rather leaden young man she had been seeing with her parents' approval. One night, he turned up and sat in the lobby of the Y while we were cooking up one of our vegetable messes in the kitchen upstairs. He rang her mobile repeatedly. Each time, Abir patiently answered his questions about what she was doing. After the sixth call, she laid down her spoon. 'I will just go down and see him for five minutes,' she said calmly. 'He's upset.'

Ten minutes later, she was back, visibly shaken. She had been seen, her ex had said, riding in a car with another man. He wanted to know who he was. When Abir refused to tell him, he had pushed her and stormed off, shouting a dark hint at her immorality at the receptionist: 'Watch out for this lady!'

For the next few days, she was pale and tearful. To discourage unwanted attentions, she stopped wearing make-up and donned a wedding ring as she hawked her CV around the city. Meanwhile, her former boss was harassing her with phone calls, questioning her right to the wages she had been paid so far. We hold a council of war over a bowl of *fuul* on the Corniche. 'Are there no employment laws against this sort of thing?' I ask, frustrated on her behalf.

'There are, but they cost a lot of money,' she replies, her face tense. *Wasta*, it seemed, was the only real option and as an inexperienced, lone woman, she didn't have much.

'For God's sake, don't let employers know that you've left your parents' home,' I counsel her. 'They will just take advantage if they know that you're vulnerable.'

She was leaning increasingly heavily on me, frequently appearing in my room in a state of panic about one or other of her problems. Often her dilemmas were fairly trivial, but Abir lived life at high-tempo, and even meeting a friend could take on an urgent, cosmic significance requiring copious amounts of support and advice.

But I had to admire her determination. 'Since I left home, I don't cry any more,' she says, as she perched on my flowery counterpane one afternoon. 'When I was at home, I used to go to my room and cry, because my father interfered in every problem. Now, when I face a problem, I keep smiling, and I think, "How can I solve this problem?"' She sniffed, on the verge of tears again. 'Maybe it's good that I face all these problems now, while I'm young. This way, I learn how to deal with myself, and with society.'

Now I was due for a weekend away from Abir's problems, to explore the Maronite heartlands in northern Lebanon. I would stay in Bcharre, the principal village and home to the Phalangist militiaman Samir Geagea. Rather more spiritually, it was also the birthplace of Lebanon's philosopher-poet Khalil Gibran, author of the international bestseller *The Prophet*.

I particularly wanted to explore the nearby Qadisha Valley, the deep, twelve-mile gorge whose southern tip starts at Bcharre and which is only accessible by foot. Fleeing Muslim persecution in the fifteenth century, the Maronites had moved their patriarchs' seat from Byblos to the valley's oldest monastery at Qannoubin. The move had been the making of them, forging an identity in which an ascetic, contemplative spirituality went hand in hand with a warrior-

43

like vigilance. 'Wadi Qannoubin,' says their official website, 'is all crag and mountain rock, soaring heights and plunging depths. It is a land still bearing the imprint of its creator, and is a source of revelation and inspiration to action. There the Maronite has been schooled in forcefulness and obstinacy, to become a man of bold initiative.'

These days, the valley was almost empty, most inhabitants driven out by war and poverty. Qannoubin was inhabited only during the summer months by an order of Antonine nuns who came back each year once all threat of snow had passed. I wanted to visit them. 'I think they are back now,' Bcharre's main hotel owner Wadih Chbat told me when I rang him from Beirut. 'And we have a new hermit here, from Colombia. He speaks six languages. When he's not praying, or working, he receives people.'

The bus bobs along the high mountain roads that lead from Tripoli to Bcharre. 'Soon I will show you a crocodile,' says the girl next to me, laughingly. Sure enough, out of the window to my left, a reptilian body stretches out along a crest of rock, its eye bulging, jaw half-open, and bony tail curling off into the distance. Around us, the world has become vertical: rock disappears into cloud or plunges into ravines and the leggy trunks of the pines stretch into shaggy green tops. Even the houses have a peculiarly vertical look, pinned to the mountainside with long columns that run from roof to ground.

Finally we arrive in Bcharre, and I step out onto the pavement with my rucksack. The atmosphere is sleepy as I walk down the main street. An elderly shopkeeper is snoozing beside his stock of fruit and vegetables and a few doors down, a young man surveys his greengrocery empire. He sports a large wooden cross, but his crisp white T-shirt and stylish sunglasses suggest that, like many of the young here, he may soon be tempted elsewhere by the city lights. After weeks of Beirut's big car culture, I stare in surprise as a Volkswagen chugs past, the body eaten away with rust, its top sliced off to reveal a cargo of mud and stone. The street is lined with them; apparently the little beetle is the car of choice here, not too grand to do a bit of farm work and reliable enough to start on a cold morning. Someone has even bought a new one, and its shiny gold paint sparkles in the mountain air.

In the heart of the village, the guardian of Gibran's house unlocks the door to his family home. Inside there is a single stone room, with a roof of cedar beams and rocks jutting out of the rough earth floor. I look at the white metal bedstead and dark wood furniture that made up the family of seven's worldly goods, and wonder aloud how ideas of such universal resonance could have come from a poor boy belonging to a small Christian sect. 'He had a big mind!' exclaims the keeper, a well-dressed woman with stone-grey hair, with evident pleasure. 'The books came from our God!'

She adds, with even greater pride: 'Here, we are Maronites.'

'Is there anyone here, even one person, who isn't?'

'No'

I make my way to the outskirts of the village and up a hillside track to the Musée Gibran, a low, white building built on the site of a seventh-century hermitage. The ticket man hands me a book and gestures to the network of galleries that houses Gibran's paintings: 'You guide yourself.' There is not another soul in the place. Alone in an art gallery. Luxury.

I walk slowly through the white stone rooms. Despite being better known as a writer, Gibran was a prolific artist in the tradition of William Blake and Samuel Palmer, and it quickly becomes clear that painting was a vehicle for a lifelong preoccupation with the relation between man and nature. The pictures are arranged chronologically, and the early ones depict a peaceable state of affairs, with archetypal figures walking naked among the rocks. The titles are equally un-

45

troubled: 'Woman and Harmony in Nature', and 'Joyful Horizons towards which Nature Invited Us'.

But in subsequent rooms the idealized vision breaks down, giving way to a titanic struggle between good and evil, separation and unity. Nature becomes threatening, indifferent, other, and now the naked figures stagger about under swirling black clouds or coil over rocks, their death-mask faces thrown back in anguish. The titles reflect this bleakness: 'Darkness of Death, the Nature-Cemetery' or simply: 'Anguish', 'Despair'. The half-man, half-beast figure of a centaur canters through the landscape. Finally, after a set of portraits inspired by a series of family bereavements, comes resolution. 'Silence', whispers one title, 'Meditation leading to Silence', another, and 'Towards Eternity', another.

In the later rooms, the images become repetitive, somehow less energized than their predecessors, and I feel my interest waning. Then, right at the end of the gallery, I stop in front of three small pencil sketches entitled 'Face of Jesus'.

The third and last of the pictures is the one that adorns the cover of *The Prophet*, a world-famous image that I have seen hundreds of times before. The other two are its prototypes, evidently part of the artist's struggle to get it right. The first has the makings of the distinctive face, its faint lineaments emerging out of the paper like a photograph in the process of development; the second is a more technical affair, highly competent but somehow lacking in life. The final version combines both elements, and something more.

I peer at it, my face right up against the picture. Close up, I can see every pencil stroke in fine detail, but instead of diminishing the effect of the portrait, something else happens. The face of the prophet seems to shimmer, its Eastern features animated by an expression combining sorrow and wisdom. Above all, it conveys compassion, as if its owner sees all human follies but can neither prevent nor condemn them. The effect is so powerful that I step back in surprise, shake my head, and move away. After a minute or so, I go back and look again. There is the same dizzying effect: the sense of the face's movement, and a feeling of being drawn in as if to a *mandala* for meditation. Puzzled, I repeat the process several times, walking back into the previous gallery to restore my sense of the banal. Each time I return to the face, the same thing happens. Eventually I give up, concluding that somehow the original has a power lacking in its reproductions.

Downstairs, I buy a copy of *The Prophet*, which I have never read. The image on the cover stares back at me: an interesting, aesthetic face, but somehow flat.

The next morning, equipped with Mr Chbat's advice and a rudimentary map, I set out for my day in Qadisha or, as it translates, Holy Valley. It is Sunday, and before I leave the village, I want to go to church. I head towards the Carmelite church of St. Joseph's, where nine o'clock mass is about to begin.

Inside, kitsch prettiness reigns. There are columns of caramel marble and walls of sky blue, and endless vases of pink and yellow flowers. A statue of the Virgin stands in an arc of fairground lights, although the full effect is diminished as some of the bulbs have blown. Regarded adoringly by four curl-headed angels, Jesus floats on a cloud above the altar in pale blue robes.

The Carmelites came to Lebanon in the seventeenth century as part of a wave of Western missionaries. Although they were Catholics following a Western rite, they adopted Arabic as their liturgical language, forming a new, hybrid church culture. Now, I was told, the locals barely distinguish between the brown-robed Carmelites and their Maronite counterparts, simply seeing them as providing a choice of venue and priest.

47

Despite its lack of music, the service has an incantatory rhythm, as the priest's intoned prayers are met by answering murmurs from the pews. The congregation is full of young families and couples. Two small boys pass the peace to the congregation with self-conscious pride, enfolding the hands of each person at the end of each pew in between their own small ones. At collection time, an ancient assistant priest shuffles down the aisles with the plastic basket. He swings violently from side the side as he goes, giving the impression that the next step will tip him over.

As the congregation trickles out, I approach Father Bernard. At first, he is diffident about talking to me. Father Georges at the Maronite church of Mar Saba down the road will know more, he says, and anyway, his French is better. But as I am turning to go, he says: *Vous voulez un café?*

He leads me upstairs to a modern room lined with sofas, and the ancient assistant sets down a tray of Lebanese coffee. Father Bernard is in his seventies, with twinkly brown eyes behind gold-rimmed glasses. He sits, his brown robe comfortably stretched over parted legs, the sun back-lighting his head through a flowery curtain. Strictly speaking, he says in his halting French, the order requires priests to move on every three years. But he has managed to escape the rule, spending the last twenty years in Bcharre.

'Have things changed much during that time?'

He shakes his head regretfully. 'No, not much. The war delayed progress a lot: other places have seen a lot of change, but here, no. Mountain people are more courageous than elsewhere, but in the end, they lost. Now they've lost political power. There's nothing to live on here—there are apple orchards, for which there's a market once a year. How can people live on that? We don't have good roads, but everyone else does. That's something for the government to do.'

'How do people you talk to every day feel?'

'They feel very bad. They are never satisfied, neither with the government, nor with the situation here. They would like a president who works for the interest of the country, and not for Syria.'

He is growing so sad as he talks about the plight of his community that I feel the need to cheer him up. 'At least, there were many young people in church this morning,' I say.

'Thank God, there has been a great return to Christianity in Lebanon,' he agrees more brightly. 'Many people come to mass, and there are also lots of people who find they have a religious vocation, both men and women. We have lay priests who help to look after people. The numbers have gone up since the war, after the horror of it.'

'But the numbers of Christians are also going down, with emigration.'

'Yes. That's what I want you to understand.' He points emphatically. 'It's only in Lebanon that the Christians have had a bit of power. In Egypt, Syria, Turkey, Iran—in all the other countries of the region, Christians count for nothing. A Muslim can have a family of twenty-five, with three or four wives, but a Christian only has about three children. Hence their disappearance. If things continue like this, there's great danger that Lebanon will become like other countries.'

As if in tune with the theme of a dying community, the ancient assistant shuffles perilously down the corridor past the open door.

'But many people in Lebanon believe in secularism now,' I console him. 'That's a guarantee of tolerance of sorts.'

'Christians believe in secularism, yes, but the Muslims, no. I accept the Muslim, but he doesn't accept me. They say one thing in front of us, but they do another. There's a lot of talk, but it's empty. They want to Islamicize the earth, so that the Christians won't be able to stay. They've already started to buy land here, in Arqa'—he gestures to the left, 'and Aley'—he points to the right.

49

Like bishop Rai, the building of the mosque next to Byblos monastery troubles him. 'It was to say, "We are here". Every day, they play discs saying *Allahu Akbar*. Every day. They don't leave us in peace.' He looks old and tired now, and his twinkle has gone. Then, as if to cheer us both up, he asks, 'Would you like to see the wine cellar?'

We go down into the bowels of the building. When the Carmelite monks came from France and Italy, they brought their viticultural skills with them. Now they have a small but thriving wine industry, hiring local labour to turn grapes from the Bekaa valley into wine. The cellar is full of plastic tubs, wooden barrels and trailing pipes, and the acrid-sweet smell of vinegar hangs in the air. Father Bernard pulls bottle after bottle from the rows of boxes, proudly displaying wines of different kinds and grades. There's dry and sweet versions of red, white and rosé. 'This is the finest quality,' he says, presenting me with a bottle of the dry red. Then we tour the liqueurs: there is Cointreau, mint, cocoa and a mysterious herb blend, bearing the promise 'Salvia Magica' on its label. 'Do you know what the magic ingredient is?' Father Bernard asks impishly. 'Sage.'

I leave the church and walk along the deserted road towards the village of Hawqa, getting hotter and hotter. Mr. Chbat suggested that I get a taxi to drop me by the path that leads down into the gorge by the church of Santa Marina, but it is a while before one stops. Even then, neither the driver nor his friend seem able to understand anything about where I want to go, and after an increasingly bad-tempered journey, I am deposited where the road runs out. I look around at my new surroundings. Below me, the bottom of the valley is filled with fruit trees, greenery and rushing water. Above, the rock is bare and stern, cutting into the sky. Halfway up the mountainside an elegant, balconied building appears to be growing out of the rock. It must be Qannoubin.

Slowly, I make my way up the winding path that leads to it, and walk through the outer gates. Inside, the monastery is in full swing, black-robed monks circulating efficiently around the pristine courtyard. Tubs of red and pink geraniums set off the pale honey stone. There's a museum containing the Middle East's first printing press, and a souvenir shop staffed by chic, supercilious sales women. Visitors wander in and out of the various attractions. I could easily be in Italy. I am further north up the valley than I intended, at St. Anthony of Kozhaya, one of the largest monasteries around. Since the rest of the gorge is only accessible by foot, I have a long walk ahead of me.

I collar one of the monks, an urbane, blue-eyed man skilfully manoeuvring a smart white car on a sandy ledge. If I follow the road for twenty minutes, I will arrive at the path leading down to the hermit, he tells me. From there, I can walk on to Qannoubin.

'How many hermits are here?'

'Two,' he says. His arm sweeps the rocky horizon. 'Our hermit is sick. He's eighty-four. He fell down and broke his legs. He couldn't stay there, so we brought him here. When he's better, he'll go back.'

I wonder aloud whether, at eighty-four, living alone among the rocks is really wise. 'What you can do?' replies the monk philosophically. Then he adds briskly: 'Okay? Have fun!' A blue eye winks at me, and he's gone.

Half an hour's climb up the winding, rock-rimmed road, and there's no sign of the path down to the hermit. The sky is leaden and, with the afternoon marching on, I'm in the middle of nowhere. Then, by the roadside, I see a tumbledown building on a desolate patch of stony earth. Only some wire-enclosed chickens and a lone, tethered donkey suggest that people are attempting to farm this arid land.

Hesitantly, I approach. Behind a corrugated iron fence, a striking-looking man is scraping the brown soil with a hoe. He wears a

51

cowboy-style black shirt and jeans, but the tanned skin and hawk nose beneath the wide-brimmed hat evoke the Indian. A woman beside him is pointing to the ground, scolding him for some oversight. But when she looks up and sees me, her face clears. *Ahlan*, she says. Welcome.

It is another half hour's walk to the path that leads down to the hermitage, she tells me; the monk, used to driving, must have underestimated the distance. Disconsolately, I turn away and resume my trudging. 'Haven't you got a car?' asks a child, pityingly, from her perch atop a wall. Then the smallholder's Range Rover roars beside me, its entire bodywork brown with rust. I climb in, and for a few minutes we bump along the narrow road, pulling up by a stony path that descends into the gorge. Gestures and a flood of Arabic convey, 'Tell the hermit that the Captain says hello,' and, waving my offer of payment away, he tells me to hurry.

In the chasm, large billowing clouds hang, as if suspended, at eye-height. I clamber down for fifteen minutes and then, rounding a rocky corner, a vista opens up. On a piece of flat, jutting rock a single olive tree stands in a carefully-tilled square of soil. A few yards away a large wooden cross looks out over the valley. The remains of a fire lie nearby. This must be the place.

But before I can make myself known, strange, chattering sounds come from the caves in the rock face above. They are distinctly human, but not like any language I have ever heard, and they sound angry. When I walk down to the olive tree and come fully into view, they stop. Five minutes lengthen into ten. From the caves above, a stick cracks.

It would be rude to interrupt a hermit in his solitary activities, I think, so I wait on. The holy man will surely come down and greet me when he is ready. Finally, aware of the lowering mist and the long walk ahead, I make a desperate bid for an interview.

Monsieur! *Monsieur*! My voices bounces back, clarion-clear, from the rocks. There is no way anyone could fail to hear me.

Il est très difficile pour moi de revenir.

The caves above return silence.

Je suis très désolée de vous déranger. Mais j'ai marché presque tout la journée pour vous voir.

My voice, echoed back, sounds plaintive now.

Some shouting issues faintly from the rocks, but I can't make it out. But, just possibly, it could be *Allez-vous en*! Picking up my rucksack, I make my way further along the gorge, reasoning that, by nature, a hermit is unsociable. But I'm half heartbroken to find, instead of a wise old man with a beard, a mad misanthropist chattering to himself among the rocks.

On the path further down the gorge, I meet a group of young Lebanese hikers. 'There's a beautiful thing there!' their leader shouts to me, pointing to the path snaking around the rock in the opposite direction. 'A man with a white beard. But hurry, he wants to pray!'

I follow his gaze. Hanging on the rock behind me is a blue sign, which reads: 'Dear visitor, the hermitage of Hawqa is strictly for praying. We kindly ask you not to camp, sleep or eat.' I follow the narrow, twisting path, through a pretty wrought-iron gate. Another gateway leads up some stone steps, and I'm in a tiny, shaded courtyard, with little doors set into warm yellow stone. It could easily be the dwelling of a storybook character. I peer into an open door—there's a tiny chapel cut out of the rock, complete with altar and miniature pews. But the place seems empty.

From the stairs below, there's a sudden clatter. 'Dario!' 'Dario!' female voices call. Two teenage girls rush into the courtyard, calling and knocking on each of the tiny doors in turn. Then, suddenly, a door swings open, revealing a bearded figure in a hooded habit. One

53

of girls immediately rushes over, and fervently raises the front of his cassock to her lips.

'And who is this?' The hermit has turned to me. Sinking onto a stone step with fatigue, I explain my purpose. 'Ah, a journalist,' he says, knowingly. The face beneath the hood is unremarkable, with a pug nose and straggly grey beard, but his small brown eyes are friendly. He knows Britain, he tells me conversationally; he has lived in Brighton. 'You're the first woman I've seen alone here,' he adds, in his halting, Spanish-accented English. 'Usually they're afraid of'—he points to the ground below, searching for a way to express its treachery—'the stones.' Although he stands formally, hands clasped over his belly, his demeanour is attentive: he has seen a need—an exhausted woman burning with questions—and has decided to meet it. I fumble for my notebook. 'Why did you come to Lebanon?'

'I chose this place because only in Lebanon are there hermits,' he replies. 'Like the old fathers.'

Father Escobar had been teaching theology and clinical psychology in Colombia when he had an epiphany. 'One day, I was in my room and I heard a voice inside my head. In one moment, I quit the life of action and went to contemplation,' he goes on. He set about learning Arabic, came to Lebanon and joined the monastery of St. Anthony. His longed-for passage to the hermit's life in August 2000, at the age of sixty four, was relatively quick. 'At last the Father Superior gave me permission to be a hermit. Usually, we must stay at least ten years in the monastery after taking vows, but after two years I got permission.'

'What is your day like?' I ask.

'I spend fourteen hours praying and three working. I have two for studying and five for sleeping, but if I am sick, I can sleep six hours.' He chuckles ironically at the leniency afforded by illness. 'Usually I

54

speak to nobody. I began speaking to you because I thought you were with my friends.'

But I'd heard local people talk about visiting him, I say, including the Captain.

'Ah, if you're a friend of the Captain's, I will speak to you!' he replies jovially. 'I talk to neighbours and to people who come for confession, young people with problems with their families.' He gestures vaguely to the girl who is sitting next to me on the stone steps, fidgeting in frustration at his lack of attention. 'But not just for talking, for bla bla bla. You are lucky.'

'We eat only once a day, never meat,' He is volunteering information, anticipating the kind of details that will interest me. 'I eat what I plant. During Lent, I eat less than usual—no fruit, milk, cookies or sugar. We have five Lents during the year, periods of fasting of up to fifty days. I chose this place because it was difficult to get here. They put in the steps after I came. I cannot go out, although once a year I must go to the monastery to renew my vows.'

'How do you find the spiritual life?'

'I am happy now,' he replies equably. 'I enjoy it. My only difficulty is the beard and the long hair—I don't like it. It's obligatory not to cut it, and it's my only problem. The other things—eating only once a day, sleeping only five hours, I don't mind.'

I put away my pad, feeling that I've trespassed long enough. But he has questions of his own. Do I know the way back? He's concerned about my long walk to Qannoubin along the steep, rocky path. Do I live in London? Am I—the inevitable question for visitors to the Middle East—married?

I am single, I tell him.

'But you are young.'

'Not so young,' I demur.

'So, in England, they are blind?'

For a moment I don't get it. Then I put back my head and roar with laughter. He joins in. It's the first time I've been flirted with by a hermit.

Late afternoon sun fills the lower reaches of the valley. The mist has lifted and the light plays on the trees, making the leaves translucent. Two nuns emerge out of the greenery, serviceable shoes striking out beneath knee-length black skirts. They are from Qannoubin, returned for the summer season. The leading nun is in her sixties, stout and energetic, with a sensible face behind large, plastic-framed glasses and a toothy smile. The other, younger and shyer, hovers behind, a hesitant curiosity lighting her face.

They are from Qannoubin, having just arrived for the summer season. 'I am researching the history of religious life from the beginning,' announces Sister Clemence, the older nun, when hearing of my project. 'When I have finished that, I will study the present.'

I was on my way to visit them, I say.

She smiles approvingly. 'No one studies the sisters.'

I think of the assured, moneyed atmosphere of the Monastery of St. Anthony: the freshly-restored stonework, the tourists circulating. 'What, they always study the men?'

'Yes.'

'In that case, I will definitely come and see you tomorrow,' I promise.

She gives me instructions for a quicker way out of the valley, a sharp left after the tiny church of Santa Marina, and a steep climb to the villages above.

'Not to be lost!' Her parting call echoes down the path after me.

An hour later, I'm hopelessly lost.

After a long climb, only a mass of rock looms above me; there's no sign of the road. It's an hour before sunset, and a thick mountain mist is already descending. Worried about the diminishing light, I retrace my steps down the mountainside. At the bottom, by the chapel, a black figure appears from behind a tree. It is Sister Clemence. 'What happened?' she asks, almost crossly.

Qannoubin lies just along the path, a rectangle of pink-yellow rock clinging to the cliff face. The easier way out of the gorge lies two hours further on. 'It is too late for you to go on,' decides Sister Clemence. 'Tonight, you will sleep here. Tomorrow, you will visit! But first we must ask Sister Mona's permission.'

She leads me through a long stone tunnel. Monks' cells line the wall on our right; on our left a deep hole recedes into darkness. 'That's where the Patriarch used to hide from the Ottomans,' she says with pride. 'How many of you are here?' I imagine a lively community of tens of nuns, filling every corner of the convent with some sort of indefinable, nun-like busyness.

'Two,' says Sister Clemence. 'We came last week. But next week, there will be eight.'

We enter the courtyard. It has a dilapidated, higgledy-piggledy air, with doors and archways going off in every direction. A chapel emerges out of the rock that anchors the building to the cliff and opposite, a balcony-fringed patio juts out into open space.

'Hooey! Hooey!' Sister Clemence approaches the frosted glass doors guarding the nuns' private prayer area with determination, adding with a glint of humour. 'Sister Mona prays all the time.'

With Sister Mona's approval for my stay granted, I am shown a Spartan bedroom with a stone floor and dove-grey walls. Tiny, shuttered windows look out onto the face of the valley opposite. Despite its bareness, the room has a cosy, secluding feel.

'I will give you my bedroom,' Sister Clemence insists, gathering up her possessions—a book about Christ and a packet of tissues. 'I will give you water, and something to eat.' She is getting into the swing of having a visitor now. 'You can lock the door, you will be safe! You are studying the life of the sisters—you will be like a hermit here!'

Sister Mona puts a clean duvet cover and pillow on the bed and fluffs them out. A comforting smell of freshly washed linen floats up into the air. Then she carries a new bottle of baby shampoo into my en suite stone bathroom.

'We are going to pray now,' says Sister Clemence, explaining that between six thirty and seven the whole of the Maronite community, wherever it is in the world, says the same prayers together. 'We will be back in half an hour.'

She looks at me curiously. 'Are you Catholic?'

'No ...' I stall. The question is difficult. How could I explain in this land of labels that while I was no longer, strictly speaking, a Christian, I was still some sort of believer?

'Anglican?'

She takes my ambiguous gesture for assent, and a toothy grin spreads across her face. 'Ah, the Anglicans are very mystic,' she says approvingly.

Slowly, a blue-black darkness descends onto the valley. The hulking forms of the mountains rise solidly, thrown into relief by the pinks and charcoals of the evening sky. Now and then a single bird swoops across the horizon. The silence is gathering, broken only by a clatter that comes from one of the valley's few remaining inhabitants working in an olive grove below.

In the stone kitchen, a monastic feast has been laid out for me. There is chicken noodle soup, bread, Baby Bel cheese, spaghetti with pine nuts and oil, cake, fruit. I pick up the tin of Zwan luncheon meat she has left as an extra measure, and examine it, smirking to myself. When Sister Clemence returns, I tentatively show her the two spoonfuls of soup left in the bottom of the pan. Are they worth keeping? She looks thoroughly shocked. 'Oh no, we don't throw anything away. We are poor persons.'

'Now,' she adds with relish. 'Would you like me to tell you about the life of the sisters?'

The three of us repair to a tiny sitting room. I sit, notebook and pen dutifully in hand, and Sister Clemence begins the instruction.

'Our work here is to receive pilgrims and to have a little experience of hermitage for six months. But after that we go back to our work in the community,' she says.

'What is your work?'

'I spent thirty years teaching; I taught French in schools.'

Her hands clasped in her lap, her gaze straight ahead, she tells of the hardships faced by the Maronite fathers; their courage as they resisted persecution by Mamelukes and Ottomans, talking as passionately as if their experiences were drawn from her own store of personal memories. 'Life was very hard for us. We were occupied by the Ottomans, and during that time we were considered second class citizens. The patriarch and the monks worked in the monasteries to earn a living and pay the taxes; there were more every year.' But despite these difficulties, the Maronites had thrived, and Qannoubin's proudest era began when their beloved patriarch Stephen Douayhi chose to make it his home.

As she talks, a second, unofficial story of the female struggle for spiritual expression begins to surface. The tiny church of Santa Marina, which had marked the turning to my abortive climb out of the valley earlier, had been built in homage to a fifth-century woman who disguised herself as a man in order to enter the monastery. As Marinos the monk, she was falsely accused of getting a local girl pregnant, and expelled. But she took on the child herself, even—some

59

said—miraculously producing milk from her own breast. When the mistake was realized, she was made a saint.

But women's attempts to live the life of contemplation were still hampered in the centuries that followed; their convents lacked the independence enjoyed by their male counterparts and, in the twentieth century, the Church authorities encouraged them to forsake the closed order and go out and serve the community. While St. Antony's had been lavishly restored by the Church, the partial re-opening of Qannoubin in 1993 had only come about thanks to money from an independent benefactor.

The nuns saw it as their duty to keep the tradition of hermitage alive. 'Sister Mona'—she gestures to her colleague who, without fluent French or English, is sitting listening quietly—'was the first one; she is permanent here, the manager. She is very strict about the time of prayer!'

Sister Mona, realizing she is being teased, flashes back an answering smile.

'How long have you been a nun?'

'Fifty years. I was very young. Now they are not allowed so young. I liked to pray in our village—I had my grandmother, who was very devoted to our Lady and to prayer.'

'Have you ever regretted it?'

'No, for me, no,' she smiles serenely. 'It is a grace. There have been some difficulties, but that is normal. I have never regretted it.'

'And Sister Mona?' I have little idea of her age. Her shyness gives her face a youthful look, but locks of grey hair fall on her forehead beneath her veil.

'Twenty years. I came at twenty-two. Because...' She searches for words—'I love Jesus!' She dissolves into girlish, almost coy, laughter.

'Are there more or fewer nuns joining the holy life?'

60

'A little bit fewer, because the young women have become free, educated,' replies Sister Clemence. 'But there are more and more young men since the war.' Her convent of two hundred, the Ecole des Soeurs at Nabatiyeh in southern Lebanon, has had six novices this year. 'For a little community it is very good,' she says with satisfaction. 'Many young people emigrated—they don't believe in a future for Lebanon. But we continue to resist, like our ancestors here.'

'How can you resist?'

'By staying. By keeping the virtues of our people, family life, and being devoted to God. Our country is beautiful, it has a historical past, and we don't have the right to leave it. But the young people can't accept that. They say, "We must have our future. We waited for years and nothing happened." It is a desperate situation.'

'What are your relations like with other communities?'

'We did a lot of good during the war,' she replies. 'There were a hundred of us in Nabatiyeh; the rest were Shiites, and they were afraid of the sisters—now they are not. We don't try to convert them; it is not good. Our aim is to be at their service, to communicate the spirit of Christianity without converting.' She smiles at the memory of one particular year when the two communities worshipped together. 'Every day we had a prayer together. There was no dogma, nothing that could hurt them, just a feeling of religious life.'

Her mood sobers as she starts to fret about the threat to the Maronite community's survival posed by the region's rising Islamic fundamentalism—a threat rooted in the mistreatment of Arabs in which the West is implicated. 'The war in Palestine, the war in Iraq—they are treated like beasts,' she says vehemently. 'We are not Muslims, but we suffer with them. The Christians are allied to the Western countries. We are divided between two worlds. We don't want the US and Great Britain to lose the war; we want there to be an *entente*.'

In Lebanon, I say, all roads lead to politics. The nuns laugh and agree, and we part for the night. 'Are you frightened to be alone?' worries Sister Clemence, offering me her mobile. I have never been less frightened in my life. The dove-grey room enfolds me, and I sleep.

'Hooey!'

Sister Clemence's promised morning call sings outside my door.

I'm already awake. I could hardly not be. Outside the little windows of my room the May morning is alive with birdsong and the rushing of water. It is another luminously beautiful day in the Qadisha Valley.

Before leaving, I look around the monastery chapel. A large fresco takes up much of one wall, painted in rich, earthy tones of terracotta and green. The Virgin Mary stands at its centre, flanked by the Father and Son; above her hovers the holy spirit in the form a swallow. But her feet, planted on the cedars of Lebanon, are rooted in the earth. A line of Maronite patriarchs look up at her adoringly. It is a visual account of Maronite cosmology, presenting Mary as the link between heaven and earth.

In front of the altar, two wooden tables have been laid out in readiness for coffins. Later that morning the convent will hold a funeral for two locals who, part of the Maronite diaspora, had emigrated to Australia. The priest and his wife had died abroad five years apart, but now they were both dead, their families were bringing their bodies back for burial in their home soil.

'How will they get the coffins up here?' I ask, mystified.

'Oh, they are strong, they will manage,' says Sister Clemence airily, flexing her black-clothed biceps to evoke the presence of muscular men.

62

I thank them and say my farewells, leaving a small donation which I realize with regret will go into the Church's coffers, rather than save the nuns more thriftiness with spoonfuls of soup. Then I set out along the valley path for the two-hour walk to the end of the gorge. Trees are swaying in the breeze, and everything seems alive with light and movement. In anticipation of the funeral party, little black flags have been staked out along the way.

I see almost no one. Recording a journey through Lebanon in the 1960s, Colin Thubron chronicles 'a time of innocence', when it was possible to vanish alone into the hills, drink from the streams, sleep under the stars and not see another soul for days. When he did encounter people, they were generally simple mountain folk, living peacefully among the rocks. War and modernity changed all that, making it, he notes in a later preface, a 'world irrevocably gone.'

But now, alone in this sun-filled, rejoicing landscape, that lost world briefly reappears.

I walk on by the bubbling river, over little stone bridges. A brown-skinned man is quietly tending a tiny plot of land by the river. His few square feet of potato plants are just beginning to flourish.

There is no sign of the funeral procession, which is now an hour and half late. Then, a car comes into view, bumping slowly along the stony track, which is now wide enough for vehicles. A dozen more follow, from beaten-up affairs to the smart Mercedes carrying the coffins. Finally, some Lebanese Maronites are coming home.

3
ISLAM IN DIALOGUE

CHRISTIAN fears about the Islamicization of Lebanon were balanced by competing claims about the tolerance of its Muslims. I wanted to explore this further, and I had one very promising lead: the name of a Shiite cleric who went out of his way to engage with other religions. Sheikh Mohammad el Hajj, my contact told me, who ran a small institute of his own in Beirut's southern suburbs, had incurred the wrath of his fellow Muslims for worshipping with Christians.

A call to the institute secures an invitation to visit and meet the sheikh. But on the day of the interview, his student-assistant Amira calls to suggest that I might like to hear him speak at a university seminar that afternoon. Her directions have the usual Lebanese vagueness—the Institute of Christian and Islamic Studies, St. Joseph's University—and so it is that I arrive, via a detour to the wrong campus, three-quarters of an hour late.

Hot and tired, I enter the cool white lecture hall and sit down thankfully amid the rows of listening people. The sheikh is in full swing, and it's immediately clear that my lack of Arabic will in no way diminish the entertainment value of his performance. His voice rises to a crescendo and then falls dramatically as he builds his argument, point by point. His mastery of timing and tone is rivalled only by a Mr. Bean-like ability to twist his face into an array of caricatured expressions: severe is replaced by ironic, which softens into benign.

The gestures that illustrate his points are a show in themselves: his hands open, questioningly, circle the air and arc together in conclusion. A finger points, arrestingly, at the audience, alights reflectively on his jaw and then both hands, with a final rhetorical twirl, come to rest on the desk before him. It's a class act, by any standards.

The audience listens attentively. They are a mixed, multi-confessional crowd: headscarves mingle with flowing tresses and the ranks of grey heads are peppered with the blue veils of two nuns and a single black, all-enveloping *chador*. In front of me, two thirty-something men in smart suits are clearly messing about, showing each other pictures on their mobile phones. We break for refreshments.

'Alex?' A dumpy, veiled woman with a kindly face is standing in front of me. Amira takes my hand in hers and sweeps me off to meet fellow followers of Sheikh Mohammad. There is Zeinab, whose blue-green eyes radiate a fierce intellectual curiosity beneath her tightly-pinned veil, and a stylish woman with flowing, bleached-blond locks and avant-garde silver jewellery. 'They will translate for you,' Amira tells me.

As the session resumes, I listen approvingly as the sheikh makes repeated references to *al akl*. How refreshing to hear such down-to-earth references to food in a spiritual discourse, I think. In the question and answer session that follows, he clearly overshadows the two other speakers flanking him, a Jesuit priest called Samir Beshara and the director of Lebanon's Sunni Religious Council, Sheikh Mohammed Nokari. He concludes a highly abstract discourse on the nature and limits of freedom with a series of hyperbolic examples, asking, his eyebrows sardonically raised: would you jump off a building to express your freedom? 'Oh, he's funny,' sighs Zeinab, as people gather themselves to leave. 'He's funny.'

65

She and Amira exchange amused glances when I share my impressions of the lecture. 'That's not the Arabic for food!' she says. 'That's *al Aql*—the mind, the spirit!'

Clambering into Amira's car, we head south through the city and plough into Dahiye. For many Lebanese, even the name—Arabic for suburbs—conjures up images of poverty and chaos. But for Westerners, the area has even ghastlier associations as the place where hostages such as John McCarthy and Terry Waite were held during the 1980s. The kidnappings were attributed to Hezbollah who later denied them, blaming the freelance militia spawned by the civil war. Whatever the truth, Hezbollah's continuing dominance over the area added to its mystique. I had heard stories of the party's vice-like grip on the community's morality—the suppression of entertainment, or even the odd beating—which occasionally filtered out.

But now, with the light fading, a grey gloom has descended and the district of Haret Hreik is a picture of suburban banality. We pull up in front of an unremarkable, two-storey house on the edge of a run-down square. Traffic roars over the flyover into Beirut and children run about in its shadows, shouting. The only indication of the building's loftier purpose is a sign which says 'Transcendental Theosophy Institute: Practical and Theoretical.'

Inside, everything has been arranged for study and contemplation. In the marble-floored classroom, rows of chairs curl reverently around the teacher's desk. A pile of books sits beside the wooden lectern—leather-bound nuggets of prayer, ethics and commentaries on the Koran—some left carelessly open, as if the teacher is about to return. The sheikh's teaching is in the tradition of Mulla Sadra, the influential seventeenth-century Muslim thinker who combined metaphysical philosophy with Shiite theology to form 'transcendent philosophy' or theosophy, a form of wisdom which is supposed to contain direct knowledge of God. It is easy to imagine the room

66

full of eager students, soaking up the spiritual truths being imparted from the front. Small, adjoining rooms have been set aside for the two sexes to pray separately.

The women show me into a sofa-lined room marked 'visitors' to await the sheikh. When he strides in, his long robes flapping about his lanky form, his demeanour is very different from the flamboyant showmanship he displayed earlier. Eyeing me cautiously, he asks a series of questions about my project and intentions. His English is fluent, and well equipped with academic vocabulary. Then, apparently satisfied and without waiting for the prompt of a question, he begins to speak.

'When—you—ask—someone—about—his—principles—philosophy—religion—he—suddenly—changes—his—attitude.' He declares, his dramatic pauses give every word a weight. 'He begins to act as if he is not himself. He starts to speak about abstractions. *I* —he drawls out the 'I' emphatically—'need to touch the truth in our community, our society.'

'Do all the Lebanese all like to live with each other? If I were you'—he puts his hand, stagily, on his heart—'I might make some psychological questions, experimentally. I want to touch the truth in everything they say—when a Muslim says he likes to live with Christians and Druze, I don't want to hear such stories. I want people in Lebanon to tell me what emotions they feel in their hearts towards each other.'

I listen somewhat uneasily. The sheikh's dark eyes rest coldly on me, and his florid style and abrupt shifts in register make it difficult to follow his meaning. Hazily, I realize he is giving me a comment on the realities of religious coexistence, along with a piece of advice on how I should approach my project. He moves seamlessly onto the institute's interfaith work and this elides, equally smoothly, into a speech on the need for tolerance in today's diverse world. His gaze

67

shifts to Amira and Zeinab, who are sitting, raptly attentive, on the sofa opposite, and I realize that I'm not, perhaps, his preferred audience. The paragraphs continue to flow. He describes his own attempts to engage with Westerners while living in Germany, makes a further statement of principle and then illustrates it with some elaborate analogies that I don't follow. Finally, he draws to a close and stares hard at me. It must be time for a question.

'Are you criticized by Muslims for your approach?'

'A lot,' he responds. 'A lot. Most of the criticism is due to ignorance. Some Muslims don't understand what we are doing.'

'What do they object to?'

'Ha!' he responds contemptuously. 'They think that they make Islam weaker when they sit with Christians, the crusaders. Not only in Lebanon, but also in Iran. They hear, for example, that girls and boys study together here. They say, if they are studying together, what are they studying? Perhaps they are studying each other.' His tone drips with irony.

'Do you ever receive threats?'

'No, no. I don't let things get to that limit. I put myself away from their bulldozers and tanks. I always step aside.'

'How?'

'If they say anything about me, I just shut my small mouth. It's already small.' Distracted by his figure of speech, I find myself looking into the depths of his beard. He's right; amid the neatly cropped hair his mouth is unusually, disproportionately small; a bit mean-looking, I can't help thinking, as he carries on talking.

'They are the evil ones,' he pronounces. The dramatic statement about his fellow Shia jolts me back to reality.

'Are they evil or are they just wrong?' I ask.

'No, when you are wrong, you ask,' he replies. 'These are ones who want to get rid of you. They are not wrong, they are evil. There are a lot of these people, in Jordan, in Iran, everywhere. They believe in bad. They are non-ethical in everything they do. I am ready to sit with these Muslims and have invited them many times to sit with me. They refused. They know that when they sit with me they are going to understand everything that I am doing, and that will hurt their intentions.'

Dimly, I realize he is talking principally about Hezbollah. 'What are their intentions?'

'They have their own goals in Lebanon—political ones,' he replies. 'Religion is serving politics. When they defend my country, I just feel respect towards them. I kneel in front of them. I respect the men of resistance as I respect nurses in hospital. But there are many problems with their social attitudes.'

But his tolerance returns when I ask about his attitude to non-monotheistic faiths. 'We were lucky to invite a Hindu female priest,' he says. 'We were very friendly, and we agreed with each other on many subjects.' While the Koran contains everything man needs to know about God, he goes on, other kinds of believers also have access to divine truths.

Huddled together on the sofa opposite, Amira and Zeinab are drinking in every word. Every now and then, when their teacher searches for the right word in English, they supply it, clearly repeating an oft-cited phrase from class. Sometimes, just a beat behind him and smiling and nodding in recognition, they chorus the last few words of his sentence.

Possibly by way of reward, the sheikh launches unexpectedly into a speech extolling the virtues of women, and how the veil is not to be seen as a sign of subordination. 'I always feel proud when I'm with the sisters in my life'—he throws a hand in the women's direction. 'My students, my sisters, my wife, my daughters.'

69

I wait for him to finish his eulogy before putting my next question. My curiosity about this strange set-up is growing, and I wonder aloud who funds it. 'The members,' he replies proudly, adding that one of the administrators mortgaged his house to pay for the building. 'That's one of the sacrifices we make for this place. We all share in the agony and'—he searches for a word, and for once his two students are at a loss. 'Ecstasy,' I suggest after a pause, with some trepidation. 'It's an expression in Eng-.'

'Okay, you're the teacher,' the sheikh interrupts sarcastically. 'Very good.'

'How many students are there?'

'Forty or fifty,' he replies. 'But there used to be seventy to a hundred. We have a filter on the door—a theosophical filtration!' He laughs, and adds seriously: 'Some people won't stay the course.'

After he's left the room, I sink back in my seat, exhausted. The sheikh's lengthy answers have made it one of the longest interviews I have ever done, and his presence has commanded unwavering attention throughout. Instinctively, I turn to the women opposite for some of the sisterly warmth I had felt earlier. But the atmosphere has changed: Zeinab is staring at me with undisguised hostility.

'What's your horoscope?' she demands. I stall, taken aback. I'm surprised that she's interested; I didn't think a love of the esoteric sat easily with devotion to the Prophet.

'I'm very interested.' The blue-green eyes stare hard.

I go with it. 'Sagittarius.'

'Oh they're strong, very strong.' My reply has obviously proved a point. 'They like money.'

'Really?' I'm not sure what is being said, but I know enough about both my star sign and finances to realize that commerce has never been a strong point. 'I've never read that.'

'Well, success,' Zeinab qualifies. 'They have very strong characters and they are sharp-tongued. Very sharp-tongued. Like my teacher'—she gestures at the empty sofa where the sheikh had been sitting. 'He is strong and sharp-tongued. He is Scorpio—they are like Sagittarius.'

I stare at her, stunned. 'Not you!' she snaps. 'My teacher—he is strong and sharp-tongued.'

Then her hostility evaporates as quickly as it came, and within a couple of sentences she is telling me to stay for a year so that she can teach me Arabic.

The two women have been studying at the institute for four years. It is rare to find women devoting themselves to religious study, and I wonder whether it will it lead to a qualification. 'It's continuous study. We will be here until we die!' replies Zeinab. 'If we don't get filtered,' she adds, her tone darkening.

She has chosen a hard way of life, she goes on, because of social attitudes. People want to know what's she's studying, and ask where it gets her, pointing out that if she didn't spend three or four hours a day at the institute, she could earn more money, or travel. But they don't understand what she's getting out of it, she explains, her eyes wide with sincerity—the knowledge of religious philosophy, and important things like how to deal with people.

As we drive back to central Beirut under the night skies, I worry that I'm keeping them from their families. 'Oh no, I'm not married,' smiles Amira, with an expression that is hard to fathom. Neither is Zeinab: in a ruse often deployed by Lebanese women, the wedding band she wears is to ward off unwanted attentions. The revelation that both women are nearing forty makes them seem more vulnerable, lacking a place in a conservative society which respects only wives and mothers. Suddenly their need for the close-knit community provided by the institute becomes clear.

71

Zeinab is shattered, her earlier feistiness drained out of her. 'I need to eat,' she says, apologizing for her faltering English. My blood sugar, too, has plummeted. With the session at the university, we have been listening, mostly to the sheikh, for almost six hours without a break. But she recovers herself enough to tell me how she came to join the institute. Although brought up in the same school of Shiism, she began, at the age of twenty-five, to ask deeper questions about religion. Her questions went unanswered, and her quest for spiritual truth went on unsuccessfully for ten, long years. Then she met Sheikh Mohammad.

He was the first religious man to answer her questions. 'Before I even asked them!' she says, her eyes widening. 'I had never had that before. It was like he could SEE inside me,'—she taps her third eye. 'You have all these questions, and then when you get—how do you say—indubitable answers—and that's the end of them—it's *helas*!' Her hand mimes the finality of this, the eureka moment of her life, her spiritual homecoming. 'When he speaks, I hear the voice of God. But when I used to talk to a certain Muslim, I could see the devil.'

I had another opportunity to see moderate Islam in practice a couple of weeks later. The Middle East Council of Churches, the umbrella body for the region's Christian Churches, was hosting a group of American students preparing for ministry. During the course of a two week tour, the group from the San Francisco Theological Seminary was to meet spiritual and community leaders from across Lebanese society and visit some of the Holy Land's key sights. Their first engagement, in the cool interior of the Near East School of Theology, was a meeting with one of the country's best known Shiite clerics, Sheikh Hani Fahes. A liberal Muslim with good connections in the

Iranian establishment, Fahes was a well-known figure on the circuit of committees trying to improve the country's interfaith relations.

Chatting quietly, the group assembles around the long seminar table towards the end of a warm May afternoon. Fahes moves among them, his portly figure so thoroughly encased in his long grey robe it's as if he's trundling about on castors. His black turban indicates his status as a *sayyed*—a descendent of the prophet—but despite these trappings he exudes an air of solidity and ordinariness. As we settle down for the talk, MECC's general secretary Riad Jarjour leans over to say something in my ear. 'He doesn't shake hands,' he whispers, tactfully omitting to say 'with women.'

From his seat at the top of the table, Fahes' speech ripples gently towards us, a series of short, elegant paragraphs delivered in crystalline classical Arabic, before being rendered into Americanized English by the translator beside him. He has a gift for epigrams that evoke hinterlands of thought, fusing philosophy, religion and politics into short, elegant formulations. 'Complexity is a beautiful thing... the society which is not diverse is less beautiful,' he avers. 'I cannot know myself if I do not know the Other—the Other is a condition of my existence.'

The American students, finally at rest after several days' travelling, listen quietly. A few droop slightly, their heads dipping towards the table.

'Eighty per cent of blood shed is shed in the name of God, and God is innocent of this,' he continues. 'Islam has no designs to impose its view of the world; we don't have any evangelism. Mission is against freedom. When we read the Koran, we don't see a mission in it—what's important is to open the way to God, and the ways are multiple.'

He concludes, and questions are invited. What message would he give to Americans? asks a young woman brightly, clearly thinking of

73

the war on terror. The sheikh, perhaps mindful of the exhaustion of his audience, replies briefly. 'Our message is a message of love. We love you, and we hope that you love us.'

In the social session which follows, a large, young American woman in shorts bounces up him and enthusiastically offers her hand. Without missing a beat, the sheikh shakes it and returns the warmth of her greeting.

Once the Americans have disappeared to their hotel rooms, the sheikh, the translator and I sit down together. Close to, Fahes' large pebble-dash glasses amplify and distort his eyes, but their expression is kindly. What do you consider key to good relations between Christians and Muslims? I ask. The cleric shifts his grey bulk in his chair and clears his throat. 'In our understanding, people themselves work out what these foundations are. For example, people fought and died together, emigrated together and so they worked out that coexistence is their only guarantee. This is one of the foundations. When they started fighting their enemy, they made peace and were strong enough to fight this enemy together. In this process they worked out some common principles and values.'

His themes—the legacy of war, the flight of people elsewhere and the emergence of a shared national identity—could have been evoked by almost any Lebanese. But there again, like the clanging of a bell, is that word 'enemy.'

'What do you mean by the enemy?'

'It's unfortunate that we have two kinds of people,' he replies. 'There are people with whom we have conflict or disagreement, but there is a chance for a kind of reconciliation. There are others with whom we want to have dialogue and understanding, but they don't want to have dialogue. We want reconciliation with the United States and the West in general, and we think the West wants the same

74

thing. We disagree with the West and sometimes the disagreement turns into conflict, just like between you and me. But with Israel all our disagreements turn into conflict. We feel a deep pain because the Christians in the Holy Land are being killed, who perhaps face more violence and persecution than the Muslims. Jerusalem used to have about 50,000 Christian residents; now it has only 7,000. In our understanding, Christians and Muslims living together guarantee success and coexistence. How can Jews live alone? I don't have a problem living with Jews, and I hope that Muslim people in the Arab world become convinced that Jews also need Muslims.'

Then, having dextrously balanced openness to the West with condemnation of Israel's actions, he shifts almost imperceptibly into a critique of Orientalism.

'We want to get to grips with the idea of *jihad* or holy war,' he continues. 'Do Westerners want to get to grips with the idea of imperialism? Do they want to continue thinking that there are superior people and lesser people? We need to talk about the balance of power, of people being stronger, more forceful than others. Let us agree that technology is for everyone, not only for Westerners to use.'

I feel a vague sense of guilt, superseded by thoughts of the masses marching against the war on Iraq and the hours I've spent tramping through West Bank checkpoints. 'It depends which Westerners!' I protest.

'Good point.' Fahes faces me directly, his attention fully focused on the question. 'There are different types of Western people. We have different Islams. The work is between moderates, so that we can all increase the space of moderation. This is what we do together. Dialogue is what produces moderate Islam. If Islam is put in a corner on its own, it reproduces itself and starts looking for what makes me different from the Other. But if it's not put in a corner by itself, it starts looking for what is common with other religions.'

75

I listen carefully to the sheikh's abstract reasoning. It was easy to see, on an intellectual level, how tolerance could flow from his claim that the West and the Arab world mutually define other. But in the realpolitik of post-war Lebanon this might mean little: some suggested that Hezbollah's new-found moderation was nothing more than political expediency and that, given the chance, they would impose Iranian-style theocracy in a flash. 'Is diversity and secularism a good in itself, or just a temporary compromise due to the impossibility of theocracy?' I ask.

Jamil! exclaims the sheikh, pleased. 'Good question,' says the translator promptly. Sheikh Fahes leans forward, his hands spread over his grey-gowned knees. 'We Arabs are ready to put the Koran aside and have a dialogue, and then re-read the Koran based on what we have discussed and concluded' he says slowly, adding with even greater emphasis: 'Dialogue would not be about what's written in the Koran, but about life. We are ready to re-understand the Koran, Islamic history and jurisprudence, based on this new relationship.'

The gentle brand of Islam he espouses, he goes on, is to be found in all sections of Lebanese society including Hezbollah, and is even respected by the authorities running Iran's theocracy. 'Our problem, of course, is the kind of fundamentalism that has been produced and reproduced by the United States,' he says, returning to theme of East-West interdependence. Then he polishes the thought with one of his rhetorical upswings: is Hezbollah more of a fundamentalist threat than Microsoft?

He nods benevolently at me and the translator. 'We make a good team for a dialogue,' he says. And then he's off, trundling away into the fading night sky.

The next day, I accompany the American seminarians on their journey into the heart of Islamic fundamentalism. In Lebanese terms, it was just a day trip to the south of the country, a pleasurable jaunt involving meeting and greeting and a bit of sight-seeing. For me, the trip was a rare opportunity to get access to the security zone. Despite the departure of the Israeli army in 2000, the Lebanese army still kept a close eye on all visitors to the area. Hezbollah, its *de facto* rulers, would regard anyone wandering around alone with suspicion. To get there safely, you needed a permit from the army, private transport and an escort trusted by the locals. The invitation from Nuhad Tomeh, MECC's deputy general secretary, solved these logistical problems for me.

My companions were the other Americans, internationalist and pacifist, the counterpoints to the strident citizens who popped up on British TV post 9/11 with sound bites about the need for a strong president. Ellen, a successful woman in her fifties, had been engaged to a Lebanese man thirty years before, but the civil war intervened and the marriage never happened. On this, her first visit since, she had met his wife and children, a poignant encounter that turned on the-what-might-have-been. But she felt it was important, she said as we sipped coffee outside the bus, to maintain human relations in this divided world. 'It's track-two diplomacy,' she said grandly. The next moment, tears welled up in her eyes and she excused herself. By contrast, David and Rachel, a young married couple with open, almost matching faces, seem untouched by worldly experience.

As soon as the minibus clears the checkpoint into the security zone, an unmistakeably biblical landscape unfolds. The road winds between green fields and the rolling hills are studded with lumps of creamy stone. It has a bucolic beauty all its own, with stubby olive groves and herds of black goats chewing the yellowing grass.

But against the pastoral beauty another, non-biblical narrative emerges, a more recent story of what has gone on in this land told by the flags and pictures planted by its inhabitants. 'Liberated Ter-

77

ritory: entered peacefully and safely, from Hezbollah' proclaims one giant hoarding. The faces of martyrs look out from stylized posters, amid ghostly illustrations of the Dome of the Rock and fleeing Israeli soldiers.

We make a brief stop at the National Evangelical School in the Shiite town of Nabatiyeh. A Lebanese paradox in microcosm, the Christian school was founded by American Presbyterian missionaries who came to convert Middle East Christians to the 'right' kind of Christianity. The headteacher's grandfather had been one of the first Greek Orthodox to convert. But now, embedded in Arab culture and multi-confessionalism, the school management had abandoned any attempt to convert its almost exclusively Shia pupils. 'No Muslim became a Christian in seventy-five years!' the head Munther Antoun tells us cheerfully.

His headmasterly duties include curbing Hezbollah when they over-reach themselves by trying to ban chess or carry weapons on school premises. 'Aren't Hezbollah a terrorist organization?' asks David, anxiously. 'That's one side of the story,' says Antoun judiciously, and furnishes him with an anecdote about receiving American ambassador David Satterfield in 1998, when no American was welcome. 'Hezbollah was mad at me, but I said, "it's better that he comes here, and he hears what people have to say himself."' He says this with pride.

Even his workaday management issues have a Lebanese twist. With 783 pupils, the school exceeds the 750 deemed to be the most that can be successfully managed by a single head. What is needed, he tells us, are heads of division who share the head's vision for the school. 'But it is very difficult to find two people in Lebanon with the same goals and objectives!' His teeth flash as he delivers the punch line.

I am taken to meet a group of pupils. Aged between fourteen and seventeen and dressed in jeans and T-shirts, they have the air of bright, well-to-do European sixth formers. 'We learned from the civil war that we must tolerate as much as we can,' says a girl with short dark curls and a voice of bell-like clarity. 'This country is built on both Christians and Muslims.'

'We shouldn't talk about Christians and Muslims, we should say Lebanese!' says her large, dark-eyed classmate cheerfully.

'How do you see the West?' I ask.

The dark-eyed boy wades straight in. 'Complicated! I will talk about two sides, the positive and the negative. People from the US, Britain and Europe are wonderful people. But the problem is with the governments. They talk about democracy, and then they come to the Middle East and ruin everything in the name of democracy.'

'There is a great difference between the government of the West, and the people of the West,' chimes the curl-girl. 'The governments are political parties—they don't have anything in mind but money. But social life is different. People work hard—they try to make their society a perfect society.'

'How do you see the values of the West?'

'The West is completely different from the East—we see things that don't fit our beliefs. For example, we see pop singers almost naked! As Muslims, we think this is wrong.' This time, the speaker is an earnest young man, with thick brown hair sticking up in tufts. The others nod, and echo him in chorus: 'it's wrong.'

'Would you like more freedom?' I ask. Surely, as teenagers…

'No.' The girl speaking is firm, decisive, one of the few wearing the *hijab*. 'We have freedom, but it must be controlled. Freedom is very precious, but there must be borders to freedom.'

Another girl gives the example of a sixteen-year-old single mother. 'It's not good for her, her friends, family or her society!' She sounds indignant. 'She will lose her future for a single mistake.'

79

'We see the problems people face in the West,' adds the curl-girl. 'Drugs, alcoholism, more than here. The young don't know the value of advice from parents and professional people.'

A tall, blond young man interjects, something clearly on his mind. 'My mother is Iraqi,' he announces. 'They cross thousands of miles and they say they are going to bring freedom. Do you think someone is spending thousands of dollars to bring freedom? They have a goal.' Having delivered his message of political cynicism, he sums up the feelings of the group: 'We can't talk about the West as one thing—we have to talk about the government and the people. They are good, but their governments offend us all the time.'

Afterwards, I am taken to admire the end-of-year craft and technology exhibition. The pupils' work is a display of ingenuity and imagination: there are dolls made out of Pringles containers, with ping pong balls for heads, wool for hair and plastic espresso cups for hats. A football has been cut in half to make two lampshades, and some broom handles sliced up and varnished to form picture frames. 'The idea is that you make something out of nothing; you don't have to pay a lot,' explains Antoun.

I stop, intrigued, in front of a model Elvis standing in a box edged with tiny light bulbs. The technology teacher flicks a switch and the lights flash while the star plays 'Silent Night' and 'Santa Claus is Coming to Town.' 'It's to demonstrate bi-directional lighting. It's very simple,' he says with pride.

Then it's back on the bus and onto the highlight of the day, a visit to Khiam, the former prison run by the Israeli-backed South Lebanon Army. Between 1985 and 2000, thousands of Lebanese prisoners were held without trial and, despite protests from human rights organizations, subject to interrogation under torture. Once the Israelis

80

had left and the prisoners had been freed, Khiam became a symbol of liberation. Now officially known as the Hezbollah Museum, it has all the accoutrements of tourism: a brown Ministry of Tourism sign, and a gift shop selling postcards of prisoners in stress positions.

In the café, a long table is laid as if for a children's tea party, with brightly coloured drinks and pyramids of fairy cakes. About fifty men flood in, an international delegation of Shiite clerics, smiling and bestowing affectionate little touches on each other's shoulders, their robes and turbans a muddy rainbow of browns, greys and greens.

Our party is guided round the narrow cells by Mohammad, who spent six years here as a prisoner. 'I consider it my mission to share with other people what happened and show how "civilized" the Israelis are,' he says tersely. His eyes are concealed by very dark glasses, a permanent necessity, he says, after his long spell without daylight.

Then we troop into the main reception hall to meet Sheikh Nabil Qaouk, Hezbollah's commander in the south. A table has been decorated with stands of plastic orange flowers and set out for a press conference. The mural behind depicts Israeli soldiers running from Islam's holy sites, surreally framed by a pair of pantomime-style red velvet curtains hanging from gold poles. Smaller versions adorn the prison windows around the room.

Perhaps in his early forties, the sheikh has striking, sapphire-blue eyes set in regular features framed by a dark beard. But he has a quality of deep impassivity which prevents him from exploiting his charisma in an obvious way.

His speech, with its ordered paragraphs and elegant pronouncements, is a model of Shia training in public speaking, its content a familiar statement of Hezbollah's political position interwoven with gestures of interfaith diplomacy. But its delivery, with a dispassionate calmness as if drawn up from some well within, is unusually compelling. 'Mr Bush has gained the title of being the greatest

81

terrorist for killing innocent people,' he concludes gently. 'Again, I welcome you and I assure you of our belief in Jesus Christ and his mother Mary. There is no home in south Lebanon that does not have a picture of Mary.'

He stops speaking. His references to the Virgin Mary, somewhat inappropriate for this Protestant audience, have done nothing to diminish the effect, and a deep silence has settled on the group. Visibly moved, a Palestinian who has been living in Canada for thirty years stands up and makes a speech of thanks. He receives in return the assurance, given with yet greater calmness, that the liberation of Palestine is nigh. For my part, after a speech carefully tailored to an American audience, I want to know how he sees the role of Britain, post-Iraq.

'Tony Blair has chosen to be allied with the American administration and Bush without being aware of might happen. British forces have been part of what are called the coalition forces and are involved in destroying Holy Places in Iraq,' he replies immediately, addressing the audience in general. Then he turns and looks straight at me with a gaze that is curiously neutral. 'Abu Ghraib has given a very bad image of the British people all around the world. I don't think that the English are better than the Americans. They are all the same in what they do to the people here.'

He spreads his hands as if in apology and nods before lowering his eyes again. As he leaves the room, he makes a point of stopping in front of me, hand on heart in the Eastern handshake. *Ahlan wa sahlan*, he says. I nod back, impressed by his courtesy but unsure whether I am witnessing the real thing or just good PR. Amid the bubble of conversation, a reporter from the Lebanese English language paper *The Daily Star* garners a clutch of quotes and hurries off, looking stressed, to file what's clearly a routine local story.

82

The American seminarians are impressed with the sheikh's performance. 'He had grace,' says Ellen. 'His heart was big enough to see round the mountain, and not only see it from one side.' The encounter has had a particularly strong impact on David. 'The thing that struck me most was how different an impression I got from the one we get from the American media,' he says. 'It makes me wonder how distorted the other snapshots of "terrorism" we get are. I was out of my comfort zone—they were things that I would probably rather not hear—but it was very good for me to hear it.' 'Are you happy to be quoted on this?' I ask. Knowing the heightened political sensitivities about the Middle East in North America, it is best to check. 'Oh yes,' he nods eagerly.

'I found what he said very clear, very straightforward and'—he pauses to smile broadly—'very right. He spoke truth. I appreciated what he said and his manner of saying it. He was so gentle and calm.' His wife agrees. 'I felt like this man who was sitting in front of us was really a brother, more so than many militant Americans.' [2]

Everyone is quiet as the bus winds its way along the hilly roads that follow the Israeli border, accompanied by the Hezbollah official who has been smoothing our passage the whole day. The large, balconied houses nestling in the cup of the hills seem mostly empty, abandoned

---

[2] Months later in Britain, I find a statement on the San Francisco Theology Seminary's homepage, claiming that the students had been misrepresented in the local press, and effectively retracting their position. Their comments were due to their fear and surprise at meeting Hezbollah on their educational trip, the statement said, and they 'sought to be courteous to all present in order to ensure their safety.' 'The entire incident,' it continues, 'appears to have been an attempt to exploit the group for propaganda purposes.'

since the Israeli occupation or still unfinished. Towards the end of the afternoon we stop high on a peak, where the UN blue line marks the internationally recognized boundary between the two territories. Below, the flat plains of the Northern Galilee stretch into the distance, while the rocky mass of Syria's Golan Heights, occupied since 1967, loom on the horizon to the left. With our feet on the soil of one country, overlooking two others, we are standing on one of the most strategic points in the Middle East.

The paraphernalia of conflict is all around us. A small, thrown-together outpost, the height of two people, bears the Hezbollah flag, while just a few yards away on the other side of the rusty border fence sits a much bigger Israeli military base, apparently deserted, bits of camouflage dangling over its concrete mass. 'Won't we get shot at?' asks one of the Americans, looking up at the watchtower anxiously.

'No, the Israelis are very easy now,' replies Tomeh, comfortably.

4

HEZBOLLAH HEARTLANDS

I AM waiting for Hezbollah to pick me up outside McDonalds.

A single soldier, machine gun slung casually over his shoulder, patrols in front of the entrance. It is mid-afternoon and the restaurant is quiet, so his only companion is Ronald McDonald sitting at the entrance, his red and yellow plastic outfit glinting in the sun. At the Armenian bar in Hamra the night before, conversation had stopped as news of Israeli air-strikes only a dozen miles from Beirut, the closest since Israel's withdrawal from Lebanon in 2000, had reached the TV screen. Now I watch anxiously as a military helicopter cleaves a path across the clear blue sky.

I was eager to meet Hezbollah properly. Despite their gruesome reputation as the kidnappers of Westerners during the 1980s, apparently these days they were pretty accessible to journalists, and keen to put their case to the world. Once I had the right contact details, it had simply been a case of requesting an appointment, a process no different from arranging an interview with a British public figure through a press officer. The service was better, though: Hassan Haider, the junior official in charge, had arranged a lift to Hezbollah's offices in Dahiyeh where I would meet the head of international relations, Nawaf al Moussawi. He had been at pains to explain what car and personnel to expect so that I, a woman alone, would not be anxious about accepting a lift with potentially dangerous strangers.

It is hard to overstate the importance of Hezbollah. Lebanon's 1.2 million Shia had been a spectacularly impoverished, direction-less minority until Hezbollah emerged as a response to the Israeli occupation in the mid-1980s. Now support for the organization, a mainstream political party with seats in parliament, far outstripped that for its secular Shiite rival Amal. In Dahiyeh and the south of Lebanon, it effectively acted as government, maintaining law and order and providing a comprehensive social welfare programme. While the state pleaded poverty, Hezbollah built schools, hospitals and community centres with its huge, undisclosed budget—around $60 million a year, some said—donated largely by Iran and wealthy Lebanese Shia.

Beyond the Shia, Hezbollah won the gratitude of the entire country for its steadfast resistance to the Israeli occupation of Lebanon. In 2000, after twenty-two years of occupation, with help from South Lebanese army proxy militia, it finally succeeded in expelling the Israelis. The Lebanese still refer to them as 'The Resistance' and, as the only Arab army ever to have defeated Israel, their reputation across the Arab world is legendary.

But despite their gratitude for this feat, the attitude of the other sects towards Hezbollah was often less than enthusiastic. Some, particularly Christians, distrusted the party's claims that it embraced coexistence, fearing that secretly it still harboured ambitions to turn Lebanon into an Islamic state backed by Iranian theocrats. They pointed out that, despite the commitment to disarm made in the Taif Accord, as the only armed group in the country, they remained dangerously capable of imposing their will. And Hezbollah's support for Syria's continued presence set them against those who would rather see her forces go home.

But all these political issues fade into the background as a smiling young man jumps out of a white Mercedes and walks towards me.

86

Haider is in his early twenties, curly-haired, with squashy, amiable features. Politely, he ushers me into the back seat of the chauffeur-driven car. On the advice of local journalists about winning the respect of the party high-ups, I have brought a token black headscarf which I start to unfurl. 'No, you don't need it. You can put it away,' smiles Haider from the front seat.

We make small talk about the growing heat of the season, my trip to the south and the border with Israel. 'By the way, we don't say Israel, we say Palestine,' says Haider reprovingly, correcting what the party considers an erroneous admission of its legal status. 'We accept the Jews—we always did—and that they can live together with Palestinians, but we don't recognize the state,' he explains.

'How, then, do you refer to Israel?'

'The enemy,' he replies simply.

The car sails into Dahiyeh, past the rows of low shops and high-rise blocks. The afternoon is sleepy and there are only a few people on the streets. Finally, after some twists and turns through back streets, we pull up in a quiet residential road in Haret Hreik. Large canvas blinds flap over the balconies of the apartment blocks.

Haider leads me into a nondescript building and up to the second floor. Behind a heavily reinforced metal door, an elegant reception room is set out with mock Louis XV furniture. Sofas and chairs, tastefully upholstered in silky green and yellow stripes, are poised on delicately wrought gilt legs. At one end, Lebanon's and Hezbollah's giant satin flags flank a framed Koranic inscription. On the wall, the disembodied faces of the Ayatollah Khomeini and Hamas' former spiritual leader Sheikh Yassin float artistically on a black background.

I sit down on one of the sofas and Moussawi makes his entrance. He is a portly man with grey hair and beard, the picture of ordinariness in his smart slacks and open necked shirt. But the interpreter

87

who follows him, a powerfully built, shaven-headed man, would look less out of place in a gangster movie. Neither of them looks remotely pleased to see me. With only the faintest difficulty, Moussawi lowers himself into the golden arms of one of the chairs. Staff appear from the adjoining rooms and set down trays of juice and water on the gold-legged table.

I attempt a conversational warm-up. Moussawi was educated in France and, like me, has a degree in philosophy. Pointing this out wins me a curt nod and a cold stare. A reference to last night's bombings by Israel gets a better result.

'Every conflict has its rules. What took place yesterday is a violation of these rules. Every violation of the rules will be dealt with in a proper manner.' He pauses and then adds, less formally: 'Before I came in, I heard of operations in the Shebaa farms area. But will our right to carry out operations in the Shebaa area be considered a retaliation or not?'

The Shebaa farms were a sensitive subject, considered by Israel to be part of the Syrian Golan Heights which it had occupied since 1967 but seen by Hezbollah as the last, offensive residue of Israel's occupation of Lebanon. While Moussawi talks in Arabic, the interpreter fixes me with a continuous, hard stare. I feel myself swallowing nervously. Perhaps asking about Hezbollah's social provision will create a more relaxed atmosphere.

'Before answering that I would like to give a historical briefing which is very important,' begins Moussawi, portentously. I sit back, and wait for him to tell the tale of Shia misfortunes. This takes some time and, as I expect, contrasts the community's impoverishment with the better deal enjoyed by the other sects. While the Maronites, Druze and Sunnis enjoyed the protection of France, Britain and the Ottoman Empire respectively, he explains, the Shia were friendless

88

until the arrival of Hezbollah. But in the end, the community had its own patron, complete with foreign sponsorship from Iran.

'Therefore it is quite normal for us to embark on removing this state of dispossession,' he concludes. The interpreter's unblinking, coal-black eyes bore into me. Moussawi outlines the growth of the social programme from its humble beginnings with a few health centres to its present, impressive scale. 'The institutions created by Hezbollah are not able to meet the needs of the people, therefore a lot more projects are needed,' he states. 'What is provided by everyone—the government, us and other organizations—doesn't cover even half the needs.'

'So, just as a joke,' the interpreter continues unsmilingly, 'I would say that if anyone would like to compete with Hezbollah in this, he would be most welcome.'

I will tell Tony Blair, I say. There's a burst of hearty, barking laughter from Moussawi.

'Is everyone entitled to services?' I ask, taking advantage of this momentary release from tension. Officially, they were open, but I had heard complaints that in reality access depended on how far the individual demonstrated loyalty to the party.

'These services are open,' Moussawi replies. 'We do not exercise favouritism on political or other criteria. They are open to anybody— we take into account the priority of the need. Since what is available is limited, the one who is the needier should get it.' He adds, making the religious underpinnings of this policy clear: 'A Muslim shouldn't sleep while his neighbour is hungry, or he isn't a believer.'

'Are there limits to Hezbollah's tolerance of people of other faiths?'

'Not at all,' he says swiftly. 'We came from a history in which we were the most persecuted and we completely understand the importance of religious freedom.' By way of illustration, he recounts how

89

the recent municipal elections had led to an electoral injustice: in the largely Maronite town of Amsheet, no Muslim had gained a seat despite a presence of 1,500, while the Maronites had gained a seat in the Muslim Baalbek where they only had a population of 500. 'That's why we are the ones who have the right to complain!' He laughs at the irony. 'Of course, we don't raise these issues. We don't want to cause conflicts and harm coexistence in this country.'

'Are there values that Hezbollah could bring to the West?'

'I believe there is error in talking about East and West, a lot of exaggeration,' he replies. 'For centuries there has been cultural exchange on both sides of the Mediterranean. I know there are some people who believe in the separation of West and East, but we don't. For example, alcohol. There is a text that says it's forbidden to drink alcohol, just as in Judaism they believe that the pig is impure, while it is a major dish in the Christian tradition. These differences exist. Some people take care of dogs, but some people in Korea eat them.'

Finding this perfectly expressed, non-judgemental statement of cultural relativism unconvincing, I try another tack. Are they concerned about the evident Westernization of Lebanon, particularly in Beirut? Seeing my manoeuvre, the interpreter grins appreciatively.

'There are some Westerners who are interested in spreading their values—for example, in the way a woman dresses. They believe that if she wears a bikini, this is a sign of modernity. But if a Muslim man studies nuclear physics, he is accused of terrorism. Let us first agree what modernity is. Is it possible that technology is part of modernity?' Moussawi is now in full discursive mode, and evidently enjoying himself. His gaze is fixed on the middle distance and the makings of a smile play about his lips as he works up to his concluding point: a distinction between 'consumer modernity' and 'productive modernity.'

'We want to create a modern society that takes the real road to modernity, not just the modernity of fashion,' he says, summing up. 'We do care about having universities that provide the best education, but there are some who are interested in having nightclubs and the best shows at the Moulin Rouge. Where is modernity? Is it a way to use all your efforts to rebuild a society, or waste everything on marginal issues? Some people believe in the modernity of fashion; we believe in a complete modernity.'

Now I am hunting around in my mind for a palatable way to put the point about Hezbollah's enduring image as hostage-takers in the West. 'If my mother knew I was here, she would be quite alarmed,' I tell him. Taking me to mean Lebanon as a whole, he looks almost sympathetic. 'I have the same impression about Northern Ireland.'

'What I mean is, Hezbollah is still seen in the West as hostage-takers.'

He looks away and spreads his hands helplessly. 'We issued statements, we denied this. What are we required to do? We said that what was done was part of things done in the Middle East war, in which there was the phenomenon of abduction. We established our movement as the resistance to defend our land, and we are not responsible for the deeds done by other groups.'

More behind-the-scenes hands place a tray of dainty cups and saucers on the table between us. As we sip our tea, Moussawi returns to his central preoccupation: the injustices committed by Sharon and Bush against the peoples of Palestine and Iraq. The frosty demeanour has returned and his tone strongly suggests that everyone in the West shares the same, hostile view of the Arab world. 'There are many people who see things differently, and are sympathetic to the plight of the Palestinians,' I tell him.

'Not sufficiently,' he returns coldly.

Back in the street, Haider leads me to a small, battered car for the drive home. 'It's mine, a simple car,' he says apologetically, explaining that the white Mercedes—the company car—is going home with the boss to the protection of a nightly garage. 'That's just because he wants to use the car himself,' I joke. He looks at me uncertainly, not sure whether to be amused or alarmed, before finally deciding to err on the safe side. 'Oh, no, he would be punished,' he says firmly.

The ordinary Shia I encountered were less hardline, more immersed in the cultural and religious miasma of contemporary Lebanon, even quirky. One of their most intriguing and endearing features, I felt, was their adoration of the Virgin Mary.

Islam considers Mary, as the mother of one of the greatest prophets, to be an important female figure with a special link to the divine. Like Fatima, Mohammed's best-loved daughter and mother of Imam Al Hussein, a central figure in Shiism, the lady of sorrows is particularly receptive to the prayers of the poor and suffering—good for a minority defined by its sense of deprivation and dispossession. Theological confluences apart, it easy to see how, in a religion dominated by the prescriptions of male sheikhs, Muslim women would naturally seek out the warmer solace offered by the Virgin.

The best place to see this syncretism in action was Harissa, the shrine to Mary that stands high on a mountain above the Mediterranean port of Jounieh, north of Beirut. When the Maronite authorities commissioned the statue in the early twentieth century, they were simply aiming to establish a monument which would demonstrate to the world the place that the Virgin held in the pious hearts of the Lebanese. They little imagined that the ten-ton white statue, poised on a cone above the sea, would become a crowd-puller, drawing coach loads up the mountainside every day. Soon the *téléphérique* was built, an impressive construction of wires and cable cars that could carry you all the way to the mountain summit.

One morning I take the bus to Jounieh and get off at the foot of the mountain. I pay my fee, push through the turnstiles and get into one of the cable cars. A man slams the door shut, and cogs and pulleys jolt noisily into action. The ride is long, vertiginous and terrifying. The mountain is steep and the cabin swings perilously, grazing trees and passing so close to the locals' windows that you can peer into their bedrooms. I wonder whether I'll have the courage for the return journey. Then, after more grinding and clanking of metal, the thing grinds to a halt and I step out into the car park. At the entrance to the grounds, a sign announces: 'This is a holy place. Here the Virgin Mary is waiting for you to pray and meditate in silence and contemplation.'

Inside the gates most of the visitors are busloads of schoolchildren. They are everywhere, lined up in crocodiles or sitting in sprawling class groups, wearing pale aertex shirts and brightly coloured baseball caps. Their teachers attempt to control them, admonishing, instructing, shushing, pointing at miscreants and dispensing hard stares. But the children's excitement at a day out is irrepressible and they are making an unholy row. Most are hopping and jumping, giggling and fighting, although a few escape from the madness by falling into cross-legged reveries and staring into space. One boy, his fingers crammed in mouth, experiments with pulling horrible new faces while a little girl plaits her classmate's hair with intense concentration.

Weaving my way through crowds and cedar trees, I enter the tiny chapel at the base of the statue. Inside, school children from the Greek Catholic order of St. Antoine are having a special service, decked in white robes with gold crosses in honour of their first year of communion. They sing hesitantly, sometimes forgetting the music so

93

completely that the voice of their teacher rises alone. Behind them, a dark, muscular man in jeans and T-shirt is singing *sotto voce*, swaying slightly, his eyes closed in bliss. Two black-caped Shia women stand at the back, surveying the scene. As they turn to go, I look into their faces to see what they make of the service, but their expressions are hard to fathom.

I go back outside and look up at the statue. The Lady of Lebanon stands on her cone of white bricks, her arms spread out in compassion at the urban sprawl below. A few solitary pilgrims are walking slowly up the spiral stairway to make their intercessions directly to the Virgin. Her form has a distinctive shape, its robes billowing around a generous female figure. At its feet is a smaller, almost perfect copy in black. A Shia woman has come to pay her respects.

Early one evening, I go out on an impromptu food run. On the way back to the Y, I stop to reassure the greengrocer's kitten, who has been intimidated onto a railing by a dog.

Three teenage boys approach me, smiling. Omar and Emir are twin brothers, with high-coloured complexions, dark curls, white teeth and long roman noses. They fizz with energy and curiosity. Their friend Ahmed, a paler version, hangs shyly behind.

'I have two cats at home, Pussy and Sussi,' says Emir, looking at the kitten I'm stroking. The three young men giggle, and hold onto each other. They want to know where I'm from, and what I'm doing. 'If you want anything: interview, translator ...' offers Omar. 'Is anyone researching gay and lesbians here?' asks Emir suddenly. 'I'm not gay,' he adds hastily, as his brother sniggers and digs him in the ribs. I doubt it, that's very controversial in Lebanon, I remind them. 'Yes, gays and lesbians have no rights here,' says Emir. 'They can't walk down the street.'

The boys are seventeen and come from Dahiyeh. The twins are Shiites, while Mohammed is Sunni. Do they consider themselves religious? 'No,' says Omar, 'I have my God, but…' He points vaguely to heaven and then earth, and his English peters out. 'I consider my parents open-minded,' says Emir, with a grin and a proud tilt of the head. Many parents in their area are very traditional, he adds. Some of them even—he taps a toned biceps set off by a stylish capped sleeve T-shirt—make the boys cover their upper arms.

As I am pen and paperless, Omar races up and down the street trying to find a passer-by with a pen, and we exchange contact details. As I write, Omar nudges his brother to do something, and Emir gives me a chewing gum.

A week later, I meet Emir at Cola bus station. He is dapper in a lime-green T-shirt and hipster pin-striped jeans. I enquire after Pussy and Sussi. He looks solemn. 'My father threw them,' he says, gesturing behind his shoulder. 'He said they made a smell in the house.' I'm horrified. What, he killed them? 'No, no,' he says, reassuringly. 'He gave them to my sisters' Christian school.' His eyes crinkle into a smile. 'When I want to see them, I go there.'

The bus negotiates Dahiyeh's long, dusty streets. It is morning, the busiest part of the day, and the shops and banks are bustling. At times, our progress is impeded as people and vehicles swirl about, crossing roads and blocking lanes of traffic. The air is full of shouting and beeping.

Eventually, we arrive and get off the bus. Emir leads me through the back streets where concrete gives way to narrow, sandy tracks in a half-urban, half-rural sprawl. As we approach his house, he worries that the electricity, only available at certain hours of the day, will have been cut off, making the planned breakfast difficult. On a corner an oddly-shaped jumble of buildings rises out of the sand.

95

Beneath various additions of breeze blocks and gaping holes in the concrete, the core of an older, more coherent building is discernible. It was built by his grandfather, he says, and now the various extensions house five families.

Inside the dark rooms, cold stone has been covered with wine-red fabrics to create the semblance of a genteel sitting room. There's a dining area, with pieces of floral fabric covering benches around a low table. But there is no disguising the bare breeze blocks that make up the kitchen walls. Showing me to the toilet, Emir suddenly sees his home through a visitor's eyes. 'My father—he is doing the house slowly. He is doing it by himself,' he says apologetically.

The boys' father sits on one of the floral benches, his hulking frame bent over the tea and *mannoush*. 'Does she have permission from Hezbollah to be here?' he asks his sons jokingly. 'If not, they will take her!'

I realize with surprise that this man is a member of a small, passionately anti-Hezbollah minority. And he is eager to volunteer his unorthodox views. 'The people who act for Hezbollah do not do it out of their hearts,' he tells me. 'They do it for money. For water, electricity, food, books, scholarships. If I go to hospitals, schools—everything—I must say I am from Hezbollah, or that I know someone from Hezbollah.'

During the Israeli occupation, Hezbollah had approached him and offered him benefits if he would act as one of their agents, but he refused. Working in the construction industry, he had found that those who built without planning permission got away with it if they were party supporters, while those who were not were penalized by the authorities. Once he was asked by a foreign broadcasting company to find them a TV studio to rent, but when Hezbollah found out, objecting to the immorality of the music, they put a stop to the arrangement. It grated with him that he could not even object to such

96

treatment. 'If I say something bad about Hezbollah, someone will come and see me at night, and ask me why I did it,' he concludes.

'Why don't you support Hezbollah?'

'I don't like them,' he replies simply. 'They are unfair with people, and they make a distinction between Christians and Muslims.'

Emir interjects, keen for me to get a balanced picture. 'And there are people who think that Hezbollah are very good—we can go and speak to them to get a different point of view.'

As we've been talking, a neighbour, a plump woman in a patterned headscarf, has come in and sat down. 'I'm not with Hezbollah, I'm with the government,' she remarks to the company in general. Having made her contribution to the political discussion, she subsides into silence and folds her hands serenely.

Omar sets up a *nargileh* and sits puffing contentedly on its long pipe. Now and then, when he thinks no one is looking, he puffs great columns of smoke out of his nostrils like a dragon. 'I don't let him do that', remarks Emir mildly.

The discussion turns to religion. 'I like Imam Al Hussain, but I don't want to kill myself for him!' says their father, his eyes twinkling ironically. I blink in surprise at hearing Shiism's central figure referred to in such familiar terms. He has chosen to send his five children to Christian schools in various parts of Beirut rather than local Muslim schools, he goes on. 'The Christians feel with people and have more mercy,' he says simply, by way of explanation.

'Almost all my friends are Christians,' adds Emir. He produces a tiny address book from his trouser pocket and shows me the names of friends which he has carefully written inside. 'See, they are Christian names,' he says. Sensing my interest, he unfolds some tiny strips of red paper from his wallet, each bearing an Arabic inscription, given to him on a school trip to Harissa. 'They are'—he hesitates, unsure how to describe them—'religious things. I keep them; I don't like to

97

throw them away.' He translates one: 'May God give us good hearts and the joy of sharing. May you be blessed today.'

Their mother comes in, perspiring faintly, and casts off her loosely draped black headscarf. Omar immediately picks it up and wraps it around it his neck. The electricity having gone off, he pours her some cold coffee. She is equally keen to present the family's Christian credentials, telling me how she came to choose her daughter's name after a special experience while pregnant. 'I was sleeping. St. Mary woke me up. She told me to call the baby Mary.'

'How did she look?'

'Like the statue at Harissa,' she replies. 'But she was speaking to me as I am speaking to you now.'

As further proof of the family's links with Christian heritage, Emir points to a silver framed picture of the Virgin Mary on the wall. 'And we have this,' he adds, lifting another picture from its stand on an occasional table. A burlesque cartoon depicts an obese woman in black underwear, flesh oozing over stocking tops, one leg hitched provocatively on a stool. 'Hey, big boy!' reads the caption. The boys watch me closely for my reaction, and the moment dissolves into laughter.

'Would you like to go out?' Emir asks. 'We could show you the mosque.' Ahmed disappears into the bedroom and returns in a smart pair of cream cords. 'All right?' he murmurs, half to himself and half to his brother, surveying his lower half approvingly in the tiny mirror on the wall. Then he combs his hair carefully. Finally, he is ready and we go out into the sunshine.

'I love walking,' proclaims Emir joyfully. 'It is my hobby.' We stride, three abreast, down the street. A horse-drawn cart pulls a tank of fuel for sale and a fishmonger has set up shop at the side of the road, trays of fish spilling out of the open boot of his car. A huge metal container offers 'free water to the people' from Hezbollah.

Emir chatters away about his lifestyle. 'I have female friends, but they are mostly older—eighteen or nineteen. He adds happily: 'not childish'. Both boys are studying for their exams, while earning some cash through jobs in restaurants and hotels. Emir pulls a bank card out of his back pocket. 'My father likes me to be independent,' he says. 'I earn money, and I put it in. Sometimes I help my parents.'

We pass beneath a large banner drawn high across the street pledging the Islamic clergy's loyalty to the people of Iraq.

'Everyone in Dahiyeh drinks alcohol,' volunteers Emir. 'But they don't like people to know.' 'I think my parents know I drink,' adds Omar thoughtfully, a trace of anxiety shading his voice. 'But I don't get drunk,' concludes Emir. 'It's only at parties.'

'Here's the mosque,' he adds, as minarets appear on the horizon. A crowd of men are gathered round its gates. But as we approach, it becomes clear that all is not well: they are throwing us looks of the deepest suspicion. We stand around for a few moments uncertainly.

'We have to go,' Emir decides suddenly.

'What are they worried about?' I want to know. 'It's to do with me, isn't it?'

'*I* don't know what they think,' he replies irritably.

We shrug it off and move on. Stepping into a little shop, I try to buy some soft drinks but Emir dives in front of me and puts the money on the counter. 'There is no difference between us,' he says, almost crossly. We resume our walking. 'Would you like to meet some of our friends?' he asks, and I nod.

'What do you think if someone is gay or lesbian?' Omar's question comes from nowhere.

Nothing in particular, I shrug, momentarily forgetting where I am. We come to rest on a raised pavement on a street corner and stand slightly apart from the dusty thoroughfare, now almost empty in the afternoon heat. 'To be frank,' says Omar deliberately, 'I am bisexual.' Then, to make quite sure I have understood, he adds: 'I sleep with boys and girls.'

I am astounded. Since arriving in Lebanon, people who were obviously gay had repeatedly crossed my path. But they went to extraordinary lengths to conceal it, even from themselves, and I'd encountered deep levels of denial. On more than one occasion, I'd pulled back from writing about someone even under a different name, having been warned that the subject might recognize themselves and have some sort of breakdown. Yet Omar seems determined that I should know.

'My father doesn't know,' he goes on, as we both survey the street around us. 'I sleep with more boys than girls. It is much easier to meet them.'

'Do you really like girls?'

He nods. 'But I prefer boys. It's about ten to one.'

'Where do people meet?' I wonder.

'Oh, there are places, *hamams*, cars,' says Emir brightly. 'There are many people like this. It is known among friends. But not to parents, and'—he gestures vaguely to the street around us—'to Society.'

As we walk on to meet their friends, I worry about publishing anything which might hurt them. 'Just change our names,' Emir reassures me. 'Write as you feel comfortable. My father can't read English.'

As if by magic, a group of teenage boys materialize out of the backdrop of the street. 'They are all bisexual,' Emir says in my ear, as they approach. They are all T-shirts and muscles, their dark eyes holding a street-wary mix of tension and fear. We go their favourite haunt, a deserted café, and sit round in a circle. *Nargileh* appear, and the young men puff on them in turn. 'Go on, ask them questions,' urges Emir. 'Ask them where they go, how they live in society.' I ask a question, but several pairs of eyes stare at me mutely.

The older member of the group, smiling and confident, explains. 'Actually, he's not gay.' He points to the boy on his left. 'And he's not gay.' He points to another boy 'They're not bisexual either,' he adds, indicating the remaining two, in case there should be any doubt. It is all of a piece with what I have observed in Lebanon before—open display followed by flat denial. Of course not, I agree with him.

'I am,' he continues cheerfully. 'I'm bisexual. And I don't have a problem talking about it. But not in front of them,' he indicates his friends. 'How could I work if people knew?'

The afternoon drifts on amid puffs of smoke. Every so often, the eyes of the younger boys flicker over me uncertainly. Yet they seem struck dumb, and say nothing to anyone. 'They're not educated,' whispers Emir in my ear, apologetically. But their older friend seems to see this contact with someone from the liberal West as a rare opportunity to openly acknowledge the gayness of the world. Do I have gay friends in London? How do I find Beirut nightlife? he wants to know. He's delighted when he learns that I've been to Acid. He pouts and sways parodically to the arabesque music drifting across the café, and exchanges a discreet caress with one of his companions.

Then Omar goes off for his private tuition in maths, his weakest subject. Emir takes me out into the street, and hails a taxi. I try to put some notes into his hand, but he pushes them away alarmed and tries to give me my fare in revenge. There's a brief scuffle in which each party tries to give the other money, fails, and withdraws. The *servis* heads for Beirut.

5

THE SECRETS OF THE DRUZE

I HAD long heard references to the Druze of the Middle East without really knowing who, or what, they were. From the battlefield of Israel and the Palestinian territories, Jews and Muslims screamed their identities at the world, identities perhaps clouded by religious or ideological fervour, but at least they had a brand. So, too, did the region's Christians. They might be a diminishing minority, but their membership of a religion claiming over a quarter of the world's population meant that you certainly knew who they were.

The Druze, by contrast, were a shadowy, unknown sect whose true religious identity was a mystery. They kept the details of their faith hidden, worshipping in private and keeping their sacred texts—the *hikma*, or books of wisdom—for the eyes of a religious elite only. The *uqqal* or 'learned' were distinguished by their black clothes and white headwear and met in closed meetings. They conveyed little of the religion to ordinary Druze beyond telling them to do good deeds and be truthful. With outsiders they practised *taqiyya*, an ancient form of concealment designed to protect a minority from religious persecution. In times of trouble, *taqiyya* involved outward conformity to the dominant religion, following its lead in prayer times and festivals. Even in a tolerant climate, they believed that a Druze should not reveal anything at odds with the beliefs of those around them. As a result, curious guests would find their questions answered in courteous generalities. Often these would be expressed in the terms of their own faith, a deft reflection of the questioner's beliefs back to him. Since the Druze only married among themselves, there was no chance of entry to this closed community. And to make matters even more complicated, some people maintained they should not be called Druze at all, but *muwahhidun*, the people of wisdom.

Leafing through some of the few books that had been published about them in the British Library, I found that this secrecy had contributed to some florid myth-making about the sect. They indulged in incest, some said, held orgies for religious festivals and worshipped a golden calf. Their fearsome qualities as warriors—they defended their mountain territories well—were attributed to a demonic alliance: some combatants (presumably the ones who had come off worst) claimed to have seen Druze equipped with horns and tails. Even the moderate account by one of the first travellers to encounter them, the Spanish rabbi Benjamin of Tudela, sounds bemused. In 1167 he wrote of 'a people called Darazyan... They have no religion, and live in the big mountains and the crevices of the rocks; no king or minister is a judge over them... And they are loving of the Jews, and they are light of foot on the mountains and hills, and no one can battle with them.'

In today's Lebanon their position is somewhat different. The country is home to the greatest concentration of the million Druze scattered across the world, where it is the one of the four main sects. While its members are excluded from the highest offices by the constitution, they have political representation in the form of MPs and a vocal dynastic leader, Walid Jumblatt, who inherited the role when his father Kamal was murdered in 1977. Despite their lack of natural allies in the wider world, the Druze won their part of the civil war, chasing the Maronites from their villages in the Chouf. Now, with more of them leaving the mountains for work or education,

103

the younger Druze were clamouring for greater openness about their faith.

But despite their growing participation in modern society, I could find little consensus about the sect's religious identity. The official view, put about by many Druze themselves, was that they were Muslims, an offshoot of Islam that had grown out of the sect's beginnings in the Shiite caliphate of eleventh-century Egypt. The Lebanese I consulted in London all had different things to say on the subject. Eyad Abu Chakra, editor of *Asharq Al Awsat* and the first Druze I ever met, seemed to confirm the official view, adding the intriguing caveat that Drusism was a faith rather than a religion. A week later, the Lebanese academic the Reverend Abu Zaid Shafik dismissed this over a pasta lunch. 'Of course they are not Muslims!' he said, waving his fork around. 'They are just pretending to be, for protection!' Then, in a café on a rainy April afternoon near his perch in the think-tank Chatham House, Nadim Shehadi flipped open his laptop and showed me some unpublished documents, his eyes glowing with excitement. The Druze religion, the papers suggested, had nothing to do with Islam but in fact stemmed from Eastern religions such as Hinduism. One claimed its roots lay in India, and shared the same spiritual heritage as the Hare Krishna. 'It's interesting, isn't it?' he said. 'Maybe you could write your whole book about the Druze!' Other scholars suggested that the roots of Drusism lay with Zoroastrianism, the ancient Persian faith that saw the world locked into a cosmic struggle between good and evil. With all these experts offering conflicting perspectives, what chance did I have of finding out the truth?

And once I arrived in Lebanon, whenever the subject of the Druze came up among Muslims or Christians, the response was always the same. 'Ah, the Druze,' the other person would say, knowingly. 'They don't talk.' My Druze friend's take on the subject was more tantalizing than helpful; like most young Druze, Abir knew little about the religion to which she belonged. 'Tell me what you find out, because I don't know,' she said, eagerly. 'I have some ideas, but I won't tell you now, because it will influence your research. When you have done some interviews, then I will tell you.'

As a first step in my investigations, I decide to visit the large Druze cemetery in the Verdun district of Beirut. The young woman in the tourist office looks surprised when I ask her to point it out on the map. 'Tourists don't usually go there,' she says, looking at me closely. 'Are you a journalist?' I've been rumbled early on, but she doesn't seem to mind. 'Of course you can go,' she assures me, adding with a friendly smile, '*I* am from the Chouf.'

Twenty minutes later I approach its high, white walls in the district of Tallet ed Druze and walk through the gates. A policeman in a sentry box at the entrance, evidently unaccustomed to having his daydreams disturbed, darts belatedly after me. 'I want to look,' I tell him with as much authority as I can muster in broken Arabic. He nods unhappily, and returns to his post.

Inside, the cemetery spreads out like an unkempt, sun-bleached meadow, dry grasses waving over the Arabic inscriptions which adorn the tombstones. Square, white mausoleums squat among them like little houses whose owners have gone away, their black front doors firmly shut. A few bear the Druze star on their roofs, each of its five points painted a different colour. Apart from the cemetery's guardian, a moustachioed man in a white fez and baggy Turkish trousers, the place is deserted, an oasis amid the sounds of rush-hour traffic.

The guardian nods me welcome, and I sit down on a bench outside a white-domed building topped with a gold star. A young woman approaches, two little girls dancing in her wake. The three of them drop their shoes at its entrance and disappear inside. I peer after them through the half-open door, but see only a glimpse of a table draped in a black and silver spangled cloth. So I wander off to explore the graveyard's furthest reaches, where the long grasses have all but taken over.

Five minutes later, I look up to see the guardian standing on higher ground looking sternly in my direction. He beckons me back onto the main path. Perhaps my notebook has aroused suspicion. In any case it is obvious that I have overstayed my welcome, and must now leave.

A few days later, I pay a visit to Sami Makarem, professor of Islamic Philosophy at the American University of Beirut, and author of one of the few books published in English on the Druze. Although he doesn't wear the religious dress, his status as an *uqqal* means he is regarded as an authority on the religion within the Druze community.

The professor, a portly man with startlingly bushy eyebrows, welcomes me into his spacious flat, full of artfully placed little armchairs and arabesque furniture in dark, carved wood. His wife, elegant in beige linen and gold jewellery, a mane of pretty pink-red hair and a collagen-sized mouth, sits in while they both size me up. Then she serves tea and biscuits, and discreetly departs.

Makarem moves rapidly into expository mode. 'Drusism is an Islamic faith; it stems from Islam,' he tells me, shifting in his antique chair. 'It was very much influenced by Islamic mysticism, they practise what the Muslims practised all the time—prayer, alms giving and so on. But these are for ordinary people. Then you have to meditate, to know God.' His gravely voice carries a suppressed chuckle which emerges disconcertingly as he arrives at the end of a point.

'It is mystical, it is secretive, for many reasons,' he continues. 'You have to feel it, live it, more than knowing about it through books.

106

That's why people may hesitate before they tell you something about Druism. They may not know about it, and if they know they may hesitate to tell someone whom they don't know about it.' He chuckles happily.

The explanation made sense. The idea of concealing spiritual truths from the harsh gaze of unbelievers was deeply rooted in many mystical traditions.

'It is more than monotheism,' he goes on. 'You can define monotheism as saying you believe in one God. But for mysticism it is not enough to believe there is only one God. There is nothing in existence but God. You are within God, and God is within you, at the same time.'

'So God is not an entity?' I find I am responding easily to his manner of a kindly teacher keen to reward the insights of his student.

'That is true.' He nods smilingly. 'You cannot think of God like he is in the Semitic religions, like an old man sitting on a throne, a king with a white beard. This cosmos, this physical existence, is nothing but the manifestation of God. You are the expression of God, I am the expression of God. That's why it's almost the same thing as in Hinduism. There is nothing outside Him, there is no other than God, this unity.' He spreads his hands, as if to acknowledge the oneness of things.

'Why is the faith organized into initiates and non-initiates?'

'Because not everybody understands these things,' he replies patiently. 'How can you really belong to the faith, if you don't understand it? Someone who does not have this mystical experience, although he is born of two Druze parents, is not really Druze until he experiences these things. Socially, I am a Druze, but spiritually I won't be. I will just be like other Muslims, Christians or Druze. When you are ready, and you understand these things, then you are initiated!'

'But how do you determine readiness for initiation?'

107

'Through feeling,' he replies immediately. Then, perhaps realizing that this begs the same question, he shifts to an easier illustration. 'I have to be ethically in line—my behaviour must be in line, my response to things. For example, I wanted to go on a trip to the mountains tomorrow, and then I found when I got in my car, it has a flat tyre. If I get nervous, I start cussing and I don't know what to do, then I am not ready. I have to be calm, to understand that these things happen. So ethical behaviour is a sign that I'm content, that I can meet the laws of nature—which are divine laws—with submission and happiness! These are conditions. I am considered initiated, but I have never passed through any...'—he searches for a word like ordination, but gives up. 'These are not dramatic things.'

'So is it just an acceptance by the community that this person is ready?'

'Yes. That's all.' An inspiration of how to convey the point to a woman strikes him. 'Like in love. How do you decide to love such and such a man? And what makes this person decide that he loves you? You go through decrees? No. Either you love him, or you don't. Either he meets your aspirations, or he doesn't. Either they accept him, or they don't. See what I mean? Of course he has to prove to them, that he is spiritually not far from them. For the Druze, initiation is acceptance.'

Still troubled by the elitism implied by the sect's jealously guarding its secrets even from its own, I ask: 'Why is access to the books withheld from ordinary people?'

'These books are commentaries on the sacred book of Islam,' he replies. 'They are written in a mystical way—they may be hard to understand for an ordinary reader. So you understand by being within this community, who are used to this kind of literature.'

108

But this *laissez-faire* approach, I object, might leave some people uncomfortably adrift. 'They don't have a place to go, books or, unless they seek them out, contact with spiritual leaders.'

'Yes, you are right,' he nods in kindly acknowledgement. 'They are left, because not everybody would like to be acquainted with this mystical nature. So it's not like in ordinary religion where the priest comes to your door and tells you have to go to the church or the mosque.

'But maybe in practice, this is wrong.' He is thoughtful now, pondering the point for himself. 'Yes, for the community it is wrong. I should not be left on my own. I should have someone tell me what is right and what is wrong. But you are not forced to mysticism.'

'So it's a path for the few, and that's just a fact of spiritual life?'

He nods. 'It's not for everybody. It's for everybody potentially. You're left to your own freedom.'

I am wondering whether this can be all there is to *taqiyya*. But the professor brushes aside my suggestion that the Druzes' careful policy has anything to do with fear of persecution by Muslims. 'Dissimulation is common to all religions,' he says. 'It is practised all over the world.'

The doorbell goes, and he takes delivery of a large bunch of pale pink roses for the hostess of a dinner he is to attend later that evening. Then he gives me some tips on talking to religious Druze in their mountain heartlands.

'First of all, they don't know much,' he advises. 'If a sheikh doesn't tell you, it does not necessarily mean that he does not want to tell you. Maybe he doesn't know the way; maybe there is a language barrier or an educational barrier.

'Because the sheikh is not necessarily someone who is learned?'

'Yes. He doesn't need to be. He did not practise the art of communication with others. And,' he lowers his voice confidentially, 'to

109

tell you the truth, not everyone who practises this kind of mysticism can be identified as a mystic. There are so many pretensions.'

Some will undoubtedly see me as an infidel, he adds. 'Yes, I think you will face some very hard times in getting answers to these questions!' He chuckles heartily to himself.

His wife, as she comes to say goodbye, is now hyper-glamorous in readiness for the dinner party. Her neck and arms glitter with jewels, and her full lips have been painted the same colour as her crimson skirt.

My interview with Professor Makarem left me oddly unsatisfied. Nothing he had said, I felt, could be considered misleading, yet I didn't have any sense of having got under the skin of the Druze condition, or of having got to grips with all this talk of secrets. His account was oddly devoid of specifics, and in many ways could have applied to a number of faiths. But I was heartened by the fact that some friends had arranged for me to meet a well-respected female initiate. The sheikha, I was told, would be happy to receive me, but would discuss social matters only, as she preferred to leave religious questions to those more learned than herself.

It would also be a rare opportunity to talk to a woman from a sect renowned for treating women as equals, both in marriage and the priesthood. 'Ask her about sex,' Abir instructs me as I set off for my appointment. 'I really want to know.'

An hour later, I'm admitted by a relative into a large apartment in a high-rise block on the outskirts of Beirut. Sofas line the walls of the sitting room where I wait for the sheikha, enough to seat at least a dozen people. There's the usual Arab kitsch: a large plastic sideboard, pots of plastic flowers, a fake gold tissue box. Only the photos of the beloved Druze leader Abu Hassan Aref Halawi, who was over a hundred when he died in 2003, suggest that this is not a Muslim house.

Then, in a glow of energy and warmth, the sheikha strides across the room, her hand outstretched. She is strikingly tall, and her height is further accentuated by her long dark robe and the white cotton veil that is draped loosely over her head. Her eyes sparkle and her voice bubbles with laughter as she enquires after my journey across Beirut, whether I need breakfast and my country of origin. 'I visited London twice before I changed my clothes!' she exclaims enthusiastically, adding—her tone lightly ironic at her younger, non-religious self—that these trips involved little more than shopping.

But as we settle into the interview, she becomes visibly tense, the shoulders of her big frame hunching as she talks. 'We are a more peaceful religion than others,' she begins tentatively. 'The way we are raised asks us to have peace inside, more than outside. We have only one excuse not to be peaceful—if somebody wants to attack us. Our religion asks us to have good intentions towards everybody, relations or far people, from our hearts. Our belief is that our relationship with God starts with a good relationship with others.'

The door bell interrupts her and a stylish woman enters, a crisp white outfit accessorized with spangled mules and a rainbow scarf. Well-cut hair falls over her shoulders. She is followed by a teenager with almost identical features. 'This is my small sister!' says the sheikha joyfully. 'She loves fashion, she loves colours.' Her gaze rests fondly on her. 'Today you see her in white, but usually she is in yellow, blue, pink...'

As her sister sinks into the sofa and becomes absorbed in punching data into her handheld computer, the sheikha resumes her account. 'Another important thing: if people have another belief, we don't have to change the way they think. Everybody is free—you are free to be a Christian, or a Jew or a Muslim. So we don't have enemies. Our

111

relationship with God doesn't interfere with what others think. It's what I think, and it's what I do and how I become nearer to God... I'm talking religiously...'

She breaks off with a light laugh, realizing she has already broken her self-imposed ban on theology. But it is already clear to me that this spiritual woman can no more refrain from expressing her faith than she can stop breathing. Perhaps, then, she will reveal some of the specifics of Druze observance, such as the mysteries of the Thursday meetings at the *majlis*. 'What are the important daily things?' I ask.

'We have obligations to others, this is very important,' she replies vaguely, citing the custom of neighbours helping a bereaved family to organize the funeral.

I ask about worship and weekly rituals and, thinking it might help to be specific, give the example of the Sunni Muslim ritual of five daily prayer times, plus Friday prayers at the mosque.

'You have to take the same pattern, but you have to add to it. It's not only about saying our prayers five times a day,' the sheikha says firmly. 'Anything I shouldn't do, I shouldn't do whether it's the time of prayer or not. No luxurious life, no smoking.'

The answer puzzles me. From what I've heard, Druze worship doesn't follow the Muslim model at all—there are no set prayer times, or obligations to go the mosque. I wonder if this is *taqiyya* in action: because I raised the example of Muslim prayer practices, this is what is being fed back to me. Perhaps I should address the matter less directly. 'Is life different for initiates than ordinary Druze?'

'Of course, it's different,' she responds. 'My intentions are more. The way I live is different. I don't need to go to parties, or any place that doesn't respect my clothes. I don't have the interest any more. If I had the same interests as my sister'—she gestures to the fashionable woman on the sofa opposite—'I wouldn't dress in black and put on my veil. It is the change of my heart that makes me change my

112

exterior clothes. So this is why we don't care for colours any more, or make-up. The unity, the whole of existence is much more important than any other thing, person, or interest. It's a feeling that you cannot express in words.' She taps her chest lightly. 'It is an inner soul feeling that leads you to live this life, an inner happiness that you don't get from all these materialistic hobbies!'

'So what are the things that help you attain this state?' I hope for details about meditation or prayer.

'To summarize the answer, cleaning your heart!' she replies. 'Can you spend all day without eating some essential nutrition? That's what we do daily. We nourish our souls with good nutrition.'

'Is it best to do this on your own?'

'You have to do it, but you have to struggle with yourself,' she says, still avoiding the question. 'We can be good, we can be bad. We have to fight the bad side in human feeling and feel the good side. This is the hardest struggle we have, deep inside. It's a job, *yanni*.'

'So what is the purpose of the Thursday meetings?'

'We encourage each other to the good side—that's what we meet about. Maybe I read a book and I didn't understand it, maybe I had a problem and I didn't know how to solve it.' She adds, confirming that idea that the Druze draw on a range of religious and philosophical texts: 'We don't read only our explanations. We read what Jesus says, what Mohammed, Aristotle, Plato says: the good wisdom. We need to take the wisdom from any high source.'

I try a direct question. 'What is special about your books?'

'If we have special explanations, it's a part only.' Her mouth closes.

I give up. I will fare better if I ask her about her own motivations and experience, I conclude. 'How did you come to change your clothes?'

113

She is immediately more forthcoming. 'I was a university girl, and sometimes I used to go to the church with our Christian friends, but I didn't think that one day I would change my clothes, until I started to read and my interest grew. My major was in social work, so I went to hospitals, saw the disabled, people who have sad lives. Maybe this made me look at life very early, at what makes happiness in life, what makes sadness.

'I wanted to know what is the meaning of Jesus? What is the meaning of Mohammed? Why are we forbidden to go out?' she continues, her eyes sparkling. 'All these questions were in mind. Like any girl at university, you feel you want to learn everything. So this moved me to know about religion. When I knew more, my inner feeling ruled me, and the way I looked at life was different. This inner change made me change my clothes.'

Seamlessly, she supplies the next question herself. 'If you ask me of the twenty-five years of my religious life, have you been happy or do you have any regrets, I tell you, I regret only the hours I didn't get my inner happiness! My family, my friends, people always want me to help them. They take my inner feeling from me—this is what I regret! If I could have my twenty-five years again, I would take all my time for my inner happiness!' She laughs ruefully.

She had hoped that the decision not to marry would guarantee her this spiritual space. 'Not getting married was my own decision; I didn't like to share family life or marriage. I wanted to live MY life, like mystics or nuns. I like to live this way!' She is exultant as she invokes her chosen lifestyle.

Then her voice plunges with regret. 'It didn't work out. My social life took a very big part. When you are in a community, people confide in you. What they don't tell their family, they tell you. Then you have to be ready for people; you can't say, "No, I don't have time." So every day you have a problem, something you are working on.'

114

'Your faith is unusual in allowing women to enter the priesthood,' I say. 'Are you really treated equally to men?'

'There are many responsibilities on men, we cannot take them,' says the sheikha airily. 'The higher decisions are theirs.'

I'm a little disappointed. 'Aren't women their spiritual equals?'

'I will ask for women's rights now!' She laughs ironically, teasing me for my pious Western feminism. 'Of course! Why not? Maybe sometimes women have more ability. Why not? They have their mind, they have their heart, they have their knowledge.'

'What about in social terms?'

'We have the same Western rights in marriage. Marriage is sometimes arranged, sometimes not. But it isn't obligatory at all—the woman must know everything about the man, she must see him, she must hear him. She must examine her feelings, if she wants him or not. If not, she can stop everything. It's very just. If she is his wife, and she says, "I hate him as a husband," she can divorce. And if the man wants to divorce her, she will get half of what he has: money, furniture. She has the right to take the house. Our rules are very advanced.'

'What are the views on sex?' There is no easy way to ask this; I have plunged in.

The sheikha is unfazed. 'People are not all the same. In ordinary life, some people like sex, some people have another interest. But religion encourages you not to be weak. It's not good for a religious man to be ruled by his sexual feelings. It's better if he can control himself. Some people have a normal sexual life, for some it's only to have children, and others live as brother and sister. Sheikh Halawi was married to a lady younger than him, and very pretty. They used to be in the same bed, and she stayed a sister. He was very close to his God, and he was capable of ruling his emotions.'

115

'I hope she was happy too,' I remark tartly, dismayed at the idea of a young woman spending her married life in celibacy.

The sheikha laughs. 'She was! He doesn't have the right to marry her if he is not frank. He must tell her if he wants to live as brother and sister. If not, it's unfair.' She repeats emphatically: 'It's unfair. But there are few people like that, very few—maybe three or four.'

I confess that my question about sex was a plant from a young Druze friend. The sheikha's laugh peels out across the room.

The interview over, she relaxes visibly, her large frame unfolding back to its natural dimensions. 'I was very frank, very frank,' she tells me, with a very direct look. Then she adds almost humbly: 'Can I ask one thing? Don't use my name. We don't like fame.'

Her sister, Salma, offers to drive me into the Chouf to visit the shrine to Job at Niha. 'I'm not busy,' she assures me, adding that the trip will be a Saturday outing for her and her daughter Hala. For me, it will be my first opportunity to see the mountainous Druze heartlands and a chance to visit one of the Druzes' main sites. They admire the Old Testament prophet for his patient suffering, and his tomb is a place of pilgrimage for those seeking spiritual help or consolation, popular with Christians and Muslims too. 'This idea of shared worship is rather strange for us in Britain,' I remark to the sheikha, as Salma goes to fetch the car.

'Many people in our sect go to churches and other shrines,' responds the sheikha. 'A lot of Lebanese people interact. You are not only a Druze in a Druze community, you have the Christian and the Muslim in the same tribe; you have the Armenian, the Ismaili. You have all your friends around you, and you grow up loving them. You go to their houses, and they come to your place. It's not strange for us, at all.'

But the civil war changed things, she adds with a note of sadness. 'Before the war, it was very nice—you never, ever had these compari-

116

sons between Druze and Muslims. After the war, if you are a Druze, you have to go to the Druze political leader to work out your thing, if you are Shia, you have to go the Shia political leader.'

We chat idly as we wait for her sister to fetch the car. Then the sheikha surprises me.

'How old do you think I am?' she asks me, coyly. 'Put a number!'

I hesitate. She seems mature, but her eyes are so sparkly, her skin so fresh and unlined. 'Forty.'

The sheikha is delighted. 'I am fifty-two!'

As Hala and I leave to rejoin her mother downstairs, we find half a dozen Druze women clustered outside the lift, their white veils and long black dresses starkly old-fashioned against the concrete, on their way to take more of her soul's time from the laughing mystic.

In no time we have cleared the concrete of Beirut and are climbing the winding roads into the mountains. The hills and valleys explode with late-spring greenery. Steering her four-wheel drive expertly around the bends, my hostess points out the main attractions. In the village of Mukhtara we pass the elegant stone arches of Walid Jumblatt's ancestral home. Further on, long walls curl around the hillside, marking the extensive grounds of the house of the Druzes' spiritual leader Bahjat Ghaith. In the country lanes, less affluent Druze are quietly going about their business in farm and construction work. Salma is umbilically attached to her mobile phone, and its loud ring regularly punctuates our conversation.

The car ascends higher and higher until finally we pull up in a car park on a mountain peak. The shrine is in a raised courtyard of pristine white stone and the midday sun blazes off it, dazzling our eyes as we mount the steps onto a plateau surrounded by sky and rock. The harsh granite slopes of the nearby mountains have only a few dots of green. It's unnaturally quiet, although the distant hum of traffic arises from the valley below.

At the entrance to the tomb, we remove our shoes, each woman donning a veil from a basket. As I put mine on, a strong perfume from a previous wearer assails me, pricking my nostrils. Salma is still talking warmly to her brother on the phone and her daughter, exasperated, reminds her of the need for quiet in this holy place.

Inside, a hefty slap of grey marble sits solidly behind golden railings. The space around it is littered with votive offerings: there are framed Koranic inscriptions, sequins glittering against black felt and someone has pinned a giant, woollen Druze star to the railings, each of its points painstakingly crocheted in a different colour. I wander around the rectangle, taking in these residues of the old animism. The place is like an embodiment of people's prayers: poignantly, someone has left two tiny T-shirts, presumably in the hope that their owner will get well. A notice from the administration requesting visitors not to deposit hair is completely disregarded, as around every knot of metalwork are twisted strands of brown, blond, grey and black.

I stop in front of a little shelf jutting out from the tomb's railings, bearing an intriguing envelope of pink satin. 'What is it?' I ask Hala curiously.

She starts as she sees looks down at the shelf and quickly bends to kiss the satin cover. Only then, devotional duty done, does she answer me. 'That's the book. We can't read it—only the initiates can.'

I continue my gentle pacing. In one of the far corners four women are sitting on mattresses staring blankly into space. A few feet away, an old woman is half-collapsed against the base of the tomb, her face etched with grief. Her hand clutches a single, scrunched tissue.

Salma is in the other corner, her vivacity gone. She sits, her legs folded under her, nursing some private sorrow. She looks out from

118

under her white veil with mournful, tear-filled eyes, and requests five minutes alone.

Ten minutes later, we are back in the car, driving back down the mountainside. 'How often do you come here?' I ask Salma, now restored to her usual chatty, smiley self. 'Usually once a year,' she replies. 'But recently, I have come more often.'

I don't pry any further, and we return to the sheikha's apartment for a hearty lunch of fish, meat and rice. A black maid, a blue scarf knotted around her head, leaves her pile of ironing to wait on us. I observe her carefully; I'm unfamiliar with this servant class, largely made up of migrant workers from the Philippines, Sri Lanka and Ethiopia. Every now and then, human rights campaigners would complain about abuses against them, but they were common in well-to-do Lebanese households. This girl looks sullen, withdrawn, her eyes permanently downcast. No one speaks to her except Hala, who calls peremptorily for her to clear this dish or that.

After we have finished, prompted by a blend of conscience and curiosity, I go back to the table and thank her. The effect is transformatory. Her face bursts into life, and she smiles.

Meanwhile, the question of the true nature of the Druze threatened to dominate my research, drowning out other aspects of Lebanon's religious life. Each time I tried to put it aside to explore how some of the country's other sects saw the world, it seemed that a new opportunity to find out more about the Druze would present itself, and intriguing questions would start tugging at my consciousness again. Now I had an invitation to spend a Sunday in the heart of the Chouf, meeting religious Druze. These initiates would be different from the

119

urban sophisticates I had met so far, rural folk whose piety had been formed in the mountains among their own kind.

I hoped that the trip would be a chance to learn more about what practising Druze believed. One key doctrine was the transmigration of souls, according to which a soul was created at the dawn of time and passed through a number of human bodies until the Day of Judgement. While this popular belief was widespread, the religious basis for the sect's being a closed community which neither sought converts nor welcomed intruders was a mystery. But warnings from the likes of Professor Makarem that even religious Druze often misunderstood their own faith were ringing in my ears, making me aware that talking to these pious folk was no guarantee of truth.

Diana Bou Ghanem was to take me to her birthplace of Ramlieh, a village known for its religious conservatism and high proportion of Druze who 'wear the clothes.' She herself had left village life behind, and lived in Beirut with a high-ranking government job. She looked the consummate urban professional, always immaculately turned out in sharp jackets and crisp shirts, and from the moment I met her I caouldn't help seeing the 1950s movie star in her chiselled features, milky skin and sleek black hair.

She was, I realized, the quintessential modern Lebanese Druze, belonging to both mountain and city, her life a delicate negotiation of modernity and tradition. She juggled her job with bringing up her two children while her husband worked in the Gulf for half the year. But despite the difficulties of maintaining a good standard of living in Lebanon, she had refused the temptation of emigration. 'I've had really good job offers abroad, but I didn't want to leave,' she tells me over coffee in her smart Beirut apartment. 'Here, my children get a good education. I don't want them to grow up in isolation; I want them to stay close to their roots. My parents and most of my family are here. My sister and brother often drop by, and we sit to-

120

gether—it's nice. And I can go to my village in the mountains; I like to see the community there. I think all these attachments are what give me my self-confidence.'

So one Sunday morning we set off, her ten-year-old son Samah grumbling about being torn away from his computer on this, his precious school-free day. Her children's loud, American-accented English puzzles me until Diana explains that her project of bringing them up as English-speakers has been so successful that they now find speaking Arabic an effort. 'I've ruined them,' she jokes. On her one day off after the six-day Lebanese week, she is still briskly efficient, phoning ahead to place orders for meat as we drive. When we stop for supplies in Aley, the large town between Beirut and the Chouf, it's clear that I've found a partner in eating.

As we wait for our snacks, I watch work in the tiny bakery closely. A tiny production line is working at top speed: a young man feeds dough balls through giant rollers at the back of the shop, flipping the flat rounds expertly onto a stone counter, and then spreading them with *zatar*. A second man scoops the pizzas onto a giant spatula and into a huge oven. A couple of minutes later they emerge, crisp and golden, and are instantly dispatched to customers at the shop front a yard away. Next door, a heavy-set man in the Turkish dress is piling *knefeh* and melted cheese into sweet milk rolls. A large round tray of cheese is kept constantly heated by a gas burner. When he gets an order, he scoops up great gloops of the cheese and loads it into the bread. The whole town seems to be preoccupied with making and getting food, with car after car pulling up and their drivers striding purposefully into bakeries and greengrocers and coming out with laden arms.

Back in the car, I try to work my way through the huge roll that Diana has bought me to sample. It has a delicate savoury-sweet-

121

ness, but is one of the richest, most filling things that I've ever eaten. Samah can't see why anyone would want to eat such a thing when burgers are available. 'Don't finish it if you don't like it, Alex,' he tells me, his tone avuncular. 'We won't be offended.'

As we speed through village after village, Diana tells me a kind of Chouf urban myth that illustrates how distinctive these local cultures used to be, isolated in their different pockets of rock. Once upon a time, about a hundred years ago, she says, there was a man who gave free rein to his witty, anthropological insights, naming whole villages after the characteristics their inhabitants called to mind. One was, he said, a village of 'colourful cocks', another of 'dogs' and another of 'hyenas'. He came to a sticky end when one community took offence and killed him.

Gradually the road narrows, and the foliage lining its white-stoned edges thickens. 'It's the end of the world,' says Diana, as we plough deeper into the greenness. Olive groves, fruit orchards and prickly pear trees jostle for space, and grasses and bushes fill every gap. Just a few houses poke out of the vegetation.

Arriving in Ramlieh, we pass the village's Holy Tree, reputed to be two thousand years old, and in whose shade a Druze prophet is said to have rested in the sect's early days. The locals had only given up the habit of tying sick relatives' clothing to its branches a few decades ago, and now the tree itself is sickly, its dead branches falling away.

At her in-laws' simply furnished house, Diana's father and mother in law fuss over their grandchildren, their bent bodies shaped by their formal black dress. We leave Samah happily munching some Western food in front of the television, and set off on our rounds.

In the house of the first initiates, membership of the *uqqal* has been handed down, parent to child. There was never a moment of decision marking their entry into the circle: the religious life just was what they did. The woman of the house, Salwa Boudaher, is chicly conservative in her tailored black jacket and elegant skirt that sweeps the floor. She ushers us onto a patio embedded in the green valley. There is no sign of the water that feeds this lushness, but its rushing sound is everywhere. A yellow canary chirps from a cage in the corner.

Salwa is wreathed in smiles for the visitors, bringing us tray after tray of refreshments. We snacks on nuts and fresh fruit, imbibe juices and tea. The pleasantries over, I am invited to ask questions. But when I do, her body folds up defensively and she shies away from eye contact. All I can see is a partial, veiled profile.

Her stepson, Jawad, a confident young man in jeans and shirt, answers most of the questions in her place. Like many young Druze, he gave up religious dress while at university in Beirut. Now, running a local eco-tourist project, he sees no need to set himself apart.

'We believe in God—that's the most important thing—and re-incarnation, and the prophets. It is important to be honest when speaking with others,' he says, his dark eyes looking at me straight-forwardly. 'We believe that when a person dies, the spirit moves from one person to another. The number of people around the world is stable—it doesn't increase, and it doesn't decrease.'

I look at Salwa and she adds, her voice low with shyness: 'The rea-son for this belief is if you imagine it increased by one per cent, there wouldn't be a place for everyone, and if it decreased, there wouldn't be enough people. How is God going to judge a person on only one life? For example, if a baby lives only one day. This person has to live so many lives in different circumstances—then they can be judged.'

'Some people are born rich, some poor, in different circumstances, so God cannot judge people according to one life,' adds Jawad. 'You should be judged on all these lives.'

I try addressing Salwa again. 'Will there be peace on earth?'

123

'Of course.' Her voice is so low it is barely audible. 'After Doomsday. We believe that heaven is not something imaginary, but it's somewhere on earth. We don't believe that heaven and the good stuff is physical—it's a state of consciousness.'

'The prophets will come back to earth at Doomsday,' says Jawad, listing the most eminent of the 164 from Salman Al Farasi and Hamza Ibn Ali, who share the same soul. 'They have been sent to all the places in the whole of the earth—to India, China. Everywhere on earth there are people who are part of our religion,' he continues. 'The age of the universe is three hundred and thirty four million years. Our religion started at this time. It was closed only a thousand years ago. All the people in our religion entered then.'

'Is there any chance that people could become Druze after this time?' We are, I realize, talking about the point the Druze became a closed sect.

His tone is both categorical and matter-of-fact. 'There are no more chances, no.'

'What will happen at Judgement Day?'

'Each and every person will be judged according to his behaviour, but the Druze people will be preferred,' he replies. 'Some people entered, and then left. They betrayed it, and will be treated the same way as the others.'

'Why was it closed?'

'We believe that this goes back to God; we don't know why it was closed,' he says simply.

'What is your relation to the Muslim faith?'

'We have our own characteristics and beliefs. Yet we are part of Islam. We are one of seventy groups. Mohammad said only a part of these will be the righteous people. They are the survivors—the preferred ones.'

124

'Is it really necessary to distinguish between the initiates and the ordinary Druze?'

'There are many opinions among us, but I think that everyone who is Druze should know his religion—it doesn't depend on his costume,' replies Jawad. 'The clothes are not a basic belief—it's a Turkish custom. I believe that the religion shouldn't be limited to those people.'

'Knowledge is a must. If you worship God without knowledge, you abuse yourself,' adds his stepmother. She is growing more confident now. 'They can read the books, but they should understand what they are reading. Some people read and just memorize—they don't know what they are reading.'

'Do you think that if people knew everything about the Druze there would be harm to them?'

'I don't think so,' replies Jawad.

I leave it there. With Diana, her daughter and several relatives looking on, I am asking delicate questions in quite a crowd.

Salwa turns to me. 'What is your religion?'

'I believe that all religions have a part of the truth,' I reply truthfully, also aware that this should constitute a safe, diplomatic answer in Lebanon.

'So you are lost, then?' It's half a question, half a statement.

'No, I'm found,' I tell her.

As we take our leave, I feel a little confused by the conflicting elements of what I've heard about the Druze faith; its universalism, with adherents scattered all over the world, sits uneasily with the elitist claims of belonging to the only righteous sect. But there is little time for reflection as we trip down the village lanes. The day takes on a holiday feel as we stop under some trees near Diana's old home. Shedding her city formality, Diana reaches up and plucks their dark red berries, cram-

125

ming them into her mouth and passing handfuls to me. 'I used to eat these as a child,' she says, her hands stained with juice.

At a house at the other end of the village, we are admitted to a bright reception room, lined with sofas and a bed with a yellow counterpane. When its owner, Sawsan Abi Ali, comes to greet us only her bespectacled eyes and rather prominent nose emerge out of the white veil drawn across her face. 'Take the veil away from your mouth', her mother tells her, a tiny, serene figure. 'There's no man here.'

Her daughter obeys. With her scrubbed-clean skin and eager-to-please smile, Sawsan has the air of a super-conscientious sixth former, certainly a prefect or even the head girl. But she's thirty-nine and the mother of several children, including the seventeen-year-old, alert-eyed young man who comes to join us.

The promptings for her entry into the religious life, in 1983, were political. 'After Israel came to Lebanon, there was a lot of fear. We got closer to our God,' she explains simply, in halting English. She has seen many changes in the Druze community in the two decades since. 'In the past, we were closed,' she says. 'But now we go to Beirut. We have many friends of other religions, especially Christians.'

'Is there anything about these changes that you don't like?'

'My kids,' she says, without hesitation. 'There are things I don't like my kids doing. In the past, mothers used to complain when their sons talked to girls. I don't have a problem with my son being different, and going out with girls. But there are limitations—he can't have a girlfriend, just be friends. This freedom is good, but it has to have some limitations—it shouldn't be in like in Europe, with people living together. I want my children to marry someone from the same religion; it would not be acceptable to marry someone from a different religion,' she continues. 'Religiously it is not allowed, and in a few years he would live in bitterness and feel it's wrong.'

126

She tells the story of a cousin who went to Russia for work and married a Russian woman. On returning to Lebanon, the family at first refused to speak to the new bride, but eventually warmed to her when they saw how good a mother she was. 'So now they like her, but they still don't like the idea,' she concludes.

Her son Assem joins in, pointing out that inter-marriages are becoming increasingly common. 'I agree with this change,' he says, his dark eyes dancing with energy. 'I don't find it bad, because every person should have contact with other people. In the end, we have the same country and we talk the same language, so we cannot divide. In the future it will be normal.'

'Would you marry outside?'

'I can imagine it—why not? We have globalization, the world is becoming a small village. We can't have a country with every sect divided. The civil war happened in Lebanon because of that. We don't want war.'

Laughter ripples around the room at his grandiose statement. But the teenager has turned everyone's thoughts to the civil war, and the brutal battle the Druze fought with the Maronites for control of the Chouf. By the time they had won, around 75 000 Christians had been routed from their homes. The experience had reawakened Maronite memories of the 1860 massacre by the Druze, fuelling the latter's reputation as warriors endowed with almost supernatural powers. 'They said we had horns and even tails!' says Assem, in amusement.

'The Druze have the reputation for being vicious fighters, but in politics they cannot do anything—they cannot lie,' says Diana. While Druze ethics permit self-defence, the obligation to tell the truth made political game-playing difficult. 'So in peace, we always lose, and in war we always win,' she adds.

127

Aiwa! sings out Sawsan in loud agreement, instinctively adopting the manner of the political rally. Then, suddenly self-conscious, she giggles.

'The Christians and the Druze are the two poles that control the whole of Lebanon,' continues Diana. 'If they clash, the whole of Lebanon will fall. We have thoughts and ways of living in common with the Maronites.' 'We have to be strong in order not to be eaten, when other people try to throw us out of our land!' agrees Assem.

Sawsan fetches a pot of *matte*, the shared drink from Argentina which has become an important group ritual for the Druze. Made of strong herbs, it is believed to have medicinal properties but, as a non-habitué, I had already discovered that even the smallest quantity had gut-wrenching properties. Internally, I blench slightly.

'We want to give you *matte*,' says Sawsan, handing me the pot for the first imbibing. 'It's not for visitors and officials—it's for family and close people.' 'It brings families together,' adds Assem. 'It makes for a conversation between families, because everyone looks at the one who holds it!'

I take the tiniest of sips through the silver straw. 'How strong do you now feel as a community?' I ask. I pass the pot back to Sawsan for the customary rinsing before the next person.

'Politically we are strong because we won the war, and everyone respects our word,' responds Assem. 'Socially and economically, we are not strong.'

'You see that our area is not very advanced,' adds Diana. 'If someone wants to go to university, he has to go to Beirut. This is part of our under-development. This is because we are a minority. There used to be agriculture, but that's not enough now. In every house there is someone who is living in the Gulf and supporting the family. My husband is living in the Emirates, working as a project manager for a construction company.'

128

'Why do you stay here?'

'We have better schools and universities in Lebanon,' she says. 'Our society—not just the Druze—believes that education is an introduction to a better future.'

'Lebanon has a very big problem now,' says Assem. 'People want to live in Europe, and they want to stay attached to their country at the same time.'

'What do you want to do?' I'm aware that this young social commentator will soon be negotiating these dilemmas for himself.

'I want to leave Lebanon.' He is cheerful and resolute. 'Every guy my age is now leaving; they want to go where they can earn money.'

I turn to his mother for signs of maternal distress. But she is smiling her goodwill smile. 'I wish him good opportunities,' she says. 'But I am afraid for the future.' The *matte* pot, having returned to her once more, rests in her clasped hands. 'I hope he will get a job here, but if not, I will accept it.'

If he does leave, it will be difficult for him marry within the community, I point out.

'I will go to the Gulf,' says Assem. 'It is hard to stay in the Druze communities in Europe, but in the Arab countries it is not that hard—there are many Druze there.' 'The problem is that the Druze are not accepted in the Arab world, not like in Europe and the US, where a guy or a girl might get along with that community,' adds Diana. 'But it's more dangerous for us to be in Europe and the US than in the Arab world. We always come back from the Arab world. Even in Brazil, in Australia, you melt. In the Arab countries you cannot melt.'

Diana's mother-in-law is calling us home for lunch over the mobile phone. As we gather ourselves to leave, Assem sums up the hopes of his generation. 'We are in the Middle East, where religion has first place. They don't look at you for the education you have, it's

129

your religion—this is the problem. In Lebanon, we have eighteen sects and every one wants power. When our country is strong, we will be united and we will be like Europeans.'

One evening I return late to the Y, exhausted by my lengthy interview with the domineering Muslim sheikh. 'Oh, they're all like that, they don't know how to have a dialogue,' Abir consoles me as I lie on my bed in the manner of a consumptive heroine. She rushes round, solicitously bringing me beer and noodles.

'Okay, I'll tell you now,' she says suddenly. Neither of us had forgotten her promise to tell me her own ideas about the Druze faith once my research was underway. Thanks to the loan of a lamp from Madame Victoria, my softly-lit room, blasted by sun and city noise during the day, has taken on an air of meditative calm.

She sits on the end of my bed, illicit beer bottle in hand. As a teenager, she begins, her father had begun to talk to her about important matters of faith. 'It began when I started studying Plato and Aristotle at fifteen. I came back from school every day, and realized that he had read all these things and knew more than I did. About once a month we discussed these things for three or four hours. Mostly, we'd begin, "what is the purpose of life?" We'd talk about why God created us—this is the most important mystery—and sometimes we'd end by saying that we don't have the right to ask this.'

It was the other side of the controlling, conservative man that had driven his daughter away. 'When I sit talking with him about philosophy and religion, he's a very open-minded person,' she continues. 'I think like I do because of him. But he can't think like that, he can't run away from his society.'

Over the years, a strange and wonderful tale about the history of the Druze had emerged out of their conversations, a new perspective on the faith which her father had gleaned from his father before him. She had never heard it mentioned by anyone else. According to the story, the Druze six books, the holy books so jealously guarded by the initiates, were not the true source of the Druze wisdom. They came about when the sect closed as a way of protecting people from persecution from other religions. By drawing on the scriptures of Islam and Christianity, the new books helped create the impression that their devotees practised a faith little different from that of those around them. Beneath the appearance of conformity, however, the *muwahhidun* did not follow a formal religion of doctrine and ritual at all. Instead, like the ancient seekers after truth that they really were, they simply sought wisdom. The impulse they followed combined the pursuit of science and spiritual knowledge, inspiring an attempt to understand the world as the creation of God.

'The wisdom the Druze believed in wasn't in the six books,' she continues. 'It was in twenty-four books that were stolen and are now found in museums, for example, in a glass case in France. People don't know what they are—it isn't known, even by Druze people. They're just presented as old books. They are the result of a long, scientific work about numbers, the principles of the creation. They were written by a group of people who had done a lot of studies—they were discoverers, brilliant people—and they discussed their discoveries and put them altogether. The equations in them are the basics, the basis of existing knowledge and technology. But people don't know that.'

She pauses and takes a swig of beer, her face only half visible in the dim light. Through the haze of my exhaustion I can hear an archetypal story in this tale of the lost books, the belief in an ur-text holding the Secrets of Everything.

Along with their scientific and metaphysical truths, she goes on, the lost books also contained the answer to the central, ethical ques-

131

tion facing humanity, that of how we should live. She is talking fast now, the words tumbling out as she tries to communicate the importance of this link between technological progress and morality. 'If the bunch of people who wrote the twenty-four books had not been stopped and continued working, so that God was gloried more, the equations and everything discovered would have been used in a good way, and not with evil aims, like the atomic bomb.'

But gradually, this fundamental truth had become forgotten, its purity clouded by the need to conform to the 'right' doctrines and practices. 'Over time, people came to believe in the six books, which are so close to other religions,' she continues eagerly. 'That's why, when you ask a Druze now, you don't know if he knows about the real religion or not, because only a few of them know. Others have just been raised to know that there is a secret—they don't know what it is. The ones who do know don't tell them, because that will be confusing for people.'

Even her father had been cautious about telling her these things. Hidden in his study, he kept a Very Old Book, off-limits to the family. Time and again, she had begged him to show it to her. 'He always says, "After your exams", or "In the summer".' Nonetheless, she had gleaned enough from their piecemeal discussions to conclude that the people of wisdom were everywhere, and not just confined to one sect. 'There are a lot of people like this, they just believe in wisdom and God and creativity,' she continues. 'And that's why people say that lots of people are Druze.'

'So it's the original mysticism, then?' I have managed to prop myself up, inspired by the picture of a non-sectarian spirituality that is emerging. Its adherents, living in societies where piety was measured in terms of observance, would be keenly aware that, if fully exposed, their faith would not qualify as a proper religion and they would risk persecution as unbelievers. Hence a policy of secrecy.

'Mysticism?' She doesn't know the word. But it doesn't matter.

In recent years, the spiritual leader of the Lebanese Druze, Bahjat Ghaith, and his son have been publishing a magazine and website dedicated to explaining the Druze faith, she adds. Maybe the publications signal a new willingness to go beyond the old, official line and finally open up to the world. I should pay the top sheikh a visit. 'Maybe there will be clues,' she tells me, sagely. 'Maybe he will talk.'

6
REVELATIONS

BUT before I meet the top man, a door into the inner world of the Druze unexpectedly swings open.

I had gone back to the Chouf to see coexistence in action. High on a mountain plateau above the Christian village of Deir el Qamar, young Druze and Christians were studying side by side, wartime hatreds apparently forgotten. Founded by the Maronites, the Catholic University of Notre Dame had opened three years before, offering the youth of the area an alternative to university in the costly, less accessible Beirut. It was an idyllic place in which to study, with clean, white classrooms overlooking rose gardens, pine trees reaching into the sky and mountain vistas stretching into the distance. In contrast to the sticky heat of the valleys below, an alpine breeze wafted across the campus.

I was given free rein in a Rhetoric class, part of the English course, to discuss students' concerns. Their teacher, Dr. Dany Badran, was an intense, articulate young man, recently returned from five years' postgraduate study in Britain. 'There are taboo topics here,' he told me when I asked him whether the institution's religious status affected the curriculum. 'Sex, politics and religion are not discussed. I teach Rhetoric, which is about discussing controversial issues, so we discuss all three.' Gathering up his papers, he added with cheerful irony: 'So far, I haven't been fired.'

In the classroom twenty-five mainly Druze students are eager to give their views. One thick-set young man with a fleshy face quickly emerges as the class spin-doctor: relationships between different sects are unproblematic, diversity is a good thing and people are attracted to the West because of the excellent social and political rights it affords, he says. His claims elicit eye-rolling and tutting from some of his classmates. The questions that are really exercising them at the start of their adult lives—the difficulty of finding an acceptable marriage partner and their future job prospects—bubble up to the surface a few times, but don't achieve any clear expression. But as I leave, a young man with delicately sculpted features stops me in the corridor. I missed something in the class, he tells me politely: the degree to which Druze society rejects marriage with anyone from another sect. Although critical of this narrow-mindedness, he adds, he himself does not intend to break with tradition. 'I prefer not to marry outside,' he says. 'You'll face social problems, and then the couple themselves will have problems.'

A sallow-faced fellow in a cream baseball cap joins in. 'The main problem is the role of the parents, telling us who to mix with,' he says.

'We have many friends from other religions, including Christian,' agrees the other. 'They don't interfere with my friends, but I think they would if marriage was a possibility. Everything except marriage!'

Having made the limits of coexistence clear, he departs.

All day long at the university of the mountains, the students seem to be on a mission of soothsaying, coming one after the other to tell me the realities of their lives. News that I'm here has travelled fast, and soon all I have to do is sit on a pine-shaded bench and wait for them. One tall young Druze strolls up, his smart shirt and dark trousers giving him the air of a young businessman. He had heard about what was said in the classroom, and wants to correct a wrong

135

impression I've been given, he says: people will certainly marry outside Druze society, but for venal motives, to get a Western passport
and a leg-up on the road to prosperity.

Prayer beads in hand, he lowers his large frame onto the bench
beside me. 'I lost two of my uncles in the war. Nobody expects my
family to forget. But we say that we are turning a new page. We don't
have anything against Christians, nor do the Christians have anything against us. But it takes time. With time, you'll find in Lebanon
that everyone will be on the same side.'

In his village of Marsa, where the proportion of Druze to Christians is seventy-thirty, the two communities have been slowly rebuilding their relationship, he explains. 'They're normal—like any
neighbours living in the same village. During the war, the Christians
went to Beirut. They came back to our village in 1997. In 1998, we
saw each other in the village, but we didn't talk. 1999 was better.
From 2000 onwards, things have been normal.'

His friend runs over and takes the prayer beads from him.

'You share them?' I ask in surprise.

'Yes,' he smiles, catching my amusement.

'Are you a religious person?'

He nods simply. 'Yes, I am a religious person.'

'Would you become an initiate?'

'No!' He tuts, smiling. 'Too much!'

A girl with long black spiralling curls has drifted up, and is leaning
against the bench, listening. 'It's not like the religious people tell us
what to do—our family teaches us how to grow up,' she says.

'I want to know about my religion,' says the young man. 'All the
youth talk about this—we say we want to know and why don't you
allow us. They don't even allow us to read the Holy Book.'

'Do you tell the initiates this?'

136

'Yeah, we tell them,' says the girl, her curls bobbing energetically. They say, "You must abide by the religion before you know. You must wear the uniform."'

'You can ask the sheikh, and he will answer you,' the young man adds. 'But on explicit things—what is forbidden and what is not.'

'They say, "cover truth",' rejoins the girl. 'They won't explain anything very clearly. They give you simple, basic things. They won't allow us to go deep into the religion until we accompany them.'

'What if you read the books alone?' I knew from Diana that it was possible, if you had money and the right contacts, to get hold of copies of the sacred texts.

'You will be responsible.' The girl's tone conveys finality and a huge sense of isolation.

'If you understand something wrong, and do something wrong, you will be punished,' adds the young man, making the spiritual consequences crystal clear. 'What follows is on our conscience.'

His thoughts turn to more practical issues. 'It's so hard in Lebanon,' he goes on. 'It's hard finding a job, hard mixing with Christians. Some Christian parties have hatred towards us. If you fill in an application for a job in a Christian organization, the first thing they ask you is: Christian or Druze? Then they ask you which political party. Then they tell you to go home. "I will call you later," they say.'

He gets up. 'I want to work.' His frustration is evident now. The business look is no accident; his degree is in business studies and he's desperate to get a job. 'Yeah, Durzi, I'll call you later.' He snorts derisively and spreads his hands in helplessness. 'It's always like this.'

Later, as the golden afternoon sun slopes across the campus, I sit with Mazen, a nineteen-year-old Greek Orthodox Christian who is studying computing. With his green eyes and an easy physicality on the cusp of boyhood-manhood, he has the kind of looks to make most teenage

137

girls swoon. His upbringing, with a mother who had taken the almost unheard-of step of converting from Islam to marry, has made him well-used to the mingling of different religious currents.

'I was thinking since I was a child that there was no difference between people,' he tells me earnestly, gazing into the middle distance through long, lowered lashes. 'I take a person for what he is, not his religion. I'm a Christian, but I don't check someone's ID to decide whether he's a friend or not. My class at school was half Christian, half Druze—I couldn't tell the difference.'

Yet while he doesn't feel any inter-religious tension himself, he has noticed how quickly tribal loyalties can surface. 'If there is a fight, all the Druze come together, all the Christians come together, all the Muslims come together.' He makes a gathering movement with his hands. 'Even if they are all friends.'

The college grounds, with their cosy high school atmosphere, suddenly take on a different light. Gangs of angry and belligerent young men form in my mind's eye, each a distinct, aggressive clan. 'Why?' I ask.

'I don't know.' The green eyes are thoughtful. 'Maybe everyone thinks, "I have to be with him, because he's my religion," not because he's right.'

'Empty brains,' supplies a Druze friend helpfully, who has been listening from the bench opposite.

'Let's say, for example, that a Christian killed one of his relatives in the war,' Mazen points to his friend. 'Or a Druze killed one of my relatives. We can't hate each other because of that. It was a war. Everyone knows the rules of war.'

There's a pause. It's been a long day, and I start to put away my pad. But Mazen prompts me. 'You've forgotten the big question—would I marry outside my religion?'

'Yes, of course,' I start slightly. 'Would you?'

138

'Yes, I would,' he says, his tone definite. 'I'm even in love with a Druze girl. But we broke up. She was afraid that if we continued, there would be a problem in the Druze community. If any Druze girl marries another religion, she's totally forbidden from her society, maybe also her family. That's the way it is with the Druze—it's a really big problem. All my friends—and I've talked to a lot of people about this—say that, in themselves, they don't have a problem with marrying outside. They are afraid of Society.'

'They say the children will not be Druze,' his Druze friend adds. 'It's recessive.' He taps his chest to indicate the inescapably biology of the matter.

I turn back to Mazen. 'Were you upset when you broke up with your girlfriend?'

'Yes.' He turns his far-away gaze directly on me and green eyes blink ever so faintly. 'Very. But I dealt with it, for her. She was right in how she thinks. That's her family, her society in the end. I dealt with it, for her. I can't blame her.' He pauses. 'That's the only problem I found with Druze society—everything else is good. They are good people, they love everyone. But when it comes to religion, there's a red line that can't be crossed.'

Then, politely conversational, he asks: 'Where else have you been in Lebanon?'

The Druze shrine to Job at Niha, I tell him. He smiles.

'He'—he points, mock accusingly, to his Druze friend opposite— 'promised me he would take me there. Me and two Muslims. He promised me!' Smiling, he looks to me to share his indignation.

Then he turns serious again. 'This is the problem with Lebanese society. The parents play a big role. I know some parents—those who were here during the war—who push their children to hate people from other religions. I know a lot of people like that from all religions. It's a big problem in Lebanese society, and the war made it bigger.

139

'The war's over now. At least'—he's laughing again now—'I hope it is!' Playfully, he swings a leg out to kick a second Druze friend who has just alighted on the bench opposite. 'If not, I'll fight him first!'

Earlier that day, as I was sitting talking to a group of students in the café, someone slid silently into a seat at the table. The newcomer's striking features and glossy black ponytail had a look of Oriental hippy-chic and a bearing beyond his twenty-odd years.

He cut across our rather limping discussion. I was not being given a true picture of the Druze, he insisted authoritatively. All this talk of their tolerance and respect for other faiths masked a conviction that theirs was the last religion of the Middle East, infinitely superior to Judaism, Christianity and Islam. Although no one dared admit it, the Druze were in fact deeply critical of other religions. His name was Ramzi Mahmoud, and he knew this from the rare books to which he had access and his mentor, a scholar and former initiate who had long tutored him in religious matters. If I care to visit him in his village of Dmit, he would arrange for me to meet this theological dissident.

A week later, I make my way once more into the Chouf. This time, it's no ordinary journey. A general strike, called by the labour unions in protest against rising fuel prices, has taken most of the taxis and buses off the roads. It takes me an hour to even find a *servis* willing to go to Cola bus station. Once I am finally on my way, a group of burly men surge out of nowhere and surround the taxi, bringing it to a halt. Their laughter has an ominous edge, making it clear that they want us—strike-breaking customers—to get out now. A fellow passenger, a workman carrying his tools over his shoulder, shrugs phlegmatically and leads me on foot for the remainder of the journey to the bus station.

At Cola groups of would-be passengers are standing around gloomily under a blazing sun. Every now and then, one or two are suddenly whisked off by one of the few working taxi drivers. But no one wants to go to the Chouf. I wait on the dusty pavement with two young men who are also trying to get to Dmit. As it happens, they know Ramzi, but don't speak English, so for the next two hours communications circulate in different languages via Ramzi on his mobile phone in the mountains.

Eventually my new-found companions blag us all a lift from a large, florid man who is profiteering from the strike by turning his tiny car into a taxi. Fingering the unexpected clutch of notes in his hand, he pushes a rich baritone out of his chest as he drives. Arabesque sounds swell above the rattling engine as the car, crammed to the gills with passengers, hurtles towards the hills. Then we are brusquely ejected onto the dusty highway. 'He's a strong man', remarks one of my travel companions philosophically as we stand under some dusty trees. A lift from an old man with a constant patter of amusing nonsense carries us up into the Chouf. Finally, on the other side of a blockade run by the strikers stands Ramzi, dapper in white jeans and a black shirt.

'They are animals,' he says grandly, waving towards the organizers of the blockade, and leads me towards his father's car.

A short drive later, and we are at the family flat. 'This is Dr. Alex,' he tells his mother proprietarily. My PhD, which had impoverished and depressed me in Britain, apparently carries some cachet here.

His mother plies us with coke and *mannoush*. She is evidently one of life's givers, a good wife and mother whose energy is focused on accommodating her family's every need, and I begin to see how her only son got to be so assured. Gently smiling, she begs to know what eating arrangements I favour. Would I like a full meal now or later? Do I prefer chicken or beef? Because of the strike, Ramzi informs

141

me, the family has decided that I will stay the night rather than risk the return journey to Beirut that evening.

Then we go out to visit his mentor, the dissident sheikh. Some years ago, Dr. Anwar Khzam had decided to leave the circle of the initiates and embrace a more free-thinking lifestyle as a lecturer in Eastern philosophy at the Lebanese University. His house is further up the mountain, and stands on a rocky plateau where every surface is bleached white by the harsh midday light. But inside, the hall is cool and dark, with elegantly carved furniture arranged over its black and white tiled floor. The professor, a rotund man in his sixties, ushers us into a small sitting room, filled with books and an air of lived-in cosiness. We sit. His wife, smiling under her loose gauzy white veil, serves little dishes of *mighli*, a rice and nut pudding, to mark the recent birth of the couple's grandson.

The professor has a distinctive way of talking, it quickly emerges, rotating his ample torso and raising his voice to a shout to emphasize certain points, a tic that would be alarming if it weren't accompanied by benevolent flashes from his bulbous blue eyes.

'Why is there a need for secrecy?' I ask.

'Ah.' His tone, as he acknowledges the validity of the question, is all comprehension. 'At this time, the Islamic community is aggressive. They don't accept us if we don't accept their way of thinking. We tend to look at morality more philosophically than other sects. So in order to keep their safety, a Druze talks with the Muslim from his way of thinking. We don't mention our point of view.'

'Is that still really necessary in today's Westernized Lebanon?' I ask doubtfully.

'Yes, it is still necessary,' he says firmly. 'If you look at what is going on in the Middle East, there is a kind of violence that has always been an obstacle to coexistence. You cannot compromise with a Muslim—you either follow him or you run away from him.

142

In Islamic communities—I'm sorry to say this, but it's the bitter truth—they cannot accept you unless you're a believer. That's why the problem with Palestine is not solved and Islamic countries are in poverty. They don't know how to compromise.'

I look at him doubtfully. I don't like this latest addition to the refrain that I have been hearing repeatedly since I came to Lebanon; it doesn't fit with the politically correct view I want to have that liberal Islam is in the ascendant. But the professor is having none of it. 'I can see this because I read Arabic,' he insists. 'They cannot have a conversation, they know nothing about dialogue.'

'Are there things that are concealed in the Druze religion?'

'Yes. There are.' He pauses, clutching his forehead, as if searching for the right way to deal with the question. 'But this is dangerous, because I don't know if I can say it clearly.'

He reflects for a moment, and then resumes. 'In every prophet, there are two sides, the positive and the negative side, especially when we are talking about the moral view of each religion. So we don't take everything that is done by Mohammed himself—he has a negative side, and he has a positive side. For example, he has nine wives!' His voice has been rising steadily and by the time he gets to his rhetorical conclusion he's shouting: 'ARE WE TO SAY THAT THIS IS A GOOD THING?'

After a pause, he lowers his voice. 'There is a bad side, *yanni*, everything in the universe is divided into two. Vice is permitted by God himself. We believe there is one God who is the source of everything: the good part and the bad part. With respect to Christianity, we believe that there are two personalities: Christ himself who was the imam and another one who is the cousin of Christ, who took on the bad side of Christianity. The one who was crucified is something other than the real Christ himself. This is inherited from the Islamic tradition, but we don't talk about it. For safety reasons.'

143

'Would it offend other religions?'

'If we preach it, yes. Islam can't stand this—you just have to look at what's happening now.'

'Why then are telling me?'

'Personally, I look at religions as a kind of regulation of human behaviour, and up to now they've been a necessity. I like to be agnostic.'

'And you are a doctor of philosophy!' He makes a charming, appealing gesture towards me. 'How could I conceal? In the Sufi way of thinking, you tell secrets to people who can understand them.'

'If I publish this, will some people be upset?'

Eh, eh, he confirms. Then he waves his hands airily, indicating that it's not a problem for him personally. 'But it will be your responsibility,' he adds firmly.

'If the religion becomes more open, what will happen to the distinction between the initiates and the ordinary people?'

'It is a matter of time,' replies the professor, now calm again. 'Time will solve this dilemma. Most people now wear the European fashion.'

'Do you still consider yourself an initiate?'

'No. I don't want to keep the wisdom apart; I want people to understand it.'

'Why are the books of wisdom kept secret?'

'If we tell the student to understand them, he will understand nothing. He should know many other sects first in order to understand his own wisdom.'

'Is there another book?'

He pauses again. I wait. I am beginning to recognize that this kind of careful, limited response, requiring a degree of pre-knowledge from the questioner, as an inevitable feature of a conversation about Druze religious affairs.

'We have another book. It's called "The Book of Points and Circles". It talks about the beginning of the universe.'

His sentences have become short and reluctant. It sounds as though he could easily leave it there, but I want to test out Abir's story of the lost books. 'Does it deal with science?'

'Yes. Geometry.'

'Are the contents already known?'

'Yes. It first appeared in the University of Tübingen in Germany. It was published in 1902. We made a comparison between it and what we have in our heritage—it is exactly the same. But at the university they didn't try to explain it.'

'Who wrote it?'

'It was written by Sheikh Takieddine five hundred years ago. He took the knowledge of the books of wisdom and the Greeks—these were the main sources. He was a big thinker.'

'The professor translated the book from German to Arabic himself,' interjects Ramzi with pride.

'It says for example that in every straight line there is a section which is a curve,' continues Dr. Anwar. 'It's a book of metaphysics because he was trying to say that everything started from a single point. It is more or less the big bang theory. It also talks about morality.'

'Are there twenty-four books?'

'The talk about twenty-four books is an assumption. The books of wisdom talk about two epistles which are not found in the Druze heritage. But we don't have them—they are lost.'

It is clear that I have gone as far as I can, and we all repair to Ramzi's house for lunch. The table groans with food. I must have said that either beef or chicken would be fine, as his mother has done both, to be on the safe side. There's a beef and mushroom casserole, fried chicken, *kofta*, *tabbouleh*, hummus, vine leaves and a big bowl of crispy, golden chips. Ramzi's two sisters, long dark hair swaying

145

against outfits of bright pink and blue, drift to the table with the vague smiles of adolescents whose real concerns lie elsewhere. But his aunt, an open, chatty woman, tells me how she and her family had returned to Lebanon after years living in California. Despite having built up a good business there, they grew sick of the long working hours, and longed for the close social ties of their native land.

'I told her some secrets!' declares Dr. Anwar cheerfully, between mouthfuls. The chips are obviously a big hit with him. The aunt nods approvingly, and they agree that too much secrecy is a bad thing. 'It makes people afraid of us,' he says. 'The reputation of the Arabs is very bad at the moment.'

'How's the food?' he prompts me. I am eating dreamily, staring into space while my mind processes this latest instalment of the Druze story, and have quite forgotten to praise the hostess. I do so, and she smiles diffidently.

After the meal, we sip coffee on the balcony. The flat overlooks a boundary between territory staked out by Druze and Christian factions during the civil war, and the railings still bear the signs of their cross fire. Confused by the professor's position on secrecy, I broach the subject again. 'Isn't it a contradiction, to say that there is still a need for secrecy on the one hand, but at the same time to reveal secrets?'

'In our time, there is a revival of Islam all over the world,' he replies. 'So it is easier for us to claim that we are Muslims, even if we sometimes speak differently. It's a political necessity, and a social necessity. The Druze are a minority—they always worry about the future. This may seem a contradictory attitude, but if you look at it from the other side, it's a kind of wisdom.'

'So secrecy is really just a political and social necessity?'

'Yes.'

146

As the last, golden hour before sunset approaches, Ramzi drives me through the surrounding hills to Russe Hill. The sprawling, pine-topped peak is one of the highest points in the Chouf and has breathtaking views in every direction. On one side, the grey outlines of the mountains recede into the distance, in another a silver band of sea shimmers beneath a bank of clouds. Looking down onto the Christian village of Cergebaal on the far side, I see two miniscule figures, one in Druze religious dress, one in civvies, deep in conversation as they walk slowly around the football pitch.

During the war the hill's panoramic views of Christian villages for miles around made it an area of strategic importance for the Druze militia. But for Ramzi, growing up after the hostilities had ended, the hill was the perfect childhood haunt, an idyllic playground with the added piquancy of its wartime legacy. 'Warriors used to come and tell us about what happened in which areas,' he says as we crunch over the undergrowth. 'To us, this place is full of beautiful memories—we used to come here, boys and girls, and drink, and smoke, and make camp. To them, this place is full of bloody memories. They talk about being here and things exploding.'

The grass mounds hide a network of tunnels which allowed the fighters to cross the hill without exposure to enemy planes overhead. Picking our way carefully over the bumpy ground, we step into the mouth of a dark tunnel and along a passage of concrete and earth. 'You can go underground and go to any spot you want on this hill,' says Ramzi with pride. Strictly speaking, he adds, visitors are not allowed up here. A disabled war veteran living in the military commander's former home keeps a look-out. 'The villagers call him and tell him, "There's a stranger entering the zone!"'

'Why would people worry now? There's nothing here to protect.'

'There's no war here now, but you never know when war could come back to Lebanon,' says Ramzi, suddenly all adult *sagesse*.

147

'Should I be here?' I am wondering whether, behind the trees, there are eyes regarding me with suspicion.

'My father's important,' he replies. 'High up in the military. I'm covered—one hundred per cent.'

We scramble over mounds, sticks cracking underfoot. I'm hardly listening as Ramzi chatters on about his romantic conquests, his Christian girlfriend. I'm entranced with the beauty of this calm, woody peak, its yellow *waszal* flowers and chalky white stone which has taken on a luminous clarity in the golden light. The scent of pine and wild sage fills my nostrils.

'You know what?' He, too, is immersed in the place and what it means to him. 'Sometimes I'd really like war to come back, because of the way we would have to live with guns and tunnels! We used to dress up as Italian mafia and go around with guns. Then we got bored of that, and wanted something more complicated.' He pauses, perhaps hearing how childish this talk of war games sounds. 'Then I realized I had to finish my studies in marketing and get my degree.'

We walk on in silence. The rays of the sinking sun slant yet lower. Suddenly he turns to me. 'How does it feel when a person grows up?'

That evening the Mahmoud family gathers on the sofas in the corner of their living room. Ramzi's father is playing backgammon with a neighbour, while his mother oversees the pot of *matte*, smiling gently as she passes it to the next taker. A neighbour, an English teacher, chatters enthusiastically to me about her faith. She describes herself as very religious, but does not go to the *majlis* because people would say she was about to become an initiate. 'I know people say we are not Muslim, but we are!' she exclaims brightly, between sucks on the *matte* straw.

On the TV behind us pictures of the day's news are unfurling. Men stagger about, bloodied from the day's rioting about petrol prices in Beirut's Shia suburbs. With at least five people killed, journalists and politicians are already grappling with the worst civil unrest the country has seen in ten years.

Eventually the family drifts off to bed. Ramzi reclines on the sofa in his pyjamas and briefs his mother on our needs for the following day. Then he picks up the thread of the day's conversation about the true nature of Druism. 'Some people know deep inside that it's not Islam,' he tells me. 'But they are afraid to say it. There's a saying in Lebanon: "Say no and you end a conversation. Say yes and you open a hundred doors!"'

'Why did the professor tell me?' I ask, a little puzzled at the privilege.

'He's ready to talk,' Ramzi replies promptly. 'There are a lot of people who are not wearing the clothes—these people must know about their religion. So why not teach Durzi people about their religion, to know what they really pray for. If Durzi people hide their religion, other sects will ask what this religion is, which creates tensions between us and other religions.'

'Are there still secrets left?'

'Yes, sure. There are some things we just can't say, because these are very debatable issues which may create tension. Dr. Anwar thinks a certain time will come when there won't be any secrets any more.'

But for now, he goes on, some things will remain hidden. 'There are certain things which, if other people knew, their lives would be affected. There are a lot of big, deep secrets about the creators of the earth, about what certain prophets did, and about some things which were hidden from their followers. We are saying that keeping some secrets may create tension, so why don't we reveal something about our relation to other religions? That doesn't oblige us to state all the secrets we have. That's just a small step. But there are more deep

149

secrets which we think it's not the right time to uncover. Each of these secrets has a certain time to be uncovered.'

'How do you know when it's the right time?'

'Do you think there is real peace in Lebanon?' He hoists himself up onto one elbow. 'We don't want to give any other religion anything that might lead to a war. Politically it's not stable in Lebanon. We don't want to be the people that start the war because of some religious point of view we have.'

The next day, Ramzi disappears to his classes and his uncle puts me into a *servis* for Beirut, paying the driver in advance. Despite the previous day's violence, the roads have quickly returned to normal. The government and Hezbollah, the effective governors of the southern suburbs, have already started the post-mortem into the riots.

Back at the Y, the strike had generated a drama closer to home. Abir's younger sister had got stuck in town, unable to get back to the Chouf because of the blockades. The obvious solution, for her to spend the night in her sister's room, was ruled out—according to the hostel's strict rules, not even family were allowed in residents' rooms. Abir had explained the situation to Madame Victoria, but in vain. The rules could not be changed.

So she devised a cunning plan. Dressed as men, the sisters sneaked past the reception at the hotel where she had formerly worked, in order to spend the night in the room of a male friend who lived there. They donned hooded sweatshirts, baggy trousers and sunglasses. 'I walked like this!' Abir strides across the Y kitchen in a mock-macho fashion. 'And made like this'—she sticks out her torso, flattening her chest—'so as to have no breasts!' She laughs, recalling the escapade. 'I walked past my old colleagues four times! It's the craziest thing I ever did!'

150

I stare at her, amazed. Had she read any of the many tales in literature and history of women posing as men in order to follow their star, or simply to survive? Abir looks blank. 'No, I've never heard this.'

Once in the sanctuary of her friend's hotel room, the pair had treated her little sister parentally, making her do her homework before the three of them watched some television. She sobers, reflecting that the youthful prank had been an adult response to a serious situation—two young women on the streets for the night. 'It was the only solution,' she says gravely.

The origins of the Druze religion go back to the events of one period in history and their central character. Al Hakim Bi-Amr Allah, the sixth and last Fatimid caliph, ruled Egypt from 996 to 1021. As chief imam, he was considered by the Shiites to be invested with the religious and political authority of the prophet Mohammed. But during his twenty-five-year reign, a minority group of Ismaili Shiites, who see Allah in the person of the imam, took this a step further and came to see the caliph as nothing less than the manifestation of God himself.

Many of the key facts of his story remain to this day shrouded in mystery. Piecing together the various elements in a way that makes sense is particularly difficult, experts say, because some of the accounts—mired in the sectarian politics of that troubled time and place—give a deliberately distorted view.

Nonetheless, Hakim comes across as a strong religious and moral reformer, determined to root out corruption in the unruly society he governed. He supported the common people, abolishing taxes and forcing the wealthy to distribute the hoards of wheat which were pushing up the price of bread. He was generous with his own wealth, founding a House of Wisdom, complete with a library and salaried

151

scholars of all disciplines. True religion, he stressed, was to do with the soul's inner state, rather than the adherence to a rigid set of prescriptions favoured by the Muslims of the time. Through a series of conciliatory gestures and reforms, he encouraged tolerance between the competing Islamic sects and the minority faiths of Christianity and Judaism. In 1017 he formalized this new approach to religion with a public proclamation. Henceforth, all those who considered themselves *muwahhidun* should openly declare and practise the new faith: Unitarianism.

Reading such accounts, it wasn't hard to detect the key features of the gentle, universal faith that Abir had spoken of, an attempt by someone frustrated with sectarianism to lead his people back to the purity of the basic spiritual impulse.

But other elements of the story painted a darker picture of the sect's founder. He could be a ruthless ruler, dispensing summary justice and executing those who crossed him. In his *Journey to the Orient*, the nineteenth-century French poet and traveller Gérard de Nerval recounts a rare meeting with a Druze sheikh, Saide-Eshayrazy. The resulting account of Al Hakim's life—presented by the sheikh as the 'whole truth' about the Druze messiah—depicts a conflicted individual who sought worldly pleasures and was destabilized by the knowledge of his own divinity which had come to him while high on illicit hash. Boosted by his new-found importance, and consumed with desire for his own sister, Al Hakim announced his intention of transgressing social mores and marrying her. The incest-shy princess foiled this plan with some skill and, mistaken for a madman while wandering the city in disguise, Al Hakim cooled his heels in a lunatic asylum, emerging to find her on the point of marrying an underling. Wearied at having his plans thwarted, he took his horse into the Egyptian desert and was never seen again.

152

Some accounts say that he died there, but recently discovered manuscripts suggest that he made it as far as the Iranian-Indian border where he spent the remainder of his years writing and meditating. Whatever the truth, his disappearance marked the end of a key period in the history of the Druze.

Emerging out of violence and chaos, the new sect was born. It took its name from one of Al Hakim's disciples, Nashtakin al Darazi, who had challenged his leader's authority and fractured the movement before being mysteriously killed in 1019. Following the divine Al Hakim's reign, news of the new faith spread as far as the Yemen and India. Then, in 1043, evangelizing came to a sudden halt. 'The gates were closed,' and no new believers were accepted. The reasons for this were unknown, but from then on the Druze were a closed sect who jealously guarded their secrets.

In a recently published book which cites material from the Druze holy books, Israeli scholar Nissim Dana marshals the evidence for the distinctive, non-Islamic character of the Druze faith. The Druze do not observe the five pillars of Islam, she points out and, most importantly, do not recognize Mohammed as the last prophet. The creed laid out in the fifth epistle in their scriptures, to which initiates must adhere, spells out a higher loyalty: 'I hereby put my faith in our Lord, al Hakim, the one, the only, and the special... I repudiate, by my own free will, all other schools of thought, fundamentals of faith, religions and opinions.'

Elsewhere in the epistles this religious exclusivity issues in literally damning condemnations of other religions. The sanctification of the cross in Christianity and the stone-throwing ritual central to the Islamic hajj are mocked as religious absurdities. On the Day of Judgement, it is declared, the other faiths will receive their just deserts: fifty curses for the Shiites and twenty for the Jews. Muslims are in for a particularly bad time. As well as being obliged to pay an annual tax

153

of twenty dinars, they will find that all their food tastes bitter. They will be in a state of perpetual discomfort from the black glass earring they will be obliged to wear in each ear: 'In summer, scorch it like fire, and in winter, chill it like ice.'

While it was unsurprising that all the unanswered questions about the sect's mysterious origins would foster a culture of secrecy, this new perspective further complicated the picture of the Druze that was slowly forming in my mind. My encounter with Dr. Anwar and Ramzi seemed to confirm the idea that the sect was a distinct faith, separate from Islam. But I was more confused than ever by what sort of religion this was—a closed elite possessed, like other religions, of its own theological quirks and an unshakeable belief in its own superiority? Or had it captured the elements of a universal spirituality, based on a mysticism lived out by ancient people and still open to all who chose that path today? The spiritual leader of the Lebanese Druze, Sheikh Bahjat Ghaith, was now spreading the word about the faith through the magazine and website he had founded. It was time to hear what he had to say.

On the morning of my appointment with the sheikh the traffic in Beirut is terrible and it looks as though I may be late. But the *servis* driver's dark eyes flash with recognition when I state my destination. *Al Akl?* he asks. *You want the holy man?* Then he drives with speedy determination, negotiating the back streets and refusing a passenger that will take us off-track. I am deposited, just in time, outside the House of the Druze Religion next to the Druze cemetery I had visited nearly two months before.

Inside, the sheikh's people are dismayed at my lack of Arabic and concerned about the sheikh's English, which he has not spoken for forty years. But after some discussion I am given the flimsiest of veils to drape over my head and led into his office.

154

The sheikh is seated at a large brown desk which, apart from some paper and a few pens, is entirely empty. He is now sixty-five, having taken up theology after a successful business career. With his big house in the Chouf and fashionable, about-town offspring, this man is no stranger to the ways of the world. But his appearance is everything you would expect of a spiritual leader, with robes of deep French blue and white and a red *pyri* form hat. A bushy white beard frames the bottom half of his face.

There is no secret, he tells me straightaway: the idea of secrecy has been handed down from parent to child and created a culture of mystery. And he is sure that I have been misled by the ignorant about the nature of the Druze religion.

'They don't know their real identity.' His rusty English sentences are short and broken with pauses, but a religious and philosophical vocabulary learnt long ago filters through. 'Sometimes if you tell them about their real identity, they don't believe it. I believe the real identity for the human being is his mind—*al Akl*.' He points to his head. 'Our real religion is the Unitarian religion. It is everywhere.'

'Is it universal?'

'Yes.'

'Then can I become a Druze?'

'No. The Druze community is a political circle, and closed. But you can be universal through your mind.'

'So can I be a Druze religiously?'

'It is a closed community. People can go out, but they cannot come in. But you can be a Unitarian whether you are a Christian, Muslim or a Druze—any religion. It's not necessary to come to Lebanon, you can be a Unitarian in China, or wherever. The real faith is in the spirit.'

At the end of each answer, the sheikh closes his mouth with an air of finality and fixes his gaze straight ahead at the window opposite.

155

His manner would make it easy for me to say my thanks and leave. But I decide in favour of careful persistence. Questions about religious scriptures get a series of fragmentary half-answers. The books were created by Druze lacking the Unitarian spirit, he says vaguely, and written by many different people. 'They talk about six books because they don't know. Twenty-four books—or one book—it's not the problem,' he says dismissively. 'You don't need books, you only need to open your mind.'

'The Druze books talk about one point in history—one man,' he adds. 'His name is Mohammed Nashtakin Darazi. He is a crook—he came to spoil the Unitarian faith!'

The sudden assertion takes me by surprise. 'Why did he do this? Did he intend to do a bad thing?'

'He did intend to do a bad thing.' He sounds irascible. 'He's from the devil!'

'Why is what he did so bad?'

'Because he made the Druze! He made the Druze community!' His voice rises in exasperation at this traitor's destructiveness. 'The Unitarian faith comes from the whole: the universal. He made this faith for a small group only: the Druze. This is imitation—this is for politicians. But for me, the faith is open. The Druze leaders want it closed to keep political power.'

'What is the position of the Druze community now?'

'The community is in a bad position because it is sleeping, spiritually it is sleeping. It will wake up—not only them—the whole world will wake up.' He has shifted into declamatory, prophetic mode now. 'The light will come, the darkness will go. In real creation, there is no darkness: it does not exist. The worlds exists, you see...' He points to the window, which is filled with sunlit greenery. I follow his gaze and, for a moment, we both stare silently at the view, mesmerized by the plenitude of existence. 'The world is now at a very complicated

156

time,' he resumes. 'We are going to the summit. There is one step to get there. If you have spirit you can go up, and if you have darkness you can go down.'

'Are you talking about Judgement Day?'

'Yes.'

'Does everyone have a chance to go up, Druze and non-Druze?'

'Yes. You have a chance through your spirit. It is between you and your creator—there is no mediator.'

'What about those Druze who say that only the Druze, the chosen people, will be saved?'

'This is imitation—they like to think like this. They understood it from their fathers, and they represent it without knowing the reality.'

Then he returns to his prophecy. 'Some person will come back and they will not know him. It will happen very soon now. Spiritual food is not made in the USA and England. But I think that people will find this food in the middle point.'

'You mean here, the Middle East?'

'Yes. The East is spirit without body; the West is body without spirit. The Middle East is the place to show the unity of body and spirit.' His gaze returns to the window.

'So it is a special place?' Despite his Delphic utterances, the idea makes a kind of intuitive sense to me.

'Yeah,' he returns. 'As we began something, so we will end it. The real light will come, to draw the darkness away—in the Middle East.'

In a sudden burst of self-revelation I tell him that I have long been drawn to the Middle East, without knowing why.

'You will understand it one day,' he says significantly. 'And not only you—everyone will understand it.'

157

The interview has drawn to a natural close, and I start to gather my things, remarking that we've managed quite well despite the problem of language. The sheikh agrees with me, but then adds, disconcertingly: 'I tell you only what you can understand. In time, you will see everything. Don't be worried—with time.'

I look at him bemused, trying to fathom his meaning.

'People are sleeping, in the West and everywhere', he elaborates. 'Maybe your book will be like a bell to wake them up'

He asks an assistant to fetch something, and I am presented with a handsomely bound book containing past issues of the Druze magazine *Adam* that he produces with his son. As I leave, he looks at me meaningfully. 'Write only what I have told you—not what everyone has said.'

Back at the Y, I leaf through the pages of the book. Pictures of otherworldly landscapes and natural wonders are interwoven with long skeins of text in Arabic and English. The range of the material is wide, with Plato, Buddha and John the Baptist featuring in poems, hymns and narrative passages. But amid the variety of sources, a single, mythic narrative emerges, the story of a lost age an advanced civilization governed by the ancient wisdom of Gnosticism. According to the story, a thousand years ago the Children of Light, overcome by the misdeeds of the Children of Darkness, were forced to sail away to Egypt. Their Atlantis sank beneath the waves, to endure only in the folk memory of true spiritual seekers.

'The term "Wisdom" never referred to a specific religion, philosophy, or text,' proclaims one passage. 'And despite all the battles that took place in history in the name of GOD, the true Wisdom of GOD has always hinted at the hidden battle inside the Soul of Adam: that part of YOU which ultimately either responds to the Light of the IMAGE OF GOD... or shuns away from it.'

158

For a while I stare at the text, puzzled by its familiar ring. Then it dawns on me how closely it resembles the self-help books which draw on Eastern philosophy and can be found on bookshops all over the West. There is even advice, delivered simply in near-perfect English, on how to solve your psycho-spiritual problems; injunctions about self-management, not giving into hatred and the best way to deal with one's dark side. Something else the sheikh said comes back to me: 'I have read everything—the Bible, the Koran, New Age things.' I think I spot his prophetic tone at work in one particular passage: 'Today, in the West there is a new current that aims at reviving the Gnostic Spirit, and this current is moving towards the East. It seems that the World is on its way to finally acknowledge its crimes against the Gnostics.'

Perhaps, then, all the elements of this fractured story were clues to the true nature of Drusism: an ancient spirituality, nurtured by the wise and open to all, regardless of tribe or place. A faith that was then inevitably hijacked by sectarianism and conflict—everything that gives religion a bad name—caught, as in the Druze account of the human condition, between good and evil. Perhaps, in its references to the good and bad sides of Jesus and Mohammad, of organized religion's tendency to self-betrayal.

Most importantly, was its ancient, peaceful side now trying to re-surface, gently and a little clumsily, in the 'middle point' where tribes and faiths collide, in today's Middle East?

It was time to leave my spiritual musings and move on to Syria. I viewed the prospect with some trepidation: ruled by the authoritarian Baathist regime and closed off from the outside world for the past forty years, it promised to be very different from liberal Lebanon. A few weeks before leaving London, I had become friends with a young Syrian who was seeking asylum in Britain. His stories of life under the regime, including his own spells in prison, had made me nervous. With thirteen different branches, the country's intelligence services were a hydra-headed affair and their agents, the *mukhabarat*, were everywhere. Although as a foreigner I hardly risked disappearing into a Syrian gaol in the way the locals did, I didn't relish the prospect of interrogation, having my notes confiscated, or being deported, all possibilities if I aroused suspicion. But confusingly, my friend's accounts of the journalistic and political work he and his friends did suggested that quite a lot was possible. It seemed that truth-seeking in Syria involved treading a delicate line, and from a distance I couldn't quite visualize where it lay. I told myself this was simply a reconnaissance trip, a first visit to get to know a difficult country on which I would avoid any involvement with the political scene.

On a domestic level I was also sailing into uncharted waters. I was to leave the sanctuary of the Y and stay with my Syrian friend's former flatmate, a young man I didn't even know. But the arrangements are made. My kindly Syrian neighbour at the Y phones her friend the bus station official to ensure my passage on the three-hour bus ride to Damascus. It is all I can do to stop her booking me two tickets. 'It is better,' she says, looking at me anxiously. 'Then you will have no one beside you.'

On my last afternoon, by way of a mini-holiday, Abir and I go to the beach. Neither of us wants to pay the fee to get into a nearby private beach, where fashion-conscious Beirutis will be displaying the latest swimwear. So we head for one of the few public beaches at the far end of the Corniche at Ramlet el Baida. It's Sunday afternoon, and the sandy shore is packed with Muslim families surrounded by beach paraphernalia. Most of the women stay fully covered even when bathing, their clothing filling with water as

160

they try to immerse themselves in the little waves at the sea's edge. One family man, crisp in Western short-sleeved shirt and trousers, strolls up and down the seashore, evidently enjoying the feel of the sun and sea air on his skin. He holds sticks of bright pink candy floss, and breaks off little clouds for his wife and children. Apart from a tiny slit for her eyes, his wife is entirely swathed in a black *chador* and feeds herself by looping her arm up under her face covering in a deft movement reminiscent of an elephant bringing trunk to mouth.

We look at them, and each other, and rapidly replace our plan of full swimwear with a compromise. Abir bears her legs, but keeps a T-shirt over her skimpy bikini top. I reveal the top half of my swimsuit, but retain my long skirt. We sit, squinting out at the sun-bleached scene, half-hidden by our hired parasol. Despite these precautions, a group of young Syrian men a few yards away lie with the necks permanently twisted in our direction, their eyes pegged on a level with our crotches. I look at them with some irritation. Over the past few weeks I've observed a negative response towards Syrian workers rising in myself a few times, generally unprovoked by anything on their part. Maybe the discriminatory attitudes that many Lebanese held towards them were getting to me, too.

But another group of Syrian men, easily identifiable with their sleek bouffant hairstyles and uniform of maroon shirts and black trousers, take no notice of us at all. 'They are *mukhabarat*,' says Abir quietly, adding with contempt: 'They are so stupid, they don't even try to hide it.' I watch the group from behind my sunglasses. The half-dozen men stand in a closed circle, talking quietly, their heads occasionally swinging round to survey the scene. They are obviously not here for pleasure, and make no attempt to blend in with the beach life swirling around them. The oldest, clearly the leader, gently tells a set of prayer beads in one hand. As he talks to

161

his subordinates his other hand slips inside his own, open shirt and fondles a nipple. Then, after a tug on the chest hair, it slides down to caress the flesh of his belly. I nudge Abir. 'Ooh!' she squeals. 'He's turned on!'

7

UNFREEDOM

DAMASCUS is a shock. The bus abruptly terminates on a street which looks exactly the same as the miles of others we've driven through and suddenly I'm on the pavement with my luggage. My phone doesn't work, as Syria has a different telecommunications system and its closed economy has prevented me from getting any more than the tiny amount of currency that my Syrian friend snuck me in London. What's more, I'm now illiterate: there's not a word of English anywhere, with every street and shop sign displaying the looping script of Arabic.

I beg the use of a local's phone in exchange for a coin and call my host. Then I wait anxiously outside a nearby hotel. Finally, a hirsute young man hurries towards me, mopping his brow and apologizing for the delay. Internally, I sigh with relief. I can tell from his face that he's all right.

At twenty-three, Gabi had more independence than most young Syrians, who were still living at home with their families. Thanks to the loan of a rent-free flat from a relative, he could live the life of a Western student, keeping his own hours and inviting what guests he pleased. His flat was in Jaramana, a suburb populated by students and middle-class families and known for its relaxed, open atmosphere. Druze and Christians strolled down its wide, dusty streets, while the main shopping area buzzed with people looking at high-fashion clothes and gold jewellery.

It wasn't chic by Western standards. Patches of scrubland interspersed the buildings and piles of dust and litter collected on street corners. On a wall above one heap of rubbish a vexed resident had written: 'Whoever left this here is the son of a donkey.'

The flat's balcony, several floors up, looked onto other apartment blocks stretching into the distance. It was a grey-and-beige scene, lifted only by the odd dash of red from an awning or a roof-top water tank. On a clear day you could see Mount Kassioun rising in sandy magnificence on the city's edges a few miles away, but too often a yellow haze of pollution hung over the horizon, obscuring the view. A variety of noises floated up from the street below: roaring diesel engines, beeping horns and the putt-putting of scooters mingled with the nasal cries of the water-seller calling over his tannoy and the clip-clop of the melon-seller's horse.

My host immediately made me welcome, giving up his bedroom so that I could have some privacy. We sat at the kitchen table, eating take-out chicken and getting to know each other. 'You know that Jack Nicholson character who is always saying, "I am tired"?' he asked. 'Well, I am like him. Sometimes I say that I was born at the age of twenty, and now I am fifty.'

In the days that followed I realized that this self-characterization as a young-old man was spot-on. Gabi liked to take life slowly, and began each morning with a prolonged session drinking coffee and reading the papers on the balcony. He had a pronounced sense of the ills of the world, and his wide oriental features took on an expression of wistful sadness when he was feeling world-weary, which was often. Apart from a supreme disinterest in the preparation of food—he would eat biscuits all day until hunger finally drove him to the sandwich shop—he ran his domestic affairs as if he had had a lifetime to

164

build up his habits, regularly and methodically embarking on various washing and cleaning tasks around the flat. The centre of his domestic existence was the computer in the living room, which served as both hi-fi and video player. He was often to be found sitting at the controls, searching for a film or bootlegging a new piece of music from a friend. His music collection was a strange hybrid affair which included Gloria Gaynor and Bonnie Tyler as well as the mournful strains of Armenia, Turkey, and the Levant. Mary Hopkin's 1968 Euro-hit 'Those Were the Days' was a particular favourite.

We were rarely alone, as his parent-free flat was a magnet for his friends, all young men slowly making their way towards university degrees. The most regular visitor was Shivan, a fair, broad-shouldered Kurd whose visiting became so seamless that he had practically moved in. Often, in the mornings, I would stumble out of my room to find him, lathered up and vest-topped, shaving at the sink in the hall. Other young men turned up in the evening and stayed late into the night, drinking bottles of Syrian beer and laughing together on the balcony.

They accepted me without question as one of their group, and I spent hours on the balcony, happy to let the swell and fall of their Arabic conversation drift over me. In bouts of English in between we discussed the state of the world and traded information about our different countries. It soon became clear that I didn't need to stand on ceremony, and I abandoned my habit of wearing a shirt or jacket to cover my arms, as I did in the street. As we all sat there in our vest-tops, engulfed by the mounting heat of the Syrian summer, a warm camaraderie prevailed.

Sometimes, when the charms of the balcony palled, Gabi, Shivan and I would go to 'the cinema', sitting in a row on the small sofa in front of the computer screen. But their cinematic tastes were incor-

165

rigibly American, and I soon grew bored of their preferred diet of *Once Upon a Time in America* and *Basic Instinct*.

Very little time was devoted to studying. 'You see, we study English literature, but we don't know English very well,' said Gabi, smiling sadly. At the university up to three hundred people crammed into a single lecture, leaving students effectively to their own devices. Gabi no longer attended them, but he bought into the mini-economy that had sprung up, in which the entrepreneurial sold transcripts of translation lectures to their peers. As exam time approached, I found one lying on the sofa. It chronicled a dialogue between the lecturer and students on the meaning of some difficult expression, a series of wild guesses to which the lecturer repeatedly replied, 'No.' It made dispiriting reading.

Nor did the lecturers have any real idea of the correct pronunciation. One teacher announced that the Queen of England had recently issued an edict instructing her subjects to henceforth pronounce the 't' in 'often'. At the other extreme, Damascus University pushed the boat out and hired an American professor on a visiting lectureship. Faced with his accent and post-modern sophistication, his students understood nothing. Gabi's bumper-sized *Norton Anthology of English Literature*, containing everything from Beowulf to Virginia Woolf, lay gathering Damascene dust on his bedroom shelf. No one read Shakespeare, who was central to their course.

But they all adored George Orwell.

Morning coffee on the balcony. The sounds of Fairuz drift out from the computer behind us. Gabi looks up from his old paper—he is in the habit of reading the comment pages of back issues rather than the day's news—and opens the discussion. 'Do you think the world is moving backwards or forwards, morally?'

His journey to political awareness had begun in the mid-1990s when the media in Syria, previously confined to state-run outfits, had opened up to the likes of CNN and the BBC. The change had brought a fresh stream of information and ideas, propelling him into new ways of thinking about politics. But after a while, with no channels to express his new-found views or to change anything, the novelty had palled. Now he was submerged by a kind of blanket cynicism, a sense that, in their different ways, the governments of both America and Syria both conspired to limit the freedom of their peoples.

'After a while you feel there are few facts in the world—like freedom, God, and how to live in the right way. I call them the columns,' he explains. 'In the East we are full of the feeling of conspiracy, in the media, in education. It's something to do with the way the government talks about things. There are great forces outside that control everything in the world, like America, and we cannot do anything.' He spreads his hands in a gesture of mock-helplessness. 'For thirty years Syria has been dependent on the idea that we have to fight Israel. The authorities need trouble to rule the country.'

Shivan interjects: 'If there was no Israel, they would say that Turkey had occupied the land.' He has a gentle voice, and talks with a sibilant lisp, sometimes softening a difficult point by batting his eyelashes. 'They demand that people should stay quiet. They say that now we have a national duty to free the land, to help the Palestinians. They say that we cannot give you democracy now—we will have to have it later.'

The roar of a passing truck almost drowns out our voices. The fumes from its diesel engine follow, pricking my nose and eyes. Gabi's thoughts turn to what really matters to most Syrians—their poor standard of living. 'Salaries are very low,' he says. Now people turned to whatever means they could to survive. 'Corruption was

167

considered a shameful thing twenty or thirty years ago. My father told me about it. Now it's a way of life.'

'To keep your place, you are obliged to be corrupt,' adds Shivan. 'Maybe you are an employee, and you see a problem with a project and want to say something. But it's easier to stay corrupt.' A louder-than-usual horn punches its way through our conversation. I grumble, in an Anglo-Saxon way, about whether it's really necessary to make such a noise.

'Maybe beeping the horn is the only thing the driver controls in his life,' Shivan says softly, his eyelashes flickering.

'We live in the past here,' Gabi is getting mournful. 'Sometimes you talk to people and you feel you are in the fourteenth century. We haven't moved on. In the West we feel that people live their moments more than here—the economic system allows this. Here, we try to catch the moments!' With an uncharacteristic burst of energy he grabs the air with his fist. 'We don't have our happiness here,' confirms Shivan.

'Does the state really stop your happiness?' I ask.

'Yes. Politics is in our blood. It is in everything.'

'How would you like Syria to be?'

'We want to build a good state with democracy, and no corruption,' Gabi answers. 'Now it's a big joke. When I look at the future, I see a big horizon, and it's always dark. Sometimes I have a dream and I see the colour of red—blood—everywhere.

'Sometimes we want to start something.' His morning indolence has given way to passion now. 'But people can't do anything here—it's the mentality. One time, a group of people I know started a cinema club. The *mukhabarat* came and said, "That's enough." They said: "It's cinema, it's just cinema." But it was finished.' He lowers his head regretfully, and adds. 'Alone, you cannot do anything. You have to gather people, and it's not allowed.'

168

Shivan's blue eyes are fixed on the hazy horizon. '"Syria is a lovely country". I hate it when Europeans say that.'

'It is, in a way.' I want to cheer them up, to go along with the standard tourist's view. But I sound unconvincing: we all know that I'm just parachuting in, soon to leave, whereas they are stuck.

'In one way,' replies Shivan, forbearing to say the obvious. 'But I think that if a foreigner could see Syria through our eyes, they would hate it.'

One evening, the boys return from the barber and take up their places on the balcony, freshly clipped and glowing with new levels of energy. On the way back they had dropped in at the internet café where they had heard news of a new form of fundamentalism which had recently emerged in Syria. Groups of self-appointed militia were taking *sharia* law into their own hands and were riding around on motorbikes, using knives to slash female pedestrians that they consider to be indecently dressed. 'It's wrong, it's disgusting,' Gabi is saying indignantly to Shivan as I sit down between them. He turns to me. 'You know I told you I saw blood, in my dreams? This is it.'

I gaze at the life going on in the flats opposite. In one brightly-lit window a couple are putting the final touches to a re-decorated room, she sweeping, he hosing, she scrubbing a cushion, he a window sill. Families sit looking out from the other balconies, children restlessly circling their parents.

Now Shivan speaks. 'If a Muslim doesn't like your way of living, he will kill you,' he says. 'They are trying to take over. We have an invasion of money here, from Saudi Arabia. They are building mosques, with no-one to go in them. Maybe we will have a revolution against Islam here. We need it. People here talk to you as if you are a Muslim. They think you must be one. But what about the minorities? What if you are Christian, or Druze, or Ismaili?'

'Which people?' I ask.

'Taxi drivers,' replies Gabi. 'It's happened many times.'

'The problem is with the Sunna, not with the Shia,' says Shivan. 'The Shia have always been more willing to let other people live differently.' I must be looking sceptical because he adds, pointing to his chest: 'I am Sunna, and I say that. I don't like religion.'

But there is, I protest, a counter-current of Sunna thought which…

'Look, Alex, I want to tell you something again,' Shivan interrupts me. 'These are thinkers. There isn't an audience for them here. It's not like in Britain.'

Gabi nods in agreement. 'Extremist Muslims aren't more tolerant here than elsewhere—they just talk as if they are.' The regime's determination to put down threats to its power from whatever quarter makes sure of that, he adds. 'They can't do anything, because of the pressure.'

In between the morning and evening sessions on the balcony I try to get to know Damascus. For the first couple of days, the boys dutifully escort me around, flagging down taxis and sitting through meetings with contacts. We sample traditional Damascene café life, listening to the storyteller at Café Naufarah, and sit in the elegant covered courtyard of Alal Bal, amid its climbing plants and rich red furnishings. Then, realizing that their lives will no longer be their own if they continue like this, they leave me to my own devices. To flag down the minibuses circulating on a prescribed route, you needed to be to read the destinations on the front. Drawing on my tenuous grasp of the Arabic alphabet, I learn to read the place names I need, although at first I have to let several go past before getting the right one.

I wander around the Old City. Its narrow cobbled streets have an ancient, almost timeless feel. I peer into the little doorways and windows, intrigued by the sight of an artisan absorbed in carving a piece of dark wood or forging a piece of bright metal, with craftsmanship handed down from father to son. The tourist books were right: it is easy to imagine oneself back in Old Arabia, the place of a thousand and one tales and an infinite, exotic Eastern richness. The covered market is less convincingly ancient. I stare in fascination at the underwear on display outside the shops: thongs with large, plastic mobile phones, birds and Santa Clauses adorning the pubic area. 'Do you like...?' asks a shopkeeper, hopefully, and I step away fast, laughing in alarm.

Elsewhere, though, Damascus is bleak and flat, an endless stretch of grey buildings, roads and traffic emitting fumes and furious beeping. The faces of Hafiz al Asad, the former president and his son Bashar, the current president, stare out from hoardings, shop windows and taxi dashboards. Large numbers of people circulate around the streets and squares, but they and I make little contact. And there's a dragging, pervasive quality that I recognize from of old, but can't put my finger on. Eventually it dawns on me where I felt it before: years before, on a trip round the Eastern bloc in the last years of communism.

As the days go past, the sense of suffocation described by the boys begins to seep into my consciousness. Making contact with local people for even the most innocent conversation about religious life proves surprisingly difficult. A spiritual thinker calls last minute to cancel a meeting, suggesting that I call back to re-arrange. When I do, his phone remains switched off, day after day. The Ismailis, to whom I've been introduced by a contact, herself an Ismaili, offer every possible assistance short of actual help. He was entirely at my disposal, said one community leader, placing his hand on his

171

heart, and would do everything he could to put me in touch with the Ismaili community. He would introduce me to his son, have me to lunch, take me on a tour of the Ismaili town of Salamiya and arrange meetings with key people. But when I broach the subject of possible dates, the offers disintegrate, gossamer-like, between my fingers. He could not, after all, invite me to lunch because he had to go and see his mother. The meetings would depend on people's availability. Did I know that religion was an extremely sensitive subject? he asked, flinty sparks flying from his eyes.

A second contact arrived at our meeting tightly clutching his wife's hand. Was I, he asked, in fact working for an organization? His smile was bright but his body was rigid in his chair as he sat, asking question after question. Was I married? And where—although I had amply demonstrated its paucity when paying the taxi driver in front of him—had I learnt my Arabic?

An hour later, after I had explained my project, background, intentions, methods and personal life in some detail, he offered to arrange a visit to a community project. But it would be the next time I was in Syria, and in the meantime communication would be difficult as his email account was out of action. As I made my way back across town to the balcony, tired and demoralized, it slowly dawned on me that, for the first and probably last time in my life, I had been taken for a honey trap.

Finally I give in to the inevitable. There is to be a demonstration for the rights of political prisoners in the heart of Damascus—a rare example of political protest—the next afternoon. Under the cover of my tourist persona I will go and observe. 'I thought you were keeping out of politics?' says Gabi, looking at me quizzically. I mutter something about just going to look, seeing as I'm here, and go to the hall to ring one of the organizers. A former political prisoner himself, he readily agrees to meet me after the demo.

172

The next day, I cautiously approach Sahat Arnous, the square in the heart of the shopping area where the protest is due to take place. There are lines of riot police, khaki-clad and tense-faced in every direction, with extra rows snaking off into the surrounding side streets. They wear white helmets and grim expressions, and each grips a baton determinedly.

The way they are organized suggests that they are protecting something, and I peer beyond them. In the leafy park in the centre of the square stands a statue of Hafiz al Asad, neatly suited in grey stone and smiling gently, his hand outstretched to the imaginary populace at his feet. The police, legs firmly astride, carve out an empty space around him. Meanwhile, ordinary people are going about their business, carefully oblivious to the riot police in their midst. Old couples are taking the evening air on park benches, while groups of women throng the brightly lit shops. There is no communication between the two groups. It is as though two parallel worlds exist side by side.

The demonstration had been organized by Syria's human rights activists to mark 21 June, the day of solidarity with political prisoners. Their exact numbers are unknown, but in four decades since the Alawite-controlled Baath party took power, tens of thousands of people have disappeared into the country's jails. When the younger Asad succeeded his father in 2000, the 'Damascus Spring' followed, a hopeful time in which the regime seemed prepared to loosen its grip. Around six hundred political prisoners were released, while a series of economic reforms inspired belief that Syria was finally opening up to the world. But as real political change failed to materialize, people continued to languish in prison, and for ordinary Syrians life went on pretty much as usual.

Nonetheless the country's tiny group of activists and intellectuals took advantage of the new climate. For years any kind of political

173

protest had been unthinkable. In the late 1990s they began organiz-
ing demonstrations on pan-Arab issues such as Palestine. Although
the protests were new, their subjects coincided with the government's
position, making them less risky. The approach paid off and instead
of the crushing response of the past, the agitators met with gentler
treatment. Now they were gaining confidence, and today's demo was
taking the culture of protest onto newer, more dangerous territory.

But with the late-afternoon sun slanting across the city, there is
no sign of the protestors. I patrol the square several times, popping
in and out of shops and affecting only the most casual interest in
this huge display of state power. By contrast, the *mukhabarat* are
all-too-visible, clutching giant walkie-talkies and staring into the
empty square with grim concentration. The combination of tension
and non-eventfulness is tiring, so eventually I sit down at a café with
a cup of tea, my tourist paraphernalia of sunglasses and guidebook
in full display.

In front of me, the white helmets continue to guard the statue.
The shoppers circulate, apparently oblivious. A toddler passes my
table and grabs at my shiny plastic teaspoon, and his mother pulls
him back with a smile. Young men stand in a café doorway chatting
idly. An acquaintance, also observing proceedings incognito, hurries
by, pushing a grin and discreet 'hi' out of the corner of her mouth.
Some police quietly lead a couple of long-haired student types away
down a side street.

An hour later, the police are visibly flagging. They stand, hip-
hitched and fidgeting, banging their batons into their hands. One
scratches his scalp by moving his helmet vigorously backwards and
forwards. Around the statue the tension holds, but behind the front-
line a row of tired-looking young men are sitting on a low wall, their
helmets lying at their feet. Others have broken rank to form little
groups, and are chatting and laughing or staring at female passers-

by. I get a hard, sexual stare from one moustachioed young officer and, fearing my time is up, flee down a side street.

Half an hour later, I go to a nearby café to meet one of the demo's organizers, Yassin Haj Saleh. The café is huge and brightly lit, with tables and chairs filling every corner. Each table is occupied by two or more men, sharing a *nargileh* or locked into intense games of backgammon. The continuous, low murmur of voices is broken by the clatter of the *tawleh* pieces hitting the sides of the boards. There's not a woman in sight, and a kind of force field seems to be in operation, preventing me from going in and sitting down amid this sea of male togetherness. I hover at the door, waiting for Yassin to spot me and introduce himself.

He's there, holding out his hand: grey hair and soft brown eyes set in a conventionally good-looking face.

'I didn't find the demonstration,' I tell him.

'We were moved. They moved us, little by little, into a side street. It took about half an hour. But they didn't beat anyone. It was good,' he adds ruminatively, assessing the success of the protest. 'It's the first time we've done that. But there were only two hundred of us: that's because people are too frightened. We're trying to start a culture of protest here, but it's difficult.' He looks around at the tables of men. 'Would you like to go for a walk?'

We leave the café and stroll through the streets. Night has fallen and the Damascene evening is in full swing. People crowd the pavements, shopping, meeting friends and taking the air. A bright crescent moon hangs high in the sky.

'How long were you a prisoner?' I ask.

'Sixteen years. I was taken when I was nineteen,' he says simply. This huge chunk of his adult life had been snatched following his arrest for membership of the outlawed Syrian Communist Party. He

175

had spent time in Syria's most notorious prison, Tadmor, and was finally released in 1996.

'There's one man who's been in prison thirty-four years,' he continues. 'That's longer than Nelson Mandela. We had never heard of him; we only found out about it two months ago. There's another man who came out six months ago, like this.' He stops in the middle of the pavement and bends his knees, so that his back is almost horizontal to the ground. 'He had an illness where his vertebrae got fused together, and it wasn't treated. Now he's out, he hasn't got a passport, so he can't go abroad to get treatment.'

Many prisoners, having found a channel for their resistance in Syria's outlawed communist parties, had been incarcerated during the 1980s, when Asad dealt harshly with opposition from whatever source. The president's increasing concern about resistance from the Muslim Brotherhood had led to the bloodiest episode in modern Syria's history, the suppression of an Islamicist uprising in Hama in 1982. The army killed thousands as it ripped through the town (estimates vary from a pro-government 3,000 to 25,000 from human rights campaigners), leaving an indelible impression on the minds of ordinary Syrians. 'Fear is in the memory of the people here. The backbone of the society has been broken,' Yassin goes on.

'Yes, it's very different from other Arab countries I've visited,' I say, thinking of the closed faces in the street, my experience with the Ismailis. 'It's hard to get people to talk to me.'

'Perhaps they are afraid of you,' he responds. 'They imagine that all foreigners are from the CIA or something. We've been educated paranoiacally here—everything that is 'outside' is regarded with suspicion.'

'Was it safe for you to be at the demonstration?'

'It's half-safe,' he replies matter-of-factly. 'You never know what will happen. That's the point about an irrational system—there aren't

176

any rules.' It was difficult to judge what was possible politically. Things had certainly changed since the 1980s, when the slightest sign of dissidence could land you in prison, possibly for decades. But no reforms had taken place and even identifying the source of power was difficult: under the new president, Syria's hydra-headed regime was not, in reality, under the control of one man.

'They know me, because I was a political prisoner,' he continues. 'But if someone unknown did the same thing, they might take him. It depends who you are.' Had they taken the well-connected writer Ammar Abdulhamid, he adds, people would speak out. 'But for other people, no one would say anything, or only a few.'

We cross Al Asad Bridge. 'Look, I want to show you something.' He stops by a roadside stall. The vendor's entire stock, laid out across a large trestle table, consists of postcards of the president. Like a celebrity in a western calendar, Bashar Al Asad is presented in different poses, here a full-length shot, there a three-quarter profile in close-up, alone and with his wife, modelling different outfits from formal evening wear to military get-up.

'There are three kinds of pictures here,' he explains, as we walk on. 'First you have Asad, his father, his brother, his wife—the Royal Family. Then you have singers and actresses, wearing few clothes, bare-breasted—these are for adolescents. Then you have Nasrallah and the late Yassin, the late Rantissi—the symbols of resistance.' The last group—the secretary-general of Hezbollah, the spiritual and political leaders of Hamas, killed by Israeli forces in Gaza in early 2004—were lauded by Syrians for their resistance to Israel.

'Why do people here put up pictures of Asad? Is it because they feel a real affection, or for show?'

'Both, sometimes,' he replies. 'It's like some people wear a cross, for protection against evil forces. Maybe if you have pictures of them you will gain protection from security.'

Issuing an invitation to lunch with him and his wife, he delivers me to Damascus' sprawling, poorly-lit bus station at Baramkeh. People are sitting placidly in the velvety darkness, waiting for the buses to fill and take them to their homes around the city.

A few days later, I make the journey to Yassin's flat in the suburbs, one of many in identikit blocks which rise out of a dip in the dusty yellow hills south of Damascus. Inside, it's a serviceable affair, with tatty cream walls and a tiled floor. His wife, Samira, a willowy figure topped by strong-featured face, sits on the yellow-covered sofa beside him, an ex-political prisoner herself. The conversation turns to my background, and the three years my father spent in a prisoner of war camp during the Second World War. Samira smiles strangely and makes a comment which I don't understand until Yassin translates it: 'She says three years is like a child's game,' he tells me. 'People here spend fifteen, twenty years in prison.'

He notices a rash of mosquito bites on my elbow just below my sleeve. 'In prison the mosquitoes were terrible,' he volunteers. 'I had lived nineteen years, and never known a mosquito and then'—the sweep of his hand indicates a plague—'I used to sleep in the day, to avoid them.' He still has the residue of a bite, a large lump on his elbow, now some twenty-four years old. Perhaps it is a stigmata, I suggest, a physical wound which carries a special significance because of the suffering it denotes. His face lights in comprehension, and he lifts his jeans to reveal marks on his ankles. 'Yes. These are my stigmata.' He mimics a rope knotting the feet together. 'Torture,' he says briskly, adding: 'Would you like to wash your hands before lunch?'

After lunch, we settle down for an afternoon talking politics. A month previously he had met a group of visiting American journalists, who had wanted to know what they could do to understand Syria better. 'I said, "Come more often!" We can save so much suffering if
178

we get to know each other. If we know each other, I won't think of killing you, or at least, I'll hesitate very much. They ought to take the initiative because they are richer, and can travel easily. We know the Americans. In a distorted way, but we know them more than they know about us. What they do affects our daily life.'

'What do we need to know about you?' I ask, realizing that from this broad perspective Britain and America are both part of the same, judgemental West.

'This is a good question!' responds Yassin cheerfully. 'The first thing is not about questions—just to come here and perhaps share a meal, or a cup of tea. You are on the right path!' He gestures to the tea and cakes on the little table before us. 'We just want them to lift the veil from our faces, because at the moment they are putting a veil over us. I don't know. Human understanding—not more than this!'

He bats away a fly, and leans forward, speaking emphatically. 'You don't know any human being unless you realize that he is as bad as you are, and you are as good as him. You can be bad tempered, he can be bad tempered! This applies to relations between nations and individuals.'

'Did you think like this at nineteen?'

'No. I don't know. Perhaps I didn't think at all. I was enthusiastic about changing things in my country. I was discovering democracy at the time. When you compared me to my friends, I was perhaps intellectual. I read a few books and could discuss things. I gave the impression of exaggerated seriousness.' He laughs ironically at his younger, earnest self.

'Do you regret the time you spent in prison?'

'No,' he says immediately. 'No. I don't say this out of heroism, or something like this. Because prison changed me deeply, and perhaps not for the worse.' He hacks into the dry Syrian cake with a fork. 'The man you are speaking to now is not the man who went into prison.

179

If it were not for my imprisonment, I would not be the same.' He smiles gently and adds: 'I prefer my situation now, more than if I hadn't been to prison.'

'You have a room no bigger than this,' he goes on, gesturing to the room in which we are sitting, 'and in it you have sixteen people. You see these people day and night. Someone's bed is next to yours, and perhaps when you are asleep a hand comes onto your face. Perhaps he drinks tea like this.' He takes his glass of tea and slurps it noisily. 'There are thousands of things that may cause friction. So it is very difficult at first. But in time, you get used to these things, and you like some of them.'

'In prison, you lose your privacy; you do everything in front of people, even changing your clothes. That's why prison is very hard for the first few months or year. Then you develop a different kind of privacy. You are still under the eyes of your friends, but your privacy is now inside you. It is not something that covers you, but it is something that you cover. There is internal privacy. You regain your self-respect.'

He leans back on the sofa, his hands behind his head, supremely relaxed. People in the West tend to guard their outer privacy jealously, I say, thinking of our highly scheduled lives and talk of personal space.

'There are two kinds of privacy, and two kinds of freedom,' Yassin responds. 'You can be a slave and not be in prison, to a dogma, a party or to fear, and you can be a really free human being in prison. I think prison did me a good turn! There was a myth in my family about me, when I was a boy of four,' he goes on. 'There was a hole in the ground'—he scoops a dip in the air with his hand—'and I used to play in it, apart from the others. I lived like this in prison. I needed my hole and that sense of being alone. If you like life to be a party, you will find prison very difficult. But if you are like me: a child who preferred to play alone in a hole, prison will be easier!'

At university he was, he says, indistinguishable from his contemporaries. But imprisonment had brought out the differences between them. One friend, superficially more lively and robust, had aged far beyond the eleven years he had spent in goal. His reflections remind me of accounts of incarceration by Primo Levi and Brian Keenan. Has he read any? He hasn't, and looks wistful at the thought of a body of literature written by people with kindred experiences. I could send you some, I offer. He lights up: 'You would do me a good turn if you did that!'

'Are things better now?'

'Yes, things are better, far better,' he replies. 'But there is something still threatening. No one can guarantee that we have left this period in the past, because there are no institutions, elected positions, no sovereignty of law, no free press, no open political system. No one can be sure that this terrible past is really in the past.'

'Is much being done to build these things?'

'Yes, we have a movement. The youth is joining the public arena. But society is still afraid. The intellectuals hesitate and the young men know what to reject, but they don't know what they want, because the opposition parties are not very attractive. We have no means to express our news and ideas. Perhaps you cannot imagine that, but we don't have a single newspaper that is free. I can write only in Lebanon, and for some websites. So we have no means to influence our destiny.'

Perhaps, I say cautiously, ordinary people don't really care about protest.

There's a pause while he considers this. 'This is perhaps true. The Syrian people are deeply depoliticized by their fear. And they need to live, to have a decent income. The annual income of Syrians is about

181

$1,000 a year, the same as in 1979. You cannot give your children a decent education. So many of them think of us as people looking for posts, or celebrity. This is one of the most complex problems we are facing—we have no means of communicating with the masses. And perhaps our discourse is elitist. For more than twenty years, there was no political life in this country at all: the regime burned the soil so that no political flowers could grow. Tens of thousands of people were killed. The economy deteriorated. The world was changing deeply and our country was put in a closed box. That's why there is a gap between people like us, and our society.'

'You have never left Syria?'

'I don't have a passport.'

I wonder where he had got his pronounced sense of this other, Western way of doing things.

'There are films, music, books,' he replies. 'The West is not something external for us. The West is known.'

A brighter view about the possibilities of reform came from Syria's artistic elite. Compared to most of the people I was meeting, Ammar Abdulhamid led something of a charmed existence. The son of a film director and well known actress and now in his late thirties, he was well-known within the country and well-connected outside. He had lived for nearly a decade in the United States, and published books of poetry and fiction in English. Recently, he had launched an Arab-English website on minority issues called *Al Tharwa*. Belatedly, the internet was taking off in Syria. Since it escaped some of the restrictions that applied to the state-regulated print press, it was a useful tool for dissidents, allowing them to raise potentially inflammatory issues without running into a head-on collision with the authorities.

When we meet in a brash, modern coffee house in the smart district of El Mezze, he strikes me more as West Coast American hippy

182

than Arab intellectual, with his check shirt and jeans and thick hair drawn back into a ponytail.

Earlier in the year, he tells me, riots in the Kurdish town of Qamishli had thrown his whole project into jeopardy. The Kurds, who made up ten per cent of Syria's population, wanted political rights, but the authorities had sent a clear signal as to who was in charge. Security forces had killed about thirty people, and unknown numbers of Kurdish activists disappeared into prison.

'I thought we would be closed down, but it didn't happen,' he says, as I sip a café latte. 'We haven't really come up against the red line. In fact we have been meeting with the First Lady and we got approval to open Kurdish schools. We're acting as a kind of conduit between minority groups and the authorities, telling the authorities what is happening on the ground. It's about being inclusive—we're talking to the authorities, like we're talking to everyone. They have the choice of whether they talk to us or not. If they tried to stop us, they would lose credibility—they want to be seen as being open. If they did close us down, I could still run the website from Beirut, for example. It's got a regional brief.'

'I suppose there's a danger the authorities might use the information you gather for their own purposes,' I suggest.

'We don't tell them any special information that isn't already known,' he replies. 'Everything is open'—he gestures to the clusters of people chatting around us—'like I'm talking to you now. We're independent, and we have to avoid taking the position of both certain Kurdish political parties, and the authorities. It's possible, if you're clear about your position from the beginning. That's what you have to do if you're doing advocacy work. So a space is opening up. To be honest with you, I can't believe it myself!' He smiles delightedly. 'I don't know how things will be in future, but every day that we continue, we get a bit stronger.'

The conversation turns to the importance of religion in political culture. A former Sunni imam and fundamentalist turned atheist, now agnostic, he has run the gamut of faith positions. 'It's a problem with the discourse—traditional Islam condemns heretical opinions,' he goes on. It tolerates Christianity and Judaism, but it puts it down—it's not a traditional source. So the reality is that the traditional language itself must be challenged.'

'I've noticed, talking to imams in Lebanon, that the same oppositional structure occurs repeatedly, the need to always have an enemy,' I observe.

Ammar nods. 'It's a rejectionist logic in its inability to cope with differences. That's why liberal reform does not work—in the end it could not work with traditional loyalties in this society. The traditional loyalty system is too entrenched. No one discusses it openly, but because of these political games no one wants to change things, because that would affect his loyalty. But today we have to.'

'Through the liberal intellectual culture?'

'Yes. But there are also problems with it, like for example, the inability of intellectuals to put up with each other. We need a clear liberal current of thought, because at the moment liberals are not coming together.'

I follow his train of thought: 'So it's about developing civil society, creating something else which lies between the government and the people.' Ammar nods again. 'How do you do that?'

'Education,' he replies. 'My own dream is to change the curriculum, to have, for example, civic education. In history, talk about the Arab-Israeli conflict would be less ideological and more factual, showing the mistakes that were made on both sides. And we should change the way we teach so that it's less on memorizing and more focused on interpretation.' He enthuses about his experience teaching children doing an environment project, in which interviews with

184

people about the pollution of a local river developed their sense of there being different views and interpretations. 'You can teach them to see the problem, and that it matters—this is education, in my opinion. And we need it particularly because fifty per cent of our population is under eighteen.'

His own plans to translate the Western philosophers such as Locke and Kant into Arabic and popularize their thought will be a contribution. 'Once you plant the seed, you can't control it.' He smiles happily. 'I know that Hobbes, for example, will be used by critics from the inside.'

I think of the academics in Britain's ivory towers, locked into churning out publications for the research assessment exercise. 'We have that kind of material widely available, and taught. But it has almost no impact on the mainstream political culture,' I point out.

'For you, it's outlived its usefulness,' he replies. 'But we need to go through that phase here.'

Back at the flat, the boys' preoccupation with how to deal with these political realities in their own lives surfaced periodically.

One night, I am sitting with Shivan on the balcony. It is past midnight and for once the street below is quiet. A huge sky arcs above us, stars twinkling in a velvety blue expanse. Shivan is talking, half to me and half into the darkness, about his plans for the future. Exhausted by late nights and the heat and pollution of Damascus, I let him muse on, hardly able to respond. At all costs, he says, he must avoid military service: a stretch of two and half years which is compulsory for all young men once they have finished their education. 'That is why I will try my best, after I finish my studies, to go abroad and never come back.'

185

He stares out in to the night. Opposite, the lights from the houses on Mount Kassioun sparkle prettily. 'I've seen people before doing military service, and I've seen them after. They change. After, they have no dignity, no thoughts, no independence. The army breaks them. Two and a half years! It's so long, another life. They have become Syrian.'

He turns to look at me directly. 'Have you noticed how the men in the street all look the same? It's military service which does that. The women are somehow more brilliant, more active, more alive.'

He was right. On my wanderings around Damascus I had noticed that Syrian men had a uniformity about them, an absence of expression in the eyes as they stood docilely on the streets and crowded buses. The women, tussling with shopping and children, seemed more connected with the business of living.

'I want a family,' Shivan muses on. 'But if I do military service, I won't be able to teach my children to have their own thoughts. I will be a bad dad, a bad father. It would be, like the song by Pink Floyd, another brick in the wall.'

Our domestic intimacy meant that I was also becoming a mother-confessor for their frustrations in other areas. Apart from the girl-friend of the only fellow in their circle lucky enough to have one, no women appeared to relieve the male monotony of life on the balcony. 'There is no sex!' was their perennial cry, whenever a potential sweet-heart came up in the conversation. Syrian society's traditional values meant that opportunities to meet women were limited and, when the two sexes did meet, young women tended to be very guarded.

Shivan's frustration with the situation had led to an early engagement to a young cousin in his hometown. Their arrangement had satisfied his libido but now, several years on, he realized that he and his fiancée had little in common. He wanted to extricate himself, but feared being dishonourable. One night, he clicked his phone shut after a long conversation with her, and turned to me, tears pricking his eyes. 'Alex, I don't know how old you are, but I think you are older, so you know more. What shall I do? She and I, we are on different planets.'

Earlier that week, after a long, softly spoken conversation the look on his face was unmistakeable as he restored his phone to its usual place on the balcony ledge. 'Was that your girlfriend?' I asked nosily.

'I love her, but no, not really,' he admitted reluctantly.

'There is no sex!' yelled Gabi from the controls of the computer inside, by way of explanation.

Shivan's true love was an Iraqi, who was also expected to marry someone else. Her parents would not accept him, a mere Syrian, as a suitor. As a result, the pair met occasionally and chastely.

In the meantime, while he waited for his future to become clearer, he intended to have some sex again. He made regular advances to the women he met at the university and they, disarmed by his charm and unusually direct approach, frequently agreed to an assignation. 'I call it the parachute approach,' he told me with pride. 'I land on their shoulders, and they are surprised.'

'Yes, and you do this.' I batted my eyelashes in rapid fire.

'Oh, you noticed that.' Shivan smiled, slightly abashed.

But these meetings were invariably abortive. Often, back in the bosom of their protective families, the young women subsequently rang to cancel. One particularly promising prospect did turn up for coffee—but she brought her brother along too.

For Gabi, less adept at negotiating his way through this minefield of social-sexual complexity, there was nothing. One day, I find him in the kitchen looking at his exam timetable, frowning and tutting. 'What, have you missed an exam?' I ask, concerned and a little surprised. 'No, it's about girls,' he replies without looking up. The time following an exam was a precious opportunity for male-female interaction, he explains, when students relieved to be at the end of their ordeal would naturally turn to each other for support.

I sit down at the kitchen table with him. 'How do you get a girlfriend here?'

Gabi pulls a long face. 'It's difficult, very difficult. I meet girls, especially at the university, but there is no sex! It never comes to anything. They are so afraid. We meet, we talk, and then at a certain point, you feel like a tension, a charge, inside them.' He taps his chest with a clenched fist. 'There are a few open-minded ones, but they are rare. It's not that sex is so important, especially for me. I have to love the girl, and it has to be right with her doing other things, like watching films and going for walks. But if there is no sex, it cannot be normal! There is always this block.' He taps his chest again, to indicate the locus of the tension, a knot of psychological and physical frustration, tangled up with the hopes and fears of the first stages of romance.

'Of course, there is sex, if you pay for it. But if you refuse to go to whores, there is nothing. And then, after a while'—he looks away in only the faintest embarrassment—'there are sex problems.'

I talk for a bit about life in the West, telling him a Bridget Jones-esque story of tens of thousands of British singles sitting alone at night in front of the television with their portions for one, of phone calls never made, of men too confused by their role or frightened of commitment to engage with women. Gabi manages a smile which is both wan and amused at that same time. 'So the situation is the same, and yet the reasons so different. They are this'—he stretches his arms so wide that one almost leaves the kitchen by the window—'far apart!'

Somehow I find myself giving the same advice dispensed by friends and self-help books back home about the importance of getting out to Meet People. 'Whatever the reasons, you have to get off the balcony, and go out and meet some women,' I hear myself say firmly.

'I know,' he replies. 'Last year, I went out a lot with friends, and met a lot of girls. But it came to nothing. It was always the same. It is a question of finding the one, the few open-minded ones.' His mind turns to practicalities and strategies. 'The university is not so good, the girls there are too young and frightened. The best place is the culture and arts, people are more open-minded in that sphere.' His mood darkens again. 'But it is so pretentious. I hate it!

'Maybe in the West, I would have success.' He brightens at the thought. 'For a while, I had this written on my computer screen: 'Some One, Some Day.'

Other times, not feeling that I had the answers to all these problems, I was less than patient. One evening, Shivan put his head round the door onto the balcony and said, 'Alex, my fiancée just rang me. Do I call her back or not?' I took a Syrian coin out of my purse, assigned each side an option and tossed it. 'Heads,' I said briskly. 'Ring her.'

It is the night before my flight back to London. I take the boys and some of their friends out for a meal, and then we go back to the flat. My taxi is booked for dawn, and they decide that they should stay up all night in order to negotiate the right fare and see me off properly. We all settle down on the sofa to while away the night hours with a film on the computer.

Another American film. A quarter of an hour later, my eyelids drooping, I retreat to bed and fall instantly asleep. When I wake a few hours later, the boys are having coffee on the balcony. First light

189

is playing across Jaramana. We go down into the street and they load my bags into the taxi. 'Is it all right to kiss you?' I look anxiously up at the blank windows of the surrounding flats, imagining all sorts of condemnatory looks. 'Will it cause a scandal?'

'No, no,' Gabi smiles serenely. 'It's all right.' I kiss them on both cheeks, climb into the taxi and then I'm off, speeding through the Syrian dawn.

8
AFTER SYRIA

IT WAS fifteen months before I made it back to Beirut. This time, the city was plastered with pictures of the dead Hariri, smiling serenely from shop windows and pockmarked walls. In some, he appeared as a ghostly figure hovering above the handsome, fleshy face of his son Saad, the young businessman who found himself catapulted into Lebanese politics as leader of the anti-Syrian alliance. Hariri senior's mosque was finished, its honey-coloured minarets and bright blue domes towering resplendently over Downtown. And Syria had gone after nearly three decades of occupation, the buildings requisitioned by its intelligence forces empty, its army packed up and driven back over the border. The street-sellers who paraded the Corniche now made their loyalty to Lebanon unquestionably clear, large red-and-cedar flags flapping above the food.

Abir was living with her Greek Orthodox boyfriend in the Christian suburb of Achrafieh near, to her great amusement, a restaurant called Hummus, Fuul and partners. 'I'm DEEP in love with him,' she told me intensely when, having picked me up from the airport, Danny disappeared into Barbar's to stock up on snacks for a late-night supper. The arrangement was top secret, and they wouldn't marry until her father accepted a suitor from another sect. 'I don't want to lose my family again,' she explained. For the moment, the couple were biding their time and making plans to buy an apartment, as a bit of property into the bargain was likely to sway the parental mind.

As we hung my clothes in her wardrobe, Abir updated me with the latest gossip. Aisha, the Arabian beauty of the Y whose life seemed laid out before her, had taken a fall: her father had embezzled funds from the bank for which he worked, and was in prison. The family was now living in the meanest circumstances and Aisha's fiancé, whom she had known since she was twelve, had dumped her and got engaged to someone else within the month. I was indeed back in Lebanon, where the tales were taller and life was larger.

Abir even had a new, typically Lebanese joke for me—a wry comment on the country's high rates of plastic surgery. One day, a rich, virtuous, elderly lady lay on her deathbed. Just as her spirit was about to depart, an angel came and promised her thirty years more life. To the amazement of those around her, the old lady sprang up, cured, and went off to book a series of operations for the latest cosmetic procedures. Months later, she emerged from her bandages and went out on the town to show off her new, youthful looks. But on her very first outing, she was hit by a truck, died and went straight to heaven. Livid, she confronted the Lord: 'You promised me thirty years more of life!' The Lord looked at her, started, and then clapped his hand to his head. 'Eugh!' He said. 'I didn't recognize you!'

I liked this new man in my friend's life. Danny was a big, fleshy young man with a sincere gaze that could quickly dissolve into giggles. He loved to relax, and could spend hours on the sofa, puffing away on his *nargileh*, watching TV. But beneath his laid-back demeanour ticked a canny business mind that was often at work, fomenting new ideas. Some of these went into furthering his already lucrative career, but he also liked to pick apart the finer points of Lebanese politics.

Most of all, he loved to cook, and he loved to eat. The couple's tiny flat didn't have a kitchen as such—it was a sink in a cubby hole,

192

with a single gas ring on a shelf—but this didn't impede the regular production of impressive meals. From the sofa Danny crouched over his own tiny calor gas stove, cooking up some sauce or frying a meat delicacy, while Abir was charged with cooking pasta or rice in the cubby hole, which invariably stuck or burned. I spend my first morning running between them, carrying a cargo of an onion or a clean knife. 'Take this to Danny,' instructed Abir. 'Take this to Abir,' instructed Danny.

When we finally sat down to eat, the table was loaded with dishes—a bolognaise sauce, little meat patties, chunks of liver and—for an extra treat, specially purchased from the butcher—lumps of white fat, fried in olive oil. 'If I had an oven, I would cook you something REALLY delicious,' said Danny, between mouthfuls.

Over the next few days, some of the realities of this subtly changed country began to seep into my consciousness. The day after I arrived, I was half-watching the television that constantly blared from the corner of the room as May Chidiac read the news. A journalist who had covered the country's political life for the Lebanese Broadcasting Corporation for decades, she was a familiar figure, visibly at ease as she smiled out of the screen in a sugar-pink top and matching lipstick. But the next day, she was lying in hospital in a critical condition, her left hand and foot blown off in a bomb blast. It was the latest in the series of targeted bombings that had plagued Beirut since Hariri's assassination earlier in the year, claiming the lives of the journalist Samir Qasir and the former Communist Party leader George Hawi. Widely believed to be orchestrated by pro-Syrian forces, the bombings were eliciting mutterings about a more sinister plot by forces trying, as usual, to make Lebanon a pawn in a bigger game of international politics. Whatever their provenance, they were a deadly reminder that Lebanon had yet to shake off its old bugbears

193

of violence and sectarianism. Meanwhile, the country waited tensely for the conclusions of the UN report into Hariri's murder.

A couple of days later, I hot-foot it down to Martyr's Square. I have heard that there is to be a demonstration by a new group of activists calling themselves *Kaffa!*—Enough!—who are campaigning for a democratic, peaceful Lebanon. I am excited by the prospect of being among the crowds, perhaps talking to some of the fervent young people whom I had seen in their thousands on my TV screen in London in the weeks following Hariri's death. But when I get to the statue—a womanly figure embodying the spirit of Lebanon, holding a blazing torch over the wounded bodies at her feet—I find only a huddle of politicians and journalists. Thirty men and one woman have arranged themselves in rows at its base, as if for a school photo, and are fidgeting self-consciously. Opposite, an almost equal number of journalists squint at them through cameras and scribble in their note-books while the spokesman reads a statement amid the smirks and shuffles of his fellow campaigners.

Afterwards, I collar him. Ryan Ashcar is the general secretary of the socialist Progressive Youth Organization. 'We are here to say, "stop the bombs," and to ask the government to put security as a priority,' he says, drawing on his cigarette. He is slightly bored by having to talk to a foreign journalist, and his sleek haircut and youthful urbanity put me in mind of something. As I walk away, I realize what: if he were in Britain, he would be a newly-elected, career-minded, New Labour MP.

I wanted to get a sense of what Syria's departure means on the ground, rather than at the level of the high politics being watched by the world. The most obvious effect was the departure of at least half of the million Syrian workers who had been doing the country's most menial jobs, chased away by the mounting hostility of many Lebanese and the tighter border controls between the two countries. But for anything else, I was stumped, so I called some local journalists for advice. One of them, Tewfik Mashlawi, edited the *Middle East Reporter*, which had provided a daily English-language digest of the region's press for almost thirty years. He gave me an appointment and some quintessentially Lebanese directions to his office—'near Sanayeh Square and a gas station.' I arrived hot and exhausted, half an hour late, having been wrongly directed to a building of the same name near a calor gas shop.

Behind a desk in the corner of a large, grey office, a white-haired man is hunched over a small transistor radio, listening intently. He doesn't acknowledge me when I walk in, and something about his complete absorption in his task makes me feel almost as if I have stumbled across an animal going about his business in his natural habitat. After a while, he swings round and fixes me with an earnest, owl-like, stare.

'The effect of it?' He speaks slowly, as he answers my question about Syria's departure, weighing out a pause between each word. 'You cannot see it on the ground.' He shuffles a pile of magazines on his desk. 'I am keeping these,' he continues with equal deliberateness, holding up a copy of the weekly magazine *Al Shiraa*. 'They follow Rustom Ghazali, and the way he dealt with the Lebanese army. Unfortunately, these stories came to be known only in the last three weeks, because they did not speak of it before.'

General Rustom Ghazali was the former head of Syrian military intelligence in Lebanon, a man with huge sway over the country's internal affairs. One such story, Mashlawi goes on, concerns a Lebanese officer called Mohammad Al Hajar who stole a public artefact, a statue from the ruins at Saida, for Ghazali. The soldier was caught,

195

tried and sentenced to two years in prison. But following a call from the general himself, he was suddenly released and restored to military office. 'These things are very, very interesting, because they show you how the Syrians manipulated affairs in Lebanon,' says Mashlawi. 'They were not known before.'

'And you, of all people, would have known about them?'

'Yes. This is the reason I want to put it out,' he says, his owl-like stare unwavering. 'We often talk about interference in Lebanon, but we don't have specific examples.'

Despite the impenetrability of the Syrian question, I can't resist a trip across Beirut to look at Beau Rivage. The Syrian detention centre lay in the well-to-do area of Ramlet el Baida, just behind the beach where Abir and I had spent a holiday afternoon the previous year watching the *mukhabarat* at work. Terrible things had gone on there, although few Lebanese had any real idea what. Organizations like Human Rights Watch had gathered evidence that this, along with other detention centres, was where Lebanon's 'disappeared' had ended up, interrogated and tortured by the Syrian intelligence services. Now, with the Syrians gone, the place had been finally returned to its owners. It was, a local journalist suggested, set to become the next Khiam: a good Middle Eastern afternoon out, a place of pilgrimage for those with a penchant for political tourism.

But as I walk away from the shoreline into Ramlet el Baida, things could hardly be more tranquil. The wide residential streets are sleepy in the mid-afternoon sun and the notorious Beau Rivage hard to locate. It is impossible to distinguish the detention centre from the several other buildings bearing the same name. I mount the marble steps of the four-star Beau Rivage hotel for directions, and the receptionist is charm itself when I ask if things have changed since the Syrians left. 'Same old, same old,' he says cheerfully. 'They didn't interfere with us here. Only if there was something wrong, like somebody drove too fast, then they interfered.'

He directs me down the road, where I'm confronted by more nondescript tower blocks. A pale-skinned policeman looks at me quizzically when I ask for the former Syrian HQ: 'You want to buy an apartment, *yanni*?' A boy of about ten is loitering nearby, and gestures to me to follow. He has one permanently closed eye sited halfway down his face, a set of thick dark lashes in the middle of his cheek.

He stops in front of an unremarkable building, twelve storeys of identical cream-coloured balconies stacked on top of each other. The blank windows give nothing away; this could be a tatty apartment block in any city in the world. A man emerges out of the innards of the building. Only two people are living there while the building is being renovated, he says and no, he doesn't know where I could find the owner. I give the one-eyed boy a thousand lira note, and leave.

Time to head east, towards the Syrian border.

The air is noticeably cooler as the bus climbs higher into the Metn, the chain of mountains east of Beirut. I am in one of the old chara-bancs that run this route, a gaily painted, high-suspension affair which noisily surmounts peak after peak until finally we reach the village of Bois de Boulogne, 1,200 metres above sea level. The air is pure and the views panoramic, the tips of the surrounding mountains melting into the clouds. The long, principal road is lined with large, stately houses and mop-headed pine trees. 'Nice, easy place,' I mutter to myself as I head for the village bakery.

But the village's air of prosperous calm belies its recent history. Before the war, Boulogne was the mountain resort of choice for well-to-do Lebanese wanting to escape the heat and humidity of summertime Beirut. Those who could afford to built gracious houses; others ran hotels, confident that the balmy climate would draw enough clients. When fighting broke out and the Syrians moved in, ostensibly to support the country's Christians and help solve the crisis, they chose the village, a strategic boon because of its sweeping views of the surrounding area, as one of their main army bases. Most of the locals left to seek a quieter life elsewhere and, one by one, their big houses and hotels were taken over to serve as barracks for Syrian troops. Only a few hundred remained to live as best they could among up to 4,500 foreign soldiers.

Georges Ghostine, a Maronite born in the village and its mayor since 1963, was one of them. He owned the large, elegant Hotel Bois de Boulogne, and he wasn't going to abandon it for anyone. Despite the fact that the hotel, roomy enough to accommodate a couple of hundred guests, remained empty year after year, he waited on for the Syrian departure. Finally, his wish was granted when, six months previously, the Syrians had packed up and left.

A small man in a large blue cardigan, a lively gaze playing beneath thick black brows, Ghostine is having coffee in the hotel lobby with his wife and a friend when I turn up for my appointment with him. 'We saw you go past,' he greets me.

'Yes, I went to find *mannoush*,' I tell them. 'I crave it on winter mornings in London.'

'Really?' They're astonished.

Ghostine and I move to a large, elegant sitting room away from possible interruptions, and he begins his story. 'I took the decision not to leave the hotel, because I knew that if I left, the army would occupy it,' he says. 'How did I manage to live all that time? That's the question—I wonder myself how I managed to keep it up.'

Initially, he believed that the occupation would end after three or four months, but it went on, even after the end of the war. 'My children said, "They are never going to leave." They lost hope. But I never lost hope.'

The family survived on savings, selling off parcels of land where necessary. Although it had few guests, the hotel stayed open, welcoming the odd friend or official brought to Boulogne on political business. I look around: money is obviously not a pressing problem; the high ceilings and well-proportioned rooms are beautifully set off by dark polished wood and immaculate upholstery. As he talks, Ghostine seems more concerned with the effects of the Syrian presence on his personal, political freedom than his finances. *On vivait dans une caserne*! he keeps repeating, energetically. 'We were living in a barracks!'

But when I press him as to what form these limitations took, I get a contradictory response. 'If we didn't get involved in politics, we had freedom,' he says, taking a sip of coffee. 'So you said nothing?' 'Of course not,' he replies, with some impatience.

Almost in passing, he mentions the political discussions he habitually held with the Syrian generals in which he spoke his mind freely, questioning their right to occupy the village. 'Sometimes they gave reasons, sometimes not.' I'm astonished at his nerve. 'Were you really able to speak to them like that?'

'I had very good relations with the top people,' he explains. 'The little soldiers didn't dare to interfere with me in the hotel. I was always very correct with them, very clear and straightforward. The Syrians aren't stupid; they know that I was sincere with them, unlike some of the opportunists they dealt with. One day a Syrian said to me, "You are very strong. You have been able to live with all these political parties, and with the Syrian army. You know how to keep your reputation."'

Then he's off, plucking at the main strings of the region's big issues with the assurance of someone who lives and breathes politics.

It's becoming clear to me how this fierce little man could keep even the occupying Syrian generals in their place. What have I discovered in the course of my research, he wants to know? He himself is quite clear as to the solution to Lebanon's problems: a division of the country into cantons along the lines of the Swiss model. The country's various sects would live side by side, yet apart, unencumbered by each other's mores and customs. His distaste for the Muslim culture is apparent, and he is visibly disappointed when I say that, no, I haven't been woken by the sound of the *muezzin* in Ain el Mreisse. I'm swept along, uncomfortably, on the tide of his convictions before finally managing to bring him back to the business at hand. 'Would you like to see what the Syrians have done?' he offers.

We get into his car, Ghostine's small frame almost disappearing below the steering wheel. He drives away from the main street, up the wooded slopes at the top end of the village. At every turn, sitting proudly on its own pine-clad mound, is a handsome, well-proportioned house in pale stone. But the gaping black holes that each has in place of windows tell of abandonment. In the bright midday sunshine the place has a creepy feel, like the opening scenes of a sci-fi film: even if you didn't know its history, you would still know that something had happened here.

In fact, the reality was rather banal. As each batch of soldiers finished their posting and returned to Syria, they took something from the houses with which to refurbish their own, poorer homes. Gradually all the fixtures and fittings were stripped away, the windows denuded of their frames. Finally, with just the bare structure of the houses standing, they had resorted to camp-style living. Black streaks from fires run up the white stone walls; a military blanket dangles from a window.

Driving slowly, Ghostine points out house after house. 'This one is being renovated,' he says, his finger waving to the left, and 'this one is not being renovated,' to the right. In most cases, it's the second option.

'Have you had many meetings in the community, to decide how to rebuild things since they left?' I ask. 'Yes, we have had meetings, meetings,' he replies, manoeuvring the steering wheel. 'But people need money to do the work. They may have been rich before the war, but thirty years of living on reserves, and they aren't any more. There have been promises of money from the government but, so far, nothing.'

He pulls up in front of a house where a shabby looking man is loitering, and the two have a brief conversation. *Mabrouk!* Ghostine congratulates him, adding to me: 'Good, he's renovating. His son in law worked in Dubai and has given him the money.'

'Do you resent the loss of all the time you spent waiting for the Syrians to go?'

'Of course,' he replies. 'I feel I lost thirty years of my life. It's a lifetime. Yes, I kept the place, but I have friends who went away to France, to London—they are millionaires now. I stayed because I kept thinking that things would change.' He indicates another pitiful building perched halfway down a slope, its eye-windows dead and empty. 'That's my sister's. She's going to renovate it.'

'Have you got the energy to start all over again?' He must be approaching his seventies; rebuilding his hotel business will be a mammoth task.

'Yes!' He's almost singing. 'I've got the energy. I haven't lost that.'

He drops me in front of Villa Jaber, the local equivalent of Beau Rivage where those who aroused the suspicion of the intelligence service were taken and questioned, held for a night or two, maybe roughed up a bit. But now Lebanese flags are draped over its freshly cleaned stone, and construction workers are busying themselves around a pre-fab house put up to facilitate the renovation. Among the trees on a nearby mound, the owners have built a makeshift altar for open-air mass. Sheets of glass cover rough-hewn logs and behind a statue of the Virgin, her head gently inclined, stands on a small stone pillar. There's a cross made of two tree trunks bonded together with cord.

I return to the house and get a nod of permission to enter from one of the workers. On the hall wall hangs an informal photo exhibition telling a story of reclamation. The glossy snapshots show people scrubbing rooms and burning Syrian slogans outside. A deliriously happy crowd picnic on the floor of a decrepit room. I wander up the wide, curling staircase. It's like a building that's been abandoned for decades; electric wires hang from sockets on the yellowing walls, and the avocado bathroom suite is the height of seventies chic. Some rooms are so dark and uninviting that I can't bring myself to step in, repelled by imagined scenes of what might have taken place in them. Turning the place back into a family home will be a lot of work.

Back on the main street, a sweet-faced café-owner provides me with a toilet and tea, refusing to take any money. Yes, she says, things have been a bit different since the Syrians left, but people still feel tense, what with the bombings. The soldiers had popped in for the odd sandwich or Pepsi, but there hadn't been much contact. She and her husband had opened the café last year, but they had yet to benefit from the increased tourism that the village's liberation should bring. 'We hope that next year, it will be better,' she smiles.

In the flat, life was dominated by the dynamics of Abir's and Danny's relationship. As before, Abir lived at a high tempo but now her moods changed frequently, and her behaviour swung between that of a grown-up embarking on marriage and career and that of a child wanting everything her own way. Her attitude to money followed the same, contradictory pattern. Her small salary did not go far, and the weight of the couple's finances fell on Danny. Conscious of the need to save for a deposit on a flat, Abir was subject to bouts of thriftiness, carefully stowing leftovers in the fridge. But an hour or two later, she was back to her high-pitched demands, lobbying her fiancé for outings, or—her constant preoccupation—a car of her own. In the supermarket she wanted almost everything that was on sale, indiscriminately piling packets of chocolate and crisps into the shopping cart, safe in the knowledge that she would not be the one footing the bill.

Her growing, multifarious appetites were worrying her boyfriend, and one night, while Abir slept, he unburdened himself to me. He was keen to settle down, he said, puffing on his *nargileh* anxiously; he had had enough of flings, but he found Abir's behaviour confusing. He wasn't clear what she wanted—at times it was a certain career, at others she just wanted to make lots of money. She professed a deep desire to study, then he wouldn't see her for a week as she went out with friends every night. She talked about going abroad in one breath and starting a family straightaway the next. 'She wants everything,' he sighed. At the back of both our minds, was the same unstated fear—that Lebanese materialism, like some big sci-fi monster, was taking over the person we loved. 'I know what Lebanese people want. They want a mobile phone, a car, and then to go out a lot to nice places,' he said, looking at me earnestly. 'What is your opinion?'

He was particularly curious to know more about his girlfriend's se-cretive religion, and was reading a book which Dr. Anwar had written earlier in his career. He took to measuring Abir's claims about the true nature of the Druze faith against some of the statements he found in it, his dark eyes expectant as he cross-examined her between

203

puffs on the *nargileh*. 'What do you believe in?' he asked her, again and again. Abir's vague replies about goodness did little to meet his need for doctrine and evidence, and he grew frustrated.

'WHAT DO YOU BELIEVE IN?' he barked.

'Just to believe in God, and be good. That's it,' repeated Abir shakily.

I was confused by the new Abir myself, and uncomfortable with the couple's tendency to call on me to adjudicate on controversial matters like whether looking at someone else constituted an act of infidelity. Finally, my head abuzz with questions and bickering, I decamp to the relative sanctuary of a hotel in my old haunt of Ain el Mreisse, pleading pressure of work.

My new domestic front at the hotel, it turned out, had its own Druze influences. The business was run by a Druze family, and the heart-stoppingly handsome young receptionist was nothing if not attentive. One day, as he helped me access the internet on the hotel computer, he pointed to the screensaver on which hovered the faces of Kamal and Walid Jumblatt, father and son, dynastic leaders of the Druze clan. 'Which one is better?' he demanded.

I paused only a second over this trick question. One, I now knew, represented the venal world of Politics, while the other the true life of the Spirit. My finger moved to the distinctive features of Kamal. My companion, sitting closer than was strictly necessary, nodded approvingly.

If there is a place that exemplifies how the shifting tides of international geo-politics have formed the people and places of the modern Middle East, it is Anjar. Spread over a gentle slope between the eastern Lebanese mountains and the verdant Bekaa valley, the village was built from scratch sixty years ago by the French Mandate authorities for the Armenian inhabitants of Musa Dagh in former Syria.

The residents of Musa Dagh's six villages already held a special place in Armenian history: not only had they escaped the 1915 genocide that killed an estimated 1.5 million of their people but, unlike other Armenian communities scattered by the diaspora, they had managed to hold onto their homeland. But in 1939 the French authorities, anxious to keep Turkey as an ally, ceded to Turkish demands for the area. To compensate the Armenian residents for the loss of their home, they bought them some land in Lebanon and built them houses. The community moved wholesale, and Anjar was born. Decades later, the village remains an exclusively Armenian community of two thousand souls, distinctive even from the thriving Armenian community in Beirut's Bourj Hammoud. No one else is allowed to buy land there, and the village has even evolved its own dialect of Anjarian, not understood by Armenians elsewhere.

The part of Anjar's history that has made the tourist books is the elegant ruin of columns and arches left by the Umayyad Islamic dynasty. But I was more interested in the village's more recent claim to fame as the headquarters of Syrian intelligence services in Lebanon, and one of Syria's main army bases. I had also heard that some members of the community even regretted the Syrians' departure, worried about their security as a tiny minority among a predominantly Muslim population.

As a taxi from the nearest town of Chtaura drops me in Anjar's main, palm-lined avenue, I wonder how I'm going to get under the skin of the place. It's a balmy October morning, and the village has an ordered beauty and spaciousness that I haven't found elsewhere. Side streets run off in neat, geometric lines, edged with low, white houses and generous, tree-filled plots of green. The hulking Anti Lebanon mountains, a natural border with Syria, rise behind the vil-

205

lage, their dry sandy sides yellowed by the sun. Signposts mark the way in Arabic, English and Armenian. But along with this atmosphere of care and calm, the place has a sense of reserve about it: there are few people on the streets, and the shutters of the white houses are firmly closed against the midday sun. Even the Orthodox church that stands at the village's far end is closed and empty.

I walk along the leafy roads to the Armenian Evangelical Secondary School to see my one contact, headteacher Reverend Rafi Messerlian. Inside the school grounds clusters of teenagers are lying languidly on the grass enjoying the lunchtime sunshine. In his cool, white office, the Rev. Messerlian talks of life with and without the Syrians. 'They were here and we, the community, shared with them their feasts,' he says matter-of-factly. 'In general, we were in a good relationship, and they didn't give us any troubles. Now they are not here. In a way nothing has changed. For the Armenians, life goes on.'

It is hard to imagine what would ruffle the calm of this man in his late thirties, with his broad, pleasant face. In economic terms, he goes on, this agricultural village has not suffered much from the loss of Syrian labour, although trade in the surrounding area has suffered and construction, largely dependent on low-waged Syrian workers, has become more expensive.

'Have you become worried about your security since the Syrians left?'

'We didn't feel our security in Anjar was threatened by their departure,' he says serenely. 'There are political tensions between Lebanon and Syria, but we are not involved, because our strategy as Armenians is that we are neutral.'

They had even managed to maintain that stance while the rest of Lebanon's sects had been dragged into conflict. 'In the civil war, we were neutral,' he goes on. 'We didn't take sides with either the

206

Christians or the Muslims. We said, "This is wrong". In the end, we were proved right—they had to sit down and talk. We try to keep good communication with everybody. We are loyal citizens here. We have our schools, we have input into the economy, and we want to have good relations with Syria, because some of our people are Syrian citizens too. We are Armenians, with people in both Lebanon and Syria.' He opens his palms, as if to say how easy it is to live out this complex, double identity and the split loyalties it involves.

'Is it difficult to stay uninvolved?' I ask.

'It's hard, because when there are tensions in this country, people want to bring you here or there,' he replies calmly. 'It's hard to keep in the balance.'

'Are people more open now that the Syrians have gone?'

Now the smile is hard to decipher. 'I don't know if they are here or not. They work in secret—that's intelligence. I think there may be intelligence in Lebanon from many countries—from Israel, the States, France—we heard there were people from Jordan,' he goes on, reasonably. 'The Syrians were here—we saw them on the street, at checkpoints. Whether they are still here, I don't know.'

His tone suggests that neither the presence nor absence of secret police in their midst, nor the provenance of spies, is of any real concern to them, the Armenians.

Then he accompanies me out of the school gates and across the road to the office of Haroutian Lakissian, a prominent community figure, on record for his fears that the loss of the order-keeping Syrian troops will expose the community to persecution from the Muslims who dominate the surrounding area. But his office is empty, the blinds down and his car gone. 'Go and see the mayor,' he suggests.

In the municipality a few streets away, I am ushered into an office where the mayor and a companion are smoking together. They look at me as if I'm a mad woman. What kind of book? Do I have a copy

207

of the manuscript to show them? The mayor has no time today—I will have to ring for an appointment next week—but they instruct their security man to drive me to the priest's house.

The priest is asleep, explains his wife. Should she wake him? She should not. She brings coffee, and we sit in her beige living room, both perplexed at how to proceed, punctuating the silence with fragments of small-talk. She is in her sixties, with dark, bird-like eyes in a pale, nondescript face and, like the place itself, she seems very self-contained. In her halting English she tells me about her high-achieving offspring, all educated at AUB in the capital, where she herself had moved in order to look after them. 'My daughter is an embryologist,' she volunteers, her dark eyes twinkling with pride. Silence falls. 'We are surrounded by Muslims,' she remarks suddenly, a propos of nothing.

'Is that okay?'

'Oh yes,' she smiles gently. 'There are no problems.'

As it emerges that the priest, even when awake, speaks neither French nor English, I begin to take my leave. But, says his wife, her sister speaks good English, and she runs a special kindergarten. If I go over to the school and ask for Miss Vicky I should find her, on her first day back at work, the week before the start of term.

The school office is full of chatting women, catching up on news after the long summer holiday. When I ask for Miss Vicky, a short woman in her sixties stands up, laughing. Yes, she has time, she assures me, and steers me over to the building that houses the kindergarten. She is wearing a top of the candiest pink I have ever seen, embellished with silver embroidery. Below her smart black trousers high, silver-buckled mules of an even deeper pink adorn her small feet. It is an outfit that has been put together with a great deal of thought, and in a spirit of fun.

208

I hear her kindergarten is special, I say politely, as we approach the building. Privately, I don't believe a word of it; I have seen lots of nurseries in the Middle East, scruffy places with a municipal feel. But when she throws open the door, my inner four-year-old gasps involuntarily and I want to rush headlong towards everything before me. Bathed in the golden light flooding through white arches, is a child's world in bright primary colours. There are slides, a Wendy house and a puppet theatre. Little trees of spring-green and tawny brown mark the passing of the seasons.

A row of polystyrene trees is growing at our feet. 'This is the family tree,' says Miss Vicky, handling a large, foam pear onto which two photos of the same child have been stuck. 'The photos show the child last year, and this,' she explains. The orchard's other trees bear alphabet fruit in Arabic, Armenian and English, curvy or angular, according to the script. The children, who join the kindergarten at two years and four months, will start learning all three languages at the age of four.

She leads me from room to room. On every floor teddy bears beat little drums against a night-blue background and the walls display charts, personalized for each child and teaching a different point. There is a birthday chart—'we know each child's birthday, and we celebrate it, whether they do at home or not,' says Miss Vicky firmly—and an attendance chart, with a stick-on plastic face for each child. She opens the door of the last classroom. 'Here, they are five, they know everything,' she explains with mock gravity, indicating the more complex information the children are now expected to absorb. On one chart giant white teeth are linked to different kinds of food, including a downcast looking tooth linked to a pile of sweets. 'If you eat junk food, you will have a sad face,' she explains with mock severity. There are corners for science, nature and art, a row of tiny dressing up clothes in brocades and velvets and a prayer corner. Everything is arranged with the utmost precision, and even the crayons are laid out in neat, colour-coordinated rows.

'Do you have problems getting funding?' I ask. They are a given for such projects, the world over.

'No,' says Miss Vicky, her pink mules clip-clopping as we walk down the corridor. 'We have money from the Calouste Gulbenkian Foundation.'

In her office Armenian artefacts line one wall. There are fishing nets and cooking pots, a tiny bread oven and a Singer sewing machine. Armenian women in high lace headdresses stare out proudly from sepia photos.

We sit down, and she tells me how, when the village was first created, there was nothing. Gradually the community developed its infrastructure, building schools and churches for its three different kinds of Christians: Orthodox, Catholic and Presbyterian. She herself has been working at the kindergarten since it opened forty-two years ago.

'No foreigner is accepted here,' she says. 'We don't want to be with other people; we want to keep our language, our traditions. No one will sell his house to any foreigner.'

'Is the survival of the community under threat?'

'No. The young people are in Beirut, but every weekend they are here with us. When they are young they are filled with our stories and traditions. We are not afraid of losing them.'

'What's the most important story?'

'What happened in Turkey, when they massacred one and a half million people. And we are telling them about our lands, now under Turkey, our Ararat—that one day we will go and take it. This is the main story we are telling them, from the kindergarten to the end.'

She is talking with such intensity that I can almost share her vision of a faraway land, the locus of the Armenians' past and future.

I wonder out loud whether it is realistic to plant such dreams of return in the minds of the young who have begun their lives here in Lebanon, in this green and balmy place beneath the mountains.

'This is not a dream,' says Miss Vicky firmly. 'We are dreaming, but we will take it.' The light humour that has infected her talk of the children's education has vanished. 'All the world knows it is our land, not theirs. Some day—not too far—we will take it.'

'How do you balance this with your Lebanese identity?'

'I was born here, and I feel it is my place. It means everything to me. It is my second country, after Armenia.'

'Has it made any difference to you, now that Syria has left?'

'Under the control of Syria, we are safe,' she replies, adding diplomatically: 'As Armenian people, we work with all these groups.'

Suddenly it all falls into place. The detachment that I sense in these intensely private people, their ability to keep their distance from politics in this highly politicized land: all derive from the unchangeable fact that in their reality the priorities lie elsewhere. Against the backdrop of their tragic past and their consuming vision for the future, living under this regime, or that, makes little difference. I intimate this to Miss Vicky.

She nods vigorously. 'Yes. This is the main cause.'

I feel I've taxed her enough, but I'm curious about one last thing. Her hand bears no wedding ring—is the kindergarten her family? The smile returns at the thought of her charges. 'Yes, I have many children.'

'Don't you ever get bored, starting again, year after year?'

The answer is categorical. 'No. Never.'

I leave her to the delicate task of forming young Armenians for the forty-third year running.

The following weekend, I accompany Abir on her weekend visit to her family in the Chouf, finally meeting her father for our long-awaited talk about the Druze. It is Saturday afternoon, the end of the six-day week, and the bus is packed with people going home to their villages. Having come straight from work, Abir is wearing a smart black suit and heels, every inch the young professional, and I sense that this is the image she wants to impress on her family. As the bus weaves higher up the mountain roads, she warns me that her father doesn't like being contradicted. 'As his daughter, I can't say, "You're wrong." I say instead, "there is this point of view that... what do you think?"'

We catch up on the events of the few days since I left the flat. 'Danny's thinking of getting his stomach stapled,' she confides. 'He saw some friends he hadn't seen for a while, and they told him he had put on a lot of weight. He's phoned to see if he can get a good price for the operation.'

I'm appalled. I could not avoid noticing that Danny had a weight problem—his walk was becoming a waddle as his limbs struggled to move freely under the pads of flesh. He was deeply averse to exercise and, when the lift to his fifth floor office broke, he stayed outside for hours rather than use the stairs, making calls on his mobile phone. Could he not consider a less drastic solution such as dieting? I suggest. For a few minutes, we have an adult, almost parental conversation, plotting weight loss strategies to help him. 'My father says, "Eat like a king at breakfast, as if you're with friends at lunchtime, and like a pauper in the evening,"' says Abir, her eyes wide. She herself will accompany him to play the only sport he likes—basketball—and learn to cook healthy, nutritious recipes, rather than leaving all the culinary decisions to him.

But her own weight was burgeoning and her attitudes to food veered wildly from a resolve to take control to a desire for immediate

212

gratification. Just a few days before, as we sipped milky coffee at Café Younis, she had been fantasizing about a potion, newly on the market, that supposedly removed a layer of fat from under the skin without the consumer having to alter their eating habits in any way. 'It's worth trying,' she said. 'It only costs five thousand lira.'

Finally we arrive in a place resembling more a small town than a mountain village and, although the bus is full, Abir persuades the driver to take a detour to her house. We hop off, and she leads me into a large building of unplastered breeze blocks. In the flat upstairs her relatives congregate in the kitchen and covered balcony and a happy bubble of Arabic chatter fills the air. I have brought a gift canister of English tea leaves and much is being made of the tea-making ritual. Abir finds a teapot of kinds, and makes up some powdered milk. 'Would you like to try some tea the British way?' she asks her nieces of two and three. The children's pebble-round eyes widen and their pony tails bob up and down. She mixes a weak, child's version, laden with milk and sugar, and small hands wrap around plastic beakers, draining them of the sweet milky liquid. 'They like it!' exclaims Abir in delight.

Her eldest brother, although in his thirties with a good job, is unmarried and still living at home. As Abir bustles around in the kitchen, he treats me to a lecture on the Ill Wisdom of Independent Living as Pursued by Young People in the West, developing his argument through a series of ordered expositions. 'They lose everything their parents have built up. This is wrong, to my way of thinking.' He inclines his head, as if saddened by this foolishness. Deciding to take the path of least resistance to what is, in fact, a coded way of expressing disapproval of his sister's way of life, I nod as he concludes each point. When I return to Abir, eavesdropping in the kitchen, she pulls a mock-straight face. 'I lived that moment with you!' she laughs.

213

It is not until darkness has fallen that her father returns from work and joins the throng, smiling benignly. Still dark-haired despite being in his fifties, he looks good for his age apart from the huge belly that lifts his checked shirt. But some residual expression behind the smile tells me that this is a man who likes to be in charge. Someone gives him a handful of lettuce leaves—he is on a diet—and still smiling broadly, he cracks a series of jokes. 'Everyone in England is very intelligent,' he announces, looking around at his assembled family. 'They speak English at the age of two or three.' Everyone sniggers. My own father has a good line in bad jokes, I tell him, and share a couple in the same format: pronouncement, pause, punch line. 'He was born in Vienna,' I pause, 'because he wanted to be near his mother. And he has a bath once a year, whether he needs it or not.' Abir's English-speaking brothers rock gently together on the sofa, chortling; her father, after the delay of having received the translation, smirks appreciatively. But not all of his jokes have humour as their aim. *Ya binti*, he says to Abir, pointedly. 'Do you recognize me? I am your father.' Abir, in disgrace for her absence from the family gathering the previous weekend which she had spent with me, smiles wearily but says nothing.

As the conversation turns to the Druze faith, the other family members gradually melt away. Her father talks at length, his exposition fuelled by the odd question from Abir, who is now taking notes in an attitude of great respect. Her eyes are wide and focused, her voice taut with emotional tension as she relays the ideas back to me. 'My father says…' begins every other sentence. It's clear that the conversation, for her, is as much about her relationship with her father as it is to do with learning about her religious roots. It's also clear that interrupting the flow of philosophy with anything as vulgar as questions would not go down well, so I sit back and let her run the show.

214

The true Druze faith, her father says, celebrates the inter-related-ness of the universe which is the oneness of God. It is up to every individual to develop his or how own path to this relationship; there is no need for religious leaders to act as intermediaries, nor for a particular place in which to worship, like a mosque or a church. No one has the right to impose moral rules on others, stipulating how they should live, and anyone can be part of the union of people who make up the *muwahhidun*. 'Baba says, this is the difference between us and the three other religions,' Abir tells me. 'The Union, and our relation with nature.'

Every so often he slides into a disquisition into the metaphysics of the universe, at one point getting up and motioning to us to follow him. Abir, her mother, and I troop obediently behind him into the kitchen. Pointing to the kettle on the stove, he explains how when the water boils, the steam evaporates, demonstrating the way in which the cosmos divests itself of unwanted energy. At another point he leaves the room, returning with a large book that he places carefully on my lap. The book, entitled *David* and supposedly dating from 1282, is a trove of ancient lore about the healing properties of plants, a testament of the *muwahhidun*'s deep understanding of the natural world. 'Good people search for good things,' he explains. I turn the pages carefully, but the densely written Arabic is impenetrable to me. 'I have never been allowed to hold this!' exclaims Abir excitedly. Feeling that I am usurping someone else's birthright, I hurriedly shift the book onto her lap.

But underneath the family politics and distracting examples I am hearing confirmation of my hunch that Drusism is, at bottom, a spiritual sensibility rather than an organized religion, one which has somehow got caught up in the realpolitik of sectarian identity. I am quietly pleased. Abir, for her part, is delighted with the proceedings. 'It's the clearest ever,' she whispers, when her father briefly absents

215

himself from the room. 'It's the first time he laid everything out like this.' For years he had been drip-feeding her with tantalizing bits of information. 'Maybe he will accept that I marry a Christian,' she adds, hopefully. 'He should do, on this philosophy,' I whisper back.

Her father, now returned and beaming comfortably from his chair, has reached a natural lull. 'Have you any questions?' asks Abir.

I do. 'How, then, did the Druze become a sect?'

'Other groups wanted to use and divide them for their own political reasons They saw a group ripe for exploitation—the people were strong warriors and also gentle souls,' explains Baba. 'With the help of Nashtakin al Darazi, they created a whole new sect.' 'They hijacked us,' supplies his eldest son helpfully from the sofa. 'There are those who want to implement certain traditions.' He is told by his father to stop butting in, and disappears. 'Since Islam was the main religion of the surrounding areas, the Druze took on its main rituals and practices,' Baba continues. 'We took the good things from the dominant religion.'

So there it was: *taqiyya*, or concealment, was a matter of placating the fundamentalists and the true faith lay safely protected underneath. 'How many people in Lebanon think like this?' I ask.

'About fifty, not more. I talk to them; I tell them about all this,' he waves his hands to show how he's not taken seriously. 'They think that I'm different from them. Bahjat Ghaith thinks like me.'

'Why then the prophecy?' I'm puzzled; all Ghaith's talk of the sect's messiah and the Day of Judgement seemed rather literalist and exclusive. Baba's and Abir's reply, delivered in tandem, is airily dismissive. 'That's just politics! He has to keep people happy, as leader of the Druze, so he has a double strategy!'

Baba finally concludes and peers at me. Am I ill? Do I have a headache? It's late, and the combination of the harsh strip light, contact lenses at the end of a long day, and a mosquito bite on my eyelid

216

must be giving me my default consumptive heroine look. I intimate some of this, and the benign smile achieves full beam. 'You have a transparent soul,' he tells me. 'You should use candlelight, it's very calming.' 'Oh, she does,' Abir says, eagerly. 'She hates bright lights.'

The conversation is over. Her father, too, is tired and needs to get to bed before an early morning business trip to Syria. Abir turns to me. 'See!' she says, exultant. 'I am a good translator! Pay me!'

'Abir!' Her father rebukes her. 'We don't talk about money when we talk Philosophy!'

The next morning is full of mountain delights. Abir's mother goes down to the scruffy plot of land that serves as the family garden and returns with her huge basket brimming with grapes cut fresh from the vine. Then she presents me with bottles of rich, dark liquid: home-made cordials extracted from the blackberries and roses that grow round about. Although she hasn't passed her driving test, Abir takes her father's car, a 1950s butterscotch classic and we go out, she, her younger sister and I. ('I hope I get a car soon,' she says, her hands resting easily on the wide, leather-clad steering wheel.) We drive about the hills, gazing at the sun-bleached landscape and downing bowls of ice-cream in the local café.

But despite my intention of having a day off, when I chat to her brother in the afternoon, the country's problems soon re-assert themselves. 'In Lebanon, the problem is that there is no unity,' he muses, leaning against the balcony window, picking a bunch of grapes off their stem, one by one. 'We and the whole world—and I mean the whole world—have tried to find something to create unity. First it was the war, and then it was hunger.'

'People say that it would be better if there were no outside interference, but I do not believe that is the case.' He laments the corruption of the leaders and people's incorrigible faith in them, no

217

matter how much they have betrayed their trust. 'I don't know why. They have minds'—he taps his head in exasperation—'but they don't want to use them. The first thing every Lebanese says is, "I'm not responsible."'

'And yet they want things.' I rejoin, put uncomfortably in mind of his sister's childlike insatiability.

'Yes, they want things. They want an easy life.' On the TV on the wall beside him, pert young Arab women are swaying and pouting, the epitome of female availability.

'But isn't Syria's departure the first step to the country fully ruling itself?'

'No,' he says categorically. Partly because of outside pressure Lebanon's leaders had been complicit with the Syrian presence, even those who were ostensibly against it. Even the mass demonstrations for Syria to leave after Hariri's death mean little, he goes on. 'Okay, you can get one million people to demonstrate. But they don't know why they're doing it! Their leaders have told them to—or someone has given them $50.'

He pauses, and I think of claims that Hezbollah had orchestrated the counter-demonstrations calling for Syria to stay.

'Politicians don't work for the people; they work for their own interests. We have to deal with that, otherwise nothing will change,' he adds, picking the last of the grapes off the stalk and inclining his head slightly. 'Ninety per cent of Lebanese don't agree with me. I'm sorry for that.'

'They think everything's getting better?'

'Yes.'

Soon after, Abir and I gather our things and head for the bus stop. On our way, we pay a visit to Abir's older, married sister. Twilight is approaching and outside her spacious hilltop flat Maya's husband is

218

watering the garden while the two little girls flit around their parents. Still in her twenties, Maya has a smooth open face and a centred air. Evidently her life, which combines motherhood and career following an early marriage arranged by her father, suits her. As we sit in the dying light, she brims with questions about how I find Lebanon, and how it compares to life in Britain.

'Have you been abroad?' I ask, conversationally

'No, not yet,' she replies. 'But you never know when you will have to leave Lebanon. It's not stable—economically, socially. There could be another war.'

A pity, I say, gesturing to our surroundings, where the soft gold light is fading into grey-pink over her mountain home. You are on top of the world.

'Yes, it's paradise here,' she agrees. 'Paradise. But They'—she waves her hand in an airy gesture which could denote the politicians, sectarian forces, or trouble-makers in general—'don't want to let it be that.'

One afternoon, I go to Diana's chic flat for tea. Diana, as usual, plies me with cake and sweets. Her husband, unexpectedly delayed from his work in the United Arab Emirates by a plane strike, launches into an enthusiastic discourse about their faith without prompting, and despite teasing from his wife and daughter. What is important, he says, is the inner belief in God, rather than the trappings of religion, such as the observance of a Ramadan fast, or the worship of a cross, for their own sake. 'God is in you, God is me, God is everywhere—not up there in some heaven.' He points to the immaculately painted white ceiling. In this sense, while the sect which is known as Druze is closed, *muwahhidun* can be found everywhere—in all countries, and even in other religions.

219

Then he stops, and looks at me keenly. 'What are you—Christian?'

I shift, rather uncomfortably, in my hosts' elegant armchair. Despite the terms of the conversation up to this point, I don't know whether, in this society of labels, he will get my position. But, amid the spiritual richness and generosity of the Middle East, it seems absurd to maintain my own policy of *taqiyya*.

'No... not really... I...'

He interrupts, smiling: 'So you are a non-believer?'

'It's not a choice between being a Christian or a non-believer,' I say, slightly impatiently. 'I'm—kind of—a pluralist.'

He looks puzzled. 'What's that—a Puritan?'

'No, it's someone who believes that all religions have something, but not one of them has the single, only, truth about God.'

His smile widens. 'So you are a Druze then?'

'Yes.'

9

EXILE FROM PALESTINE

THERE was one group who struck me as occupying a blind spot in Lebanon's multi-confessional dream. The Palestinians were, in a sense, the country's nineteenth confession, a minority of around four hundred thousand who were as much a part of the country's recent history as its other, officially recognized, sects. But since their flight from the newly-created state of Israel in 1948, they had been an unwelcome addition to Lebanon's diversity. The government, in an attempt to discourage them from becoming permanent fixtures, refused them the right to own property and restricted their right to work. The people, while sympathizing with the plight of the Palestinians in general terms, resented their presence in the country, blaming the PLO for its role in the civil war. With the situation dragging on for decades and no resolution to the Israeli/Palestinian conflict in sight, ordinary Palestinians were paying the price. Crammed into a dozen refugee camps and other illegal encampments, most Lebanese Palestinians eked out a miserable existence.

For me personally, the Palestinians were the indirect reason why I was here. My first experience of the Middle East had come, years before, with a summer spent teaching in a West Bank refugee camp. Perched amid the Judean hills, Al Fawwar was more like a backward rural village than a camp, and a deeply conservative place. Our

Palestinian hosts had tried to curtail the movements of us Western women, while the small British charity running the project pressurized us to wear the *hijab*, to the disapproval and amusement of the locals. I had struck up a friendship with a respectable but atypical family, a triumvirate of three women whose men folk were mostly dead, divorced or imprisoned. Devout Sunni Muslims, they were some of the most tolerant, accepting people I had ever met, and their friendship drew me back to see them many times.

Camps in Lebanon, however, were uncharted territory. Some of them, like the notorious Ain el Hilweh, were dangerous places that could ring with militia gunfire, and permission from the Lebanese army was needed to gain entry. You couldn't just wander in and garner a few invitations to tea, as you could in some West Bank camps. I would need help to get access to the Palestinians of Lebanon.

The minute I hear her friendly, capable tones over the phone, I know I've found it.

Sylvia Haddad runs one of the small, local charities dedicated to alleviating Palestinian poverty; as a Palestinian with Lebanese citizenship she is also a member of an even smaller minority, one of the few to have made it into mainstream Lebanese society. She gives directions to her office, the most precise I have ever had in the Middle East, plus a tip: 'It's the ugliest building in the street. You can't miss it.' Soon I find myself with Sylvia in the second-ugliest block, after a detour into a yawning chasm of a building opposite. 'You found one uglier?' She leans out of the window and looks down the street with interest. 'Show me!'

As we sip coffee, she tells me how she decided that charitable work would be the best expression of her Presbyterian faith, giving up a 'cushy job' teaching English at the Lebanese American University to head the Joint Christian Committee for Social Service. 'I got 'stuck with this,' she says, with mock distaste. 'Seven years, I've been doing it.'

She gives me a potted history of the Palestinians in Lebanon. The first Palestinians came during the Arab-Israeli war of 1947-48, followed by another wave in the 1967 war. Then the PLO, having been ejected from Jordan for allegedly trying to overthrow the monarchy in 1970, moved its power base to Lebanon. Its growing strength and government-like status in the south of the country worried the Lebanese, and when the tensions between them and Phalangists resulted in war, the Palestinians became a scapegoat for many of the country's problems. There was also a typically Lebanese religious-political reason why government and people agreed that they should not be welcomed as citizens: as a population mainly made up of Sunni Muslims, the Palestinians risked upsetting the already delicate sectarian balance.

Once in Lebanon, many Palestinians found themselves obliged to uproot themselves again. In 1974 Nabatiyeh camp was destroyed by Israeli warplanes; a couple of years later, the beginning of the civil war put paid to the camps of Tal el Zaatar and Jisr el Bacha. A few managed to emigrate, but most settled in the unofficial camps or 'gatherings' dotted around the country.

Meanwhile, a Byzantine situation was developing with their status as refugees. As the only refugees in the world to have an agency devoted to meeting their basic needs, shelter, healthcare and education was provided by UNRWA—the United Nations Relief and Works Agency. But to qualify for these benefits, you had to be a Registered Refugee. Not all candidates had the paperwork to prove their provenance and situation, leaving around 30,000 Non-Registered Refugees. This group, at least, won recognition and travel documents from the Lebanese government with help from the Red Cross.

223

But over the past few years, a third, shadowy group started show-ing up on the philanthropists' radar. The Non-IDs had no identity papers and therefore no rights. Afraid of being caught by the authori-ties and imprisoned for illegal residency, they scraped a living on the camps' black economy, or begged from relatives. Although they were difficult to identify, there was thought to be about five thousand of them. Even Sylvia, working with the Palestinian community, had been surprised to learn of these faceless, nameless folk. 'I knew there were some people, but such a big number?' she concludes. 'I thought I knew about these things.'

'I have some very nice brochures somewhere,' she adds, getting up and hunting through the piles of publications documenting the refugees' plight on the table. Then she goes to the bookcase and rifles through the shelves.

Eventually she gives up and sits down, resuming her story of the Lebanese Palestinians. 'They were very educated, about ninety per cent of them, when they came. But now there is no more ambition in the camps. We'—she speaks emphatically but whether as a member of Lebanese society or as a member of the wider world that fails to resolve the Middle East crisis, I can't tell—'are killing their ambi-tion. They say, "even if we study, we can't work." If you go and ask the young men, "What are you going to do?" they say, "I'll paint a wall." Their big dream is to buy cigarettes. This is very disturbing for us as Palestinian leaders.'

As a result, attendance at the free classes which teach agricultural and other lucrative skills is suffering. 'They are not coming. I have the funding, I have the teachers, I have the equipment. I have eve-rything. But I don't have the beneficiaries,' she says. 'The Islamic groups are moving in—we, the NGOs, are moving out. The Islamic fundamentalists are funding them and all their dreams of going to the next world. They promise them: "You will have all your happiness there,"'

She gets up and rummages through a pile of papers on the table again. 'Very, very nice brochures,' she murmurs abstractedly. 'I'm mad at myself.'

A few days later, Sylvia drives me to one of the charity's flagship projects, the Sabra Community Centre. Squeezed in a row of thrown-up buildings on the edges of a muddy food market, the centre's location just outside Shatila camp gives it an added kudos in the eyes of the refugees.

Inside it's break time at the kindergarten and a score of small children are running frenetically around a giant plastic slide. In one of the adjoining rooms, the morning's hairdressing class is getting underway. The beauty business is booming among the Palestinians, and young women jump at the chance to learn a trade which combines the pleasure of preening each other with the respectability of working at home or in small salons.

In the centre's office Sylvia introduces me to the director Aida who, smiling and talking to several people at once, is unwinding a tightly pinned scarf to reveal a chic, layered haircut that wouldn't look out of place on a TV make-over show. 'She how pretty she is?' says Sylvia, adding *sotto voce* to me: 'She wears it all the time. Even if a boy of twelve comes along, she puts it on. But if I make a hullabaloo—just to annoy her—she will take it off.'

Sitting beside the desk is an older woman, watery dark eyes shining fiercely out of soft, papery skin. 'I am chair of the volunteer committee,' Yousra Daiffallah tells me proudly, brandishing a book of receipts with some ferocity. 'Some people, they take money for this work.' She casts a sidelong glance at Aida. '*I* don't take money.'

225

She leads me to one of the adult education rooms. Inside, four teenage girls are sitting lumpenly around a table waiting for a literacy lesson. For one reason or another, they have fallen out of the education system, and are not attending either a private or an UN-RWA-run school. Yousra explains her charges' backgrounds in the professional, diagnostic style of her former role as headmistress. One girl is made to open her palms, revealing scales of white, peeling skin, the signs of a recessive genetic disorder. 'She's from one family,' she explains, joining her index fingers in illustration. 'Her mother and father too close.' Her teachers had taken exception to this consequence of a marriage of first cousins. 'They think it is some illness,' she says. 'They ask her to leave.'

'And this girl don't learn.' She taps her pen hard on the table, indicating a plain-faced girl who is smiling benignly, apparently unfazed by having her inadequacies highlighted so starkly. 'She can't speak good; she can't hear good. No school take her. She likes the hairdressing job. After she finishes, she will find job in a salon.'

Next door, the hairdressing session is in full swing. The room is packed with female bodies, and young women rush around excitedly, putting combs and clips in and out of their navy smocks. Yousra ticks off the one older member of the class, a stylishly dressed woman with a wedding ring, for not wearing hers. 'I will give her minus marks,' she says severely. The wayward thirty-something and I exchange looks of amusement and she catches my hand. There isn't much equipment—only one sink and a couple of hairdryers—but everyone is busy. A couple of students mix up bowls of colorant and daub it along sections of black hair. Another girl's face contorts with the effort of trying to manoeuvre skeins of exceptionally long, thick, hair between brush and dryer. Every now and then a dispute breaks out, and the teacher, a fleshy young woman with a centred air about her, adjudicates.

226

I sit, warm and comfortable in this steamy female atmosphere, taking it all in. Suddenly, a pretty girl, snub-nosed, pale-skinned and auburn haired, is beside me, alive with curiosity. 'Where are you from? America?'

I look shocked. 'Certainly not. Britain.'

Layal is disappointed: she has an uncle in America. But, she adds, smiling shyly, she has another in Britain. We chat in pidgin-English until it is her turn for the make-up chair. Lying back and closing her eyes, she gives herself up to it while a crowd gathers to watch. A determined teenager, pushing her sleeves back and chewing gum furiously, applies herself to the task of making her classmate beautiful. First she rubs foundation vigorously into her face; then, concentrating intently, she builds up layers of eye-shadow from a palette of pinks and browns. As a swathe of thick black kohl is swept across her eyelids, Layal seems almost asleep. Generous quantities of mascara and blusher, and her lips are outlined with a dark pencil. Finally, the process is complete and she is awake again. Now her face is a mask of Arab beauty, its delicate quality obliterated by the bold strokes of colour that have re-defined her features.

My turn. I am tired today, and it is so relaxing to lie back and have fingers work over my skin. A crowd hovers above me, surveying progress appraisingly. Several times there is disagreement about what my make-up artist is doing and, after some discussion, she is obliged to apply more or scrub some off. Eventually, I am deemed finished and allowed to sit up. Layal's face swims into focus above me. 'Very beautiful,' she pronounces with satisfaction. I go to the mirror on the wall and start back in shock. The face looking back at me is almost a pantomime character; its eyes heavily ringed with glossy black and its cheeks a candy pink. Every area of skin has been covered in some line or powder, except under my eyes, where the concealer I usually wear has been completely removed, to reveal dark

227

shadows. The overall effect is rather ageing, with the beginnings of crows-feet thrown into relief. For some reason, the process has made my hair stick out rather wildly.

The girls gather round me eagerly. Now they want to do my hair. 'Please!' says Layal, looking up at me beseechingly. 'Just a brushing!'

I head back to the office, via a trip to the toilet to wash off some of the heavier colour, and find Aida pinning her headscarf tightly under her chin in readiness for the outside world. We set off to tour Shatila. The streets are hung with streamers and red paper lanterns in readiness for the holy month of Ramadan, due to start in a few days. '*This* is Shatila,' Aida keeps telling me emphatically, as we hurry through the streets, dodging pools of water and fallen fruit from the market stalls. '*Here* Israelis came.'

We plunge into the gloom of the camp proper. Thick electrical wires festoon the narrow alleyways and the sky has become a slit between the houses, which have been built up to accommodate each new generation. We duck into one doorway and two elderly women, almost as wide as they are tall in their floor-length floral dresses, greet Aida affectionately. The house is damp and dark, the only light coming from a high slit window. Male faces stare out from photos stuck on the stone walls, memorials to the 1982 massacre in the camp by the Israeli-backed Phalangist forces. 'She'—Aida points to one of the women, who is smiling hospitably—'lost five men.'

Then we are away again, and she whisks me through a maze of dark alleyways until we emerge into an open square in the south of Shatila. Blocks of flats with pleasantly creamy façades stand at its edges, perceptibly better than their higgledy-piggledy neighbours. 'They were built by UNRWA,' Aida tells me. In one of them, her husband Hasan Bakir is working away in a room he has rented as an office. Forbidden by Lebanese law to work as an engineer, he turned

228

to journalism and now works as camp correspondent for the newspaper *Al Quds*. Even this is only due to the paper's status as Palestinian, he explains; government restrictions on Palestinians' right to work mean he would not be permitted to pursue his career on Lebanese titles.

'Hasn't the relaxation in the law improved things?' I ask. Two months earlier, there had been a breakthrough, as the ban on fifty of the seventy forbidden jobs had been lifted.

'Nothing happened,' replies Hassan. 'No Palestinian has benefited from this rule. Palestinians have to have a permit—if I want to work, it will cost a lot of money.'

'My impression is that people are always studying the Palestinian situation here, but nothing really changes,' I observe.

Hassan smiles resignedly. 'We were talking about that yesterday,' he says. 'We talk a lot, and do a lot of research, but none of it has improved our situation. We have many NGOs here, and the situation in the camps is going back.'

At the moment, he goes on, he is researching a story about a ship that went missing with its cargo of Palestinians trying to emigrate to Europe illegally. 'There were about sixty of them on the boat; they didn't find any of them. I want to know everything about them.' He plans to enter his investigation into a journalism competition run by the British Embassy, for the prize of some much-valued training. For last year's competition, he had embarked on the sensitive subject of Palestinian weapons in Lebanese camps. 'But I neglected it; I got threats from some Palestinian factions,' he smiles. In any case, the prize had gone to a journalist from Ramallah for an investigation into a sexier subject: corruption in the Palestinian Authority. We both smile ruefully at the vagaries of journalism.

The locals' more immediate concern is the flood water that engulfs the ground-floor flats every winter as Shatila's over-burdened sewage and water system overflows. Sitting on the sofa, the young man who lives there describes how the water level rises, covering the furniture and making normal life impossible. 'When the water came, I sat and smoked my hubble-bubble. I couldn't do anything,' he says, proud of his stoicism. Aida is keen to get back to the office, but as we leave the next door neighbour also wants to tell a foreign journalist about the scandal of the flooding. Nadia Abdeen has one of those strident, staccato voices that afflict some Arabic speakers. 'Every year we are afraid of the water!' she yells in fury from her porch. 'All the people go to UNRWA, but they don't do anything.' She points to her sofa, visible through the half-open door. 'Last year I threw it. It was dirty water.' She wrinkles her nose in distaste. 'This is new. I buy it. I am afraid for it now. Not only the seats—the carpets, clothes, beds.'

As if on cue, a truck drives up to the edge of the square, two men get out, remove the drain covers, and start poking long metal probes into the bowels of Shatila.

An hour later, I'm in Sylvia's apartment, where she has invited me to join her and some relatives for lunch. It is a world away from the camp, spacious and tastefully furnished, the walls adorned with impressionistic, lyrical renderings of the Lebanese mountains. Sylvia had bought the pictures years before as a way of helping an impoverished painter too proud to accept charity. After his death, Omar Onsi became one of Lebanon's best-known artists.

The atmosphere is relaxed and cosmopolitan: there is an elderly couple and their son visiting from the States, part of the Christian diaspora, plus a Beirut-based cousin whose accent slides intriguingly between American and Scots. I feel obliged to explain the remains of my heavy *maquillage* to this genteel, Westernized company. 'I thought you looked different,' remarks Sylvia, casually. Courteously, the entire party gives up the Arabic they had been speaking when I arrived and moves effortlessly into English.

Sylvia's husband Fouad disappears into the kitchen to dress the *tabouleh*. 'He has to do it,' she explains. 'He won't trust it to anybody else.' Dish after dish is brought to the dining table by their smiling Sri Lankan maid. I eye her curiously, mentally comparing her with the downtrodden creature I saw in the Druze sheikha's house. The young woman has the figure of a supermodel set off by a lime green mini-dress and her coils of thick, straight hair are piled stylishly high. She seems delighted to be there, and is thanked at every turn by at least one of the guests. Then we are off, piling our plates: after the *mezze* there is cinnamon chicken, creamy potatoes with parsley, stuffed vine leaves, followed by a wobbly pink blancmange made of strawberries and *labneh*.

Fouad is the polite host, enquiring after my project and my experiences in the Middle East. But when he reveals that three weeks before he had returned from his first visit to Jerusalem since his family fled to Lebanon in 1948, my own meagre experience pales. 'For the first time in fifty-seven years,' he repeats, spooning *tabouleh* into his mouth. 'I have mixed feelings about it.' Riveted by this glimpse into ancient Palestine, I almost stop eating to listen. Having spent five days at the family wedding in Nazareth, Fouad revisited some childhood haunts with his sister. They had gone to the house where they grew up, a rented place rather than the ancestral homes that so many families abandoned. 'We went to the house and knocked on the door,' he says, matter-of-factly. 'The Israelis were very welcoming, very friendly. They permitted us to take photos, video, everything.'

But he had found the experience unsettling. 'You know, Alexy, if you go back to a place after fifty-seven years, you expect to see people and places you know.' He looks grave, and a little sad. 'But there was

231

no one—no one exists anymore.' He had found some buildings he recognized, but that was all. The huge YMCA building in east Jerusalem where had spent so much of his youth was empty and lifeless.

'If you ask me, "Would you go again?"' He poses the question that I, still imagining this lost time and place, am forgetting to ask. 'No. What for? No relatives, no friends, nothing to do. To sit in a hotel? No—I would not go back. My anxiety to return has been fulfilled.'

Throughout the meal, my eye has been drawn to a curious construction on the sideboard—a paper model of an elegant, traditional Ottoman house in a square enclosed by walls of paper stone, a Lebanese flag on its façade. As the guests drift away from the table, I go to examine it properly. A mass of figures and objects fills the courtyard: there is a man in a fez puffing on a *nargileh*, and an outsized version of the brown, pink-breasted birds that populate Beirut's parks and gardens. 'It's something I play with; I made it during the civil war,' explains Fouad, seeing my interest. 'I made the house from a kit.' He has coloured in its roof and doors and filled its windows with red transparent paper that light up at night. 'But I need to get a new battery,' he says, fingering the wires and empty battery clamps. Decades of cutting out little paper figures from magazines has peopled this little world. 'Here's my eldest daughter.' He indicates a figure on the balcony. 'And here's my youngest.' He points to a papery young woman standing near the fish pond.

'But I can't find Sylvia,' he adds vaguely. I'm not surprised, I think to myself, she's probably out at a meeting. We hunt through the paper forest, to no avail. 'And I usually have this on the roof, but it fell down,' he says, producing a blue paper banner which reads, in large, bold letters: 'LEBANON'.

⊗

'The south is very nice,' says a friendly young man next to me on the bus, 'since the Israelis left.' He used to live there, he says, but is now in Beirut, working in Starbucks. 'Is it good?' I ask doubtfully. 'Oh, yes,' he smiles, and offers me a cigarette. Acres of banana plants, their large rubbery leaves spread out to catch the sun, sail past the windows. He gathers crucial information about me to satisfy the neighbouring passengers' curiosity. 'Meeting. NGO. In Lebanon for two weeks.' They smile and nod approvingly.

I am en route to Qasmieh, one of around thirty 'gatherings' or illegal camps where the Palestinians forced for one reason or another to leave the dozen official camps end up. Despite this miserable *raison d'être*, Qasmieh's location on the coast in a fecund region between Saida and Tyre is beautiful. As the bus heads south, grove after grove of lemon trees, and *bala* trees heavy with clusters of orange fruit fill the fields by the roadside.

The bus drops me at a petrol station, apparently in the middle of nowhere. Anxiously, I look up and down the dusty road until my contact drives up in a white car. Ali Hweidi, the Lebanese representative of the Palestine Return Centre, is one of those highly groomed Arab men found throughout the Middle East who possess a mysterious quality for staying immaculate no matter what the conditions. No dusty refugee camp, no desert wind, seems to have any impact on the crisp and spotless shirt, the immaculately groomed hair and moustache, the highly polished shoes. Trotting along beside them, travel-creased and filmed in a light sweat, I often feel put to shame.

Ali is well versed in the needs of Western visitors, having worked for the Save the Children Fund for twelve years. He has a passion for Byron, Shelley and Keats, and our tour has been carefully planned to take place after his exams for his literature degree.

We pull up by the mosque on the gathering's borders. Inside one its community rooms Sheikh Ibrahim is sitting in a plastic chair, wearing a long beige *shalwar kameez* and skull cap, his rather flat, Asiatic features framed by a trimmed beard. Pictures of Mecca and the Dome of the Rock relieve the plain white walls. 'Soon we will go to the kindergarten,' says Ali. 'Now you can ask the sheikh some questions.'

It is the first day of Ramadan, so I decide to start by asking the cleric what this means to him. The sheikh likes this question. He smiles faintly. 'We are very happy because Ramadan is from Allah, and in Ramadan we are learning the will and patience.' Ali translates, as the sheikh's fingers lightly tell a set of prayer beads. 'It is not only about the worship of Allah; it is also a teaching for the self. The wise men say, "If the self is hungry, the spirit will be nourished." The ultimate goal of the fasting is to feel hunger with the poor people. Briefly, fasting is a school, and religious believers believe in fasting—Christians, Jews and Muslims.'

'How long have you been here?'

'Twenty years,' replies the sheikh. 'I came when I was twenty; now I am forty.'

'Has there been a change in the quality of spiritual life here during that time?

Sheikh Ibrahim shifts in his chair while he considers this question. 'In general, people here are close to religion. Sometimes people forget Allah, but if they have a problem, they go directly to God,' he says, after a moment. Recent years have seen a rise in religiosity. When he first came, there were only two or three men who had been on the *hajj*, but now there are about hundred, although some of that, he admits as an afterthought, is due to the rise in population.

'How do see the situation of the Palestinians in Lebanon now?'

'In general we are optimistic that at one time we are going back to our homeland. But daily life is miserable, and we feel the world is treating us in a tyrannical way. The Lebanese government is better

234

than other Arab countries, because it gives the Palestinians the right
to express themselves.'

'Could you envisage living side by side with the other sects in
Lebanon?'

'Nothing can equal going back to our homeland,' replies the sheikh
promptly. 'We are living now side by side with others, but we prefer
to go back to our homeland.'

Next door, two classes of four and five year olds are hamfistedly
drawing with crayons under the watchful eye of their young female
teachers. Some are swamped by the kindergarten uniform of pink-
and-white checked smocks. Showing off his charges, the sheikh
smilingly asks them some questions, and they chorus back, stumbling
and tailing off. Then we examine their artwork which is pinned along
the walls. Some are standard infant produce—houses with triangle-
roofs, set between a sun and a tree. But others are explicitly political,
with tanks and Palestinian flags. One has been annotated: 'the right
to return: the rising sun is Palestinian freedom.'

It reminds me of the month I spent teaching in a summer school
in a Palestinian camp in the West Bank, years before. The adolescent
girls were attentive and hardworking, eager to grasp this rare opportunity to improve their English. But the boys of the same age were
unfocused and undisciplined, picking fights and finding even the
simplest exercise a struggle. Finally, as a long shot, I suggested they
draw a picture. For once, silence reigned in Classroom Testoster-
one. Each gangly teenager was completely absorbed as he applied his
coloured pencils to a crisp sheet of A4. The results made me stretch
my eyes: most had drawn representations of the Dome of the Rock,
following their longed for, first-ever visit to Jerusalem as part of the
programme a few days before. My one model pupil, a cheerful, co-
operative soul, produced a detailed rendering of a standoff between

235

Israeli soldiers and the local boys in which he had taken part, during one of the regular incursions made by Israeli tanks into the camp. He had been fearless in his own encounter with a tank. *Allahu Akbar*! he told its occupants. 'Come here and say that!'

But here in Lebanon, the content of the children's drawings is more a result of teaching than direct experience. Attendance is low in this, the mosque kindergarten, explains the sheikh, because the Palestinian political parties often persuade parents to send their children to their own kindergartens, sometimes providing a bus as extra encouragement. 'But the curriculum is the same in both—concerning the culture, the national issues, the flag, the map. The only difference is that here, there is religious teaching—a few prayers, and some reading from the Koran.'

It is close to midday, and both men are starting to worry about my planned visit to the mosque. 'The time is moving,' says Ali. 'People will come to the mosque. They will say, "Who is this woman? And why is she not wearing..."' He motions to his head. I have a scarf, I say, pulling a long piece of creamy fabric out of the handbag Abir has lent me, a Tardis-like affair with surprising capacity. Exchanging a look with the sheikh, Ali gestures that it would, after all, be as well to put it on. I wrap it round my head, pushing my fringe back as an extra gesture of good will. Unlike my previous experience with the elasticated poncho in the Omari mosque, I feel no resentment.

'The sheikh expresses admiration that you take account of these things,' says Ali as the three of us, having removed our shoes, mount the stairs to the mosque.

Upstairs the vast floor unfolds repetitively in a sea of blue prayer mats laid seamlessly together, all pointing towards the *kibla* at the front. 'They were a gift from Iran,' says the sheikh. My guides indicate the curtained-off section for women, who attend the mosque only during Ramadan, and the chamber where the men perform

236

their pre-prayer ablutions, rows of low white basins and taps. Some shelves house the collection of Koranic recitations and lectures which make up the mosque's audio library, and Ali reads out a few of the titles: 'Woman and the Islamic Family', 'The Uprising is Guarded by Allah', 'How the Young Should Spend their Vacation', and 'Silence and the Risk of the Tongue'.

We finish the tour just in time. A couple of elderly men with sticks, knitted white caps hugging their skulls, are painstakingly making their way up the stairs, having factored in so much time to allow for their disability that they are early. We say our goodbyes in the midday sun. 'These are for you.' The sheikh is holding out his prayer beads.

I am thrown into a panic. Al Sheikh's own prayer beads? But I am touched by the gesture, and for some reason I do want them. 'It's all right,' says Ali, reassuringly. 'And he apologizes that he can't offer any refreshments because of Ramadan.'

Driving further into the gathering, every track is bordered with fruit trees: oranges and lemons, bananas and prickly pears push through wire fencing. Then the car comes to an abrupt halt in a large, open square of dust. I blink, trying to take in my dramatically different surroundings. Shacks of corrugated iron frame the square, positioned for all the world like cottages around a village green. But there is no colour in this landscape, only a muddy sameness as the grey of the metal houses shade into the beige of the dust.

Ali speaks to a woman standing in a stone gateway, and we step over the threshold into her courtyard. Inside it's a disconcerting mix of the paradisial and the squalid: a vine crawls overhead, and kittens are tumbling between the plants. The house in the centre of this little world is constructed around two small sets of stone walls; the roofs and other walls are all corrugated iron. Fatima, a tired-looking, middle-aged woman, waves us in to her household. The place

237

is immaculate, with scrubbed down stone and wall hangings placed with geometric precision. Leads trail, connecting the TV and ghetto blaster to the electricity supply. From behind a set of inner stone walls in a corner comes the sound of a man washing and hawking.

Gently, Ali teases out Fatima's story. The family—Fatima, her husband and their six children—lived originally in Tal El Zaatar camp north-east of Beirut. But when the camp was destroyed at the beginning of the civil war, they moved to Damour, then to another gathering called Mar Elias in the Bekaa before settling in Ain el Hilweh. But they could not afford the rent on their house and so, eleven years ago, they moved to Qasmieh. The stone for their current dwelling came courtesy of her brothers, and the corrugated iron—ten sheets of it—was a gift from the European Community. 'Thank you, EU, thank you,' says Ali with heavy irony, casting his eyes heavenwards. The resulting building is like a furnace in summer, with water seeping in under the walls during the winter.

As we leave, a final question occurs to me. 'What one thing would make your life better?' I expect the usual grand talk of the Homeland.

'I would like a house,' she says.

Ten minutes and some alleyways later, we are in a youth club run by the French charity Enfants Réfugiés du Monde. Boys in their late teens sit around a table, their long curly hair tied back in trendy ponytails. But their eyes flicker uncertainly as we come in, and their demeanour lacks any kind of teenage swagger.

The social worker who runs the club, Hannan Hassan, is in her thirties and lives in the nearby gathering of Kfar Badda. Unusually, for such a conservative community, the youth club is for both sexes. 'You know the traditions here,' explains Ali. 'The parents are not happy to allow their daughters to go and share their activities

238

with males. They faced a lot of problems with this, and they still do. But there is a need for people to express themselves through talking, sports. We try to encourage the girls to communicate with the men here, because sooner or later they will go into society, maybe to university,' adds Hannan. 'We invite the parents here to see the activities to soften the ground—we discuss education, health, and social matters with them, in order to build trust.'

'What is their favourite activity?'

'Sport, sport, sport!' she grins.

It is classic youth work, dealing with the disaffected and the school drop-outs, trying to instil in them the basics: time-keeping, teamwork, and self-esteem. But the real challenge is building hope for the future.

'All of them here are ambitious to leave the area because of the economic situation,' says Hannan. 'They think if they go abroad, they will become rich quickly. There is no chance for Palestinians to work, because if they graduate from the university and get an engineering or a law degree—what is next? He sees that some of the engineers are driving cars or working in the fields, so ambition is frustrated. So he plans to work abroad—maybe illegally, through'—she hesitates, searching for the right word—'a mediator.'

'Oh my God!' I exclaim involuntarily, as I suddenly realize that she means a trafficker. As if all this misery isn't enough.

Ya Allah! Hannan teases me, before continuing: 'A lot of people lost their money through people like this. They promised to get them abroad, but in the end they stole their money. They give false names and addresses, and people believe them, because they are eager to leave.'

But surely people know better than to hand over large sums of money to strangers, I protest.

239

Ali shrugs. 'I know. But I can't blame them—these are simple people. And often these men—they might be Palestinian, or Lebanese—spend a year working with the community, to gain their trust first.'

'One of my brothers paid $2,000 to this man for the hope of going to Germany,' says Hannan. 'This man asked him to visit this office in Beirut, but when I tried to go, I found it was a false address. The money was everything that he had saved in his life.'

Somehow Ali and I slide into a discussion of the whole situation, while Hannan looks on serenely. All these dreams for a life elsewhere while whole lifetimes are slipping by, half-lived... I can't bring myself to suggest that the Right to Return might be hopeless, but perhaps so much focus on it might distract from the need to improve life in the here-and-now?

'We believe in that,' responds Ali. 'We ask UNRWA and the international community to help improve the daily life of refugees inside the camps. But at the beginning of this year Sharon put a proposal to the EU to try to make the camps better so that people would forget the right to return.'

'The only solution is to go back,' he goes on, increasingly passionate. 'We believe that this generation may face a lot of difficulties, but the next generation it will change. We have our own rights, not eliminable by any negotiations or power, or any realistic policy, because one power is strong and one power is weak. We have many examples to follow in history.'

'How is your brother now?' I ask Hannan, as we turn to go. Her smiles widens. *Mumtaz.*

'See?' says Ali, with a flourish of pride in the recovery power of his people. 'Flexibility!'

240

On the way back to Beirut in Saida, I hunt for food. I have barely eaten today and my blood sugar level can't take it much longer. Plus I am haunted by memories of a difficult assignment in Palestine during Ramadan, where food was so hard to come by that the weight fell off and the strength to climb Jerusalem's hills left me. But although I swear I saw a young woman in hijab eating *mannoush* with *zatar* on the bus this morning, now there is no street food to be seen.

A man sitting outside a shop catches my questing look. *Mannoush? Al youm?* He looks down the street doubtfully. Then our eyes meet, and we chant in unison: 'RAMADAN!' But one of his neighbours sells me a few *fatayer*, popping an extra one into the bag for good measure. I hover in the shadows at the back of the bus station, cramming the spinach and pastry apologetically into my mouth. Although the locals will not expect non-Muslims to observe the fast, there's no need to wave the food under their noses, having the smell fill the bus. 'You can eat it!' You can eat it' shout some young men from a nearby wall. 'Is it good?' The driver tries to persuade me to mount the bus, picnic and all, and when I shake my head, someone else brings me a plastic chair and insists that I sit.

A few days later, I visit Mar Elias which, with nearly a thousand people crammed onto 5,400 square metres, is the smallest Palestinian camp in Lebanon. I make my way between walls of breeze blocks along a series of narrow, winding alleyways and stop for a moment to stare at one of the tumbledown buildings, lost in admiration at this *oeuvre* of found objects. There are bits of wire fencing, pieces of cardboard, torn fabric—anything that could be, has been conscripted into the business of making a home. Further down the narrow alley, a father and son have laid out the parts of a bicycle for repair and are staring at them in concentration. On a corner, a pair of ginger kittens are boxing each other's ears.

In this maze it only takes a couple of minutes before I'm lost. A teenage boy in a Che Guevara T-shirt politely offers his assistance, and a few minutes later I'm in the white air-conditioned office of the Palestinian Human Rights Organization.

Project manager Mohammed Najjar is an earnest young man whose slow, pause-laden English is, I soon realize, the hallmark of a precise mind, given to clear distinctions and careful judgements. I've sought him out as one of the few campaigners looking at the situation of non-IDs in any depth.

The problem came to light, he tells me, in 2001 when a Palestinian called Hosni Hargar took fright at being asked to show papers he didn't have at an army checkpoint, fled, and was shot. 'At that time, the non-IDs were not known—their life was hidden,' he says. The case highlighted the plight of the whole group and campaigners began to document their situation and campaign for changes.

'Were they happy to talk to you?'

'No, at the beginning they were very suspicious. A lot of organizations started to work on them, and they felt they were a target group for people who wanted to make a business. But now we have a good relationship.'

The non-IDs' advocates, he goes on, are trying to persuade UN-RWA to recognize them as genuine refugees by helping them to find documentation from overseas that would prove their status. But the real solution was political: only if the governments of the Middle East gave the Palestinians official ID carrying the same rights as citizens would the problem be solved. They were lobbying the Ministry of Interior on this, but so far with little success.

'Why is government so reluctant to address the issue?'

'This could affect the balance of the sects. They don't look at this issue as a humanitarian issue. They look at it as a political or religious issue.'

'Are you worried about them becoming more radical?'

'We, as Palestinians, are worried about it.' He is almost statesman-like in his gravity now. 'If the PLO stops funding them, of course they will be fundamentalists because they have nothing to lose. Of course, they will be very dangerous if the PLO stops the funding, and the situation is as it is now. There are four to five thousand of them, and they are still young. If you put them in a corner, what can they do? They will replace the earth with paradise.'

Solving the problem is key to Lebanon's stability, he goes on. 'Here, there is a hidden contract between the members of all the same sects—this will affect the Palestinians on the ground, and the Sunni Muslims. For this reason it's very important to find a fair solution for them, not only with the Lebanese government but also with the Egyptian, Jordanian and Syrian governments, UNRWA and the international community.'

My questions are answered and the problem of the non-IDs, unjust and unresolved, hangs in the air between us. But I'm curious as to how this grave young refugee, with no prospects of entering the professions, acquired the skills for this kind of work.

'I studied law.' The gravity has gone now; his face is lit with pleasure. 'At the Lebanese University.'

'But you knew you wouldn't be able to practise as a lawyer?'

'Exactly. But I did it, because I like to study law.'

'No one likes to study law for its own sake,' I protest.

'Me!' he points to his chest, his eyes alive with enthusiasm. '*I* do.'

On my last afternoon in Lebanon, Abir and Danny take me to Jeita Grotto, one of the country's biggest tourist attractions. Despite the lure of one of the world's biggest collections of stalagmites and stalactites, I wasn't very enthusiastic about the outing. The network of

243

caverns running deep into the mountainside had been discovered by an American in the nineteenth century; now the mercantile authorities were exploiting its commercial possibilities to the full. The visitor attraction imposed a hefty entrance fee, a photo ban and a large dose of tourist kitsch, with a cable car and miniature train to transport you the absurdly short distance from the car park to the gift shops. But it was, I consoled myself, a natural wonder, and one of the few public spaces in Lebanon that hadn't been claimed by a sect.

'I spent twenty minutes in the shop getting this valued,' remarks Abir as we get into the car, tapping the watch on her wrist. The Rolex had been a gift from her fiancé. 'It's worth $1,500 as it is, but it would be $3,000 if it was new,' she adds with satisfaction. 'I'll kill you if you sell it,' says Danny, shifting the car into gear. We head north out of Beirut, into Nahr al Kalb, the Valley of the Dog.

Arriving at Jeita, we park in the tree-covered gorge, pay at the turnstile and swing in the cable car to the mouth of the mountain. We walk along a tunnel and through some glass doors. Then we step into a rocky cathedral, and my breath is taken.

Great vaults of rock swoop overhead. In every direction are little arcs and caverns, creating a sense of receding perspective. Each is sculpturally distinct, its detail lit by strategically placed spotlights of gold and rose. The concrete path beneath our feet winds deeper into the mountainside, promising further wonders. I look down. A split in the rock reveals a river coursing through the lower cavern, illuminated by a bright, otherworldly green. The crisp air outdoors has given way to a warm, womb-like dampness.

'This is from Nature,' says Abir, giggling at this reference to the now well-worn theological debate that has been disrupting the harmony of her household. '*This* is God.'

'It's made by water,' adds Danny, ever the empiricist.

'Worship of rock was one of the first religions,' I muse, staring down into the cavern below. The pink stone of Petra, the temple built by the Nabateans to the gods of the mountains, floats across my inner vision, replaced by one of the masses circling the black stone of the Kaaba at Mecca. The doyen of comparative religion Mircea Eliade put it succinctly: 'The Arabs adore stones.' Instinctively, I reach out and touch a knobbly stalagmite growing by my elbow. Its clamminess is puzzlingly familiar until I remember the time I put my hand through a dark hole in Haram al Sharif in Jerusalem and touched, along with my thrilled Palestinian pupils, the sacred Dome of the Rock.

We wander deeper into the cleft. Strange forms and textures play out across the rock; there are waxen clubs and phallic symbols, clumps of mushrooms and long smooth sheaves of something: parchment or, perhaps, Lebanese bread. Then, rounding a curl in the path, we hit a bank of hundreds of round, bud-like shapes growing out of the rock face. 'Oh, nice!' exclaims Abir. 'Roses!'

I head off for a moment alone, unwilling to get caught up in the couple's issues in this of all places. But they call me back. From the bottom of a large rock pool under a little bridge, hundred of coins glisten with the promise that their donors' wishes will be granted. Abir and Danny are rummaging in their pockets. 'That's for Druze,' I say, momentarily vexed at this childish petitioning of the divine for small favours. 'Not *muwahhidun*.'

'Superstition,' agrees Danny.

But we all throw a coin in nonetheless, me a shiny English penny, each of us keeping our wish a secret.

Further along, a tiny tower of Babel rises in a rocky enclave, each arch-laced tier smaller than the previous one. A few yards away a Buddha sits staring meditatively ahead, his belly spilling out over his knees. I wander on, peering at dark crannies and brightly lit montages of sparkling stones. There, sitting on a boulder with his back to me, is the quite distinct form of a man praying: a Maronite from the Qadisha Valley, in all probability. This temple of rock is reflecting the glories of Lebanon back to me. High up, on a vaulted arch, some mop-headed pines stand out in relief against some smoother stone.

The guide, a middle-aged bespectacled man in denim jeans and jacket, befriends us, highlighting sight after sight. 'Look, there's a man praying,' he says, pointing to my Maronite. He indicates some markings on a panel of stone, high on the cavern wall, as if hanging for display. Apparently it shows a man and woman in a tender embrace. 'Romeo and Juliet,' he says. I stare hard at the wall, but can't for the life of me make out the forms of the lovers. What I do see, quite clearly, is the outline of Santa Claus in his sleigh, proudly pulling the reins of his frisky reindeer.

He has been working there ten years, he says, but never a day goes by without him finding some new treasure in this infinitely varied world. He has taken a shine to Danny and follows us with fresh insights and bits of information, ignoring the other tourists. The shapes have been formed by calcium carbonate-rich water dripping over the limestone for millions of years; grease from repeated pawing by human hands changes its colour, he explains. *Mazbut*, says Danny after a while, trying to steer us gently away.

Finally we break free and start to walk back, giggling as we spot more and more of our favourite things in the cavernous sides. 'Abir's seeing bags of money,' teases Danny. 'Don't go getting any big ideas now!' He and I, for our part, are increasingly detecting the presence of food. It's almost two hours since lunch and we are spotting patches of cauliflower and broccoli growing in odd corners although, worryingly, there is no cake.

Then, examining a rocky stretch above our heads, we are all brought up short. 'Harissa!' we exclaim, almost in unison. There she is, our

Lady of Lebanon in miniature, a tiny, cloaked figure atop a cone, halfway up the rock face. It's almost as if some sculptor has been commissioned to create one of Lebanon's principal symbols here, in the heart of the mountain. 'It really is,' says Abir, staring.

'It really is!' I breathe after her, astonished.

At the exit, the golden sun of late afternoon and a riot of greenery beckon us back to the real world. The guide's footsteps sound behind us. 'Did you see Harissa?' he asks excitedly.

10
ISRAEL RETURNS

IT SURPRISED everyone. War returned once more to Lebanon, a new conflict spinning out of a clear July sky. Instead of the busy tourist season that they had been expecting—predicted to be the most successful ever—the Lebanese found themselves under bombardment by the Israelis. Beirut's Rafik Hariri airport, symbol of the country's reconstruction, was an early target, followed by roads, bridges, factories, schools, hospitals and homes. As Hezbollah and the Israeli Defence Forces waged war across the border, the south took the brunt of the destruction: a million people fled their homes and parts of villages were razed to the ground.

In London I watched the news with an interest bordering on the obsessive. As well as the progression of the war, covered largely by reporters parachuted into Lebanon for the purpose, there was an increasingly heated domestic debate about Britain's role to follow. It seemed that this unexpected conflict had awoken a new public awareness of the part played by the West in the Middle East's fortunes. There were meetings and demonstrations, calls for the British government to back a ceasefire and condemnation of what was seen as its complicity with Israel's disproportionate response to the Hezbollah kidnappings that had triggered the war. My own feelings mounting, I wrote messages of support to Lebanese friends and contacts. The replies were prompt, gracious and restrained. Texts and emails to

Abir went unanswered, however, and when one night the news reported that Achrafieh had been hit, I panicked and rang her mobile. Danny answered. 'Don't worry, everything's cool,' he said. 'She's in the mountains, but we're fine.' He added, as if to allay my anxiety completely: 'That bomb was a mistake.' He sounded even more laid-back than usual: it was after midnight in Beirut and I could almost feel the *nargileh* smoke coming down the phone line.

Meanwhile, the Lebanese conflict had come home in a very real way. The evacuation ships sent by the British government to rescue its citizens brought back a number of Lebanese with British passports. Around sixty of them, having arrived at Stansted airport with nowhere to go, became the responsibility of the small, rural district council of Uttlesford in Essex. With local housing in short supply, they were being put up in student accommodation at the University of Essex until other arrangements could be made. When I went to Colchester to seek them out, they were immediately recognizable as they sat in the square outside their student rooms, one of them puffing away on a *nargileh*. A child was promptly dispatched to fetch me a coffee, and soon I was doing the rounds, hearing tale after tale of this sudden exile. There were the Charaff Deens, a Shia family who had fled bomb-struck Tyre and were determined to make a new life for themselves. At sixteen and twenty-one, the two daughters spoke brightly about their plans for further education and a teaching career, while their father, in his fifties, said he had had enough of struggling in an economy paralyzed by conflict. Only their mother, smiling and silent throughout the conversation, seemed to have little idea of what a future in Britain might hold—it was the first time she'd every been away from her own mother and extended family, and she spoke no English. 'She didn't want to come at first, but we made her accept it,' explained her eldest. Then there was Rafik, an intense young man who had lost his two mobile phone shops to the war and was desperate, from the off, for a new job and girlfriend in his adopted country. 'Lebanon is finished,' he declared bitterly, envisaging a new life in Europe. A few days later, when I went back to interview the group for an article, he had changed his mind. 'I think that, when everything is fine in Lebanon, I'll go back,' he announced, his dark eyes earnest, and looked astonished when I reminded him of his former plans. 'I LOVE Lebanon,' he declared. 'I miss my family. I've found that there is no life without family.' Suddenly, the quintessential Lebanese refrains were rising amid cloudy Essex skies and the mudflats of the River Colne.

What I was witnessing, I realized, was the next wave of the Lebanese diaspora in the making, with all its ambivalences and conflicting desires. The war had plunged into these people's lives, possibly changing their course for ever.

In a much lesser way, the war had mucked up my plans, too. I had thought that the trouble and expense of my Lebanese adventure was over, and was moving onto some other, neglected areas of my life. But now, with the country half in ruins, my book, too, was incomplete. Although it had only lasted a month, the conflict had changed the face of Lebanon. There were the twelve hundred people who had died, the damage to the fabric of the country which would, it was estimated, cost $7 billion to put right, and the million cluster bombs dropped in the last three days before the ceasefire, leaving a deadly legacy for years to come. But it wasn't just the physical costs; it was also Lebanon's sense of itself as a country on the path to peace and prosperity that had been damaged, its confidence that its days of bloodshed were firmly in the past. And, in the weeks that followed the war's end, it became clear that the conflict had opened up a new fault line which re-arranged the pieces of Lebanon's sectarian jigsaw. Two very different visions of the way forward now deeply divided the country.

One side, known as the 14 March Coalition after the big anti-Syrian demonstration that had taken place in the wake of Hariri's killing, embraced a vision of Lebanon characterized by a thriving, business-driven economy and a liberal society in a country free of Syrian influence. Instead, it sought allies with the West and politically moderate Arab regimes such as Saudi Arabia, the main investor of the Hariri years. Since it was backed by the Sunnis, as well as large sections of the Christian and Druze population, it represented the political elite, including Prime Minister Fouad Siniora. In the other, competing vision held by Hezbollah and the Shia (the Opposition), Syria retained a key role as an ally in the cause of pan-Arabism and the all-important struggle against Israel. Without a strong line of defence, they argued, Lebanon would become an emasculated outpost for Israel and her Western allies, its people subjugated. The two sides no longer fell into the neat sectarian terms of Christian versus Muslim that had governed the period of the civil war: the disagreement placed the Sunni and Shia on opposite sides. And, in a surprise shift of allegiance, the Christian leader of the Free Patriotic Movement and former general Michel Aoun, with his eyes on the presidency, had given Hezbollah his political backing, taking many of the Christians with him.

While these differences centred on Syria's departure the previous year, the war had brought them to a head, fuelling the grudge that each side held against the other. Many 14 March supporters blamed Hezbollah for dragging them into a new conflict they didn't want; the Hezbollah camp, for their part, felt they deserved a greater share of political power for having once more saved Lebanon from destruction by Israel. As the country tried to recover from the conflict, the disagreement played itself out at the political level. Every week brought fresh calls from the Opposition leaders for a political shakeup which could bring down the Siniora government, and answering

251

statements from Siniora and Saad Hariri defending the status quo. It was as if, the external pressure off, Lebanon was retreating to the time-honoured internal wranglings that had long defined its internal politics. Meanwhile, ordinary Lebanese looked on this bickering between their political masters with despair. Rafik was particularly gloomy: 'The political situation is very bad. The war is over, but another will be beginning again soon,' he said, echoing the widespread fears of a new civil war that were rippling across the country.

So, a few weeks after the airport has re-opened, I put myself on a flight to Beirut. It has been difficult to get a seat, and the plane is packed with Lebanese eager to return after a period of enforced absence. Even in the air, it is not long before the new tensions manifest themselves: next to me is a Lebanese émigré on his annual visit home, taking a break from heading up a Canadian science lab. An air hostess dispenses Lebanese papers and, as we stare at a picture of Nasrallah addressing an adoring crowd, his animosity spills out. The weekend before, the Hezbollah leader had come out of hiding to make a brief, upper-body appearance, declaring that the recent conflict had resulted in a 'divine victory' over Israel. 'This militia,' says my companion passionately, 'I hate them.' He can't even bear to say their name. 'That's why I'm in Canada; I can't live with these people.' His finger jabs at the image of the Hezbollah leader. 'I walk down the street, I see his picture, I'm offended.' I realize that since he is a Maronite, a degree of antipathy is to be expected, but the level of his hostility seems extreme. Soon he is citing figures to support his case, and it is brought home to me how key a role statistics and demographics play in Lebanon's sense of itself: 'a hundred per cent of Christians are against them, a hundred per cent of the Sunnis. The Shia—maybe seventy-five per cent are for.' There's a pause. 'Nasrallah must be in collaboration with the Israelis,' he adds as a final thought. 'Why else did they not kill him?'

In the taxi from the airport, I lean back and watch Beirut's night sky speed past. The roadside is brightly lit with illuminated advertising hoardings, now filled with Hezbollah material. Each carries the slogan 'Divine Victory' in Arabic, English or French on a tomato red background beneath an iconic image of a man, woman, child or a piece of military hardware.

A day later, I set off for Beirut's southern suburbs to see some of the damage for myself. Hezbollah's clean-up operation in Dahiyeh was in full swing, enabled by their dedicated reconstruction unit, the Jihad al Benaa, The Holy War for Reconstruction. The government, by contrast, was taking its time to make crucial decisions about compensation and get its own reconstruction effort going, a fact that was not lost on the Lebanese. Everyone, including some of those most opposed to the party's ideology, seemed to agree that Hezbollah's levels of organization and commitment were impressive. 'It's like they've got an inner strength,' said one Christian friend admiringly.

The conflict had created a new bureaucracy for journalists, and the party's head of media Hajj Hassan Rahal sounds vaguely weary when I ring; it has evidently been a long summer, dealing with the sudden interest of the world's press. 'There are certain regulations,' he tells me. 'You need to get permission from the Ministry of Information to do your work.' There follows a day's fretful scurrying about, requesting accreditation from London, collating documents and photos for the requisite letter from the Lebanese government. I'm staying at the same family-run hotel as before, and news of my intentions to visit post-war Dahiyeh elicits clucky concerns from the motherly cook-and-cleaner. 'Don't go alone,' she says. 'And don't

253

say you are British—they don't like the British there any more. Say you are French.'

There is little sign of destruction as the *servis* heads towards the district of Beer Al Abed, where Hezbollah have set up a new office following the destruction of the one I had visited previously in Haret Hreik. I get off at the mosque, as instructed by Hajj Rahal's assistant Madame Wafa, and ask for directions. A series of locals point me to the fourth floor of a gloomy apartment block. Behind a heavy door, two expressionless young men sitting at a reception desk wave me into an empty room. There's nothing in it except a shiny empty desk and a couple of detached computer monitors on an old filing cabinet in the corner. But the party has not lost its love of opulent curtains, I notice: neatly framing the desk, a pair of satin drapes hangs from a pole embellished with gold fittings. Two large tasselled bell-pulls hold them elegantly back from the window, revealing the free-wheeling electricity cords dangling on the outside of the building. I sit, and the minutes tick by.

Madame Wafa enters, chocolaty brown eyes crinkling in a warm smile. I explain myself, sensing behind them a shrewd intelligence assessing my intentions. Having established that I have the right paperwork, she expedites my request efficiently, taking the copies of my press card and the letter of accreditation from the Ministry of Information I have brought. But I hesitate to give her the grease-soaked copy of my passport that has been sitting next to my latest snack. 'It's been next to some *mannoush*,' I explain apologetically. Madame Wafa smiles understandingly. 'We will get another.' She waves my passport at the corner and it is promptly snapped up by a young man who returns a minute later with a clean photocopy.

She dispatches another young man to accompany me to the nearby reconstruction site where I will meet the man in charge of the operation, Dr. Bilal Naim. I follow the back of the young man's head as

254

we weave rapidly through the streets, which are full of people doing their Saturday shopping at the fruit and vegetable stalls. He does not speak or look at me as he ploughs into the next neighbourhood of Haret Hreik, prayer beads between his fingers, only once looking back to see if I'm keeping up.

Rounding a corner, I gasp. It's a different world, a cross between a disaster zone and a massive building site. In front of a backdrop of multi-storey buildings in a state of semi-collapse, bulldozers are hard at work, twisting and lifting, kicking up clouds of white dust from the piles of concrete they're manipulating. The men beetling about on the ground are wearing protective paper masks, but most people are just carrying on with ordinary life around the chaos. Apparently oblivious to the dust, a young woman in a first-floor apartment is vigorously scrubbing a window pane.

I follow my escort towards a huge yellow marquee. At its entrance hangs a sign, another piece of post-war branding. It's a trendy affair with the cheerfully ironic 'Extremely accurate targets!' blazoned across the red and white design. It could almost be part of the marketing for a hair gel sold by some ethically responsible company in London. In the marquee's long entrance lobby are rows of brown plastic chairs, and a young boy is wiping the film of dust from them with a damp cloth with the eagerness of someone desperate to earn the approval of his elders. Further on in the main reception area, a dozen men are sitting, chatting or reading the paper. Usually the space would be full of coffee and smoke, but it is Ramadan and the ashtrays on the plastic tables are empty. Everyone looks subdued. My guide melts away wordlessly but several of the men, hands on heart in the oriental handshake, approach me with smiles. 'Where are you from?' asks one. I expect a remark about Tony Blair or Britain's recent position on the war, or a least a change in expression. 'You are welcome,' he replies amiably. 'Dr. Bilal will be here in ten minutes.'

'How many flats were destroyed in Dahiyeh?' I ask.

'About five thousand,' he replies. 'Look around. Feel free.'

Outside, I take a closer look at the destruction. It's not so much the look of it that's hard to grasp, but the sheer scale. It's gigantesque, like a landscape in which the rises and dips of landmass are made entirely of urban rubble. Ten-storey apartment blocks have melted like chocolate in the summer heat, the huge slabs of concrete that make up their floors and walls bending pliably downwards. Pipes and girders stick out in all directions.

I wander towards a crater which is the size of a small reservoir, filled with mound upon mound of rubble, and stop to watch a young man climbing precipitously down into it. When he's reached the bottom of one pile of rubble, he embarks on another, descending further and further into the crater's depths. Then, at a point which is not the quite the lowest, he stops and starts methodically going through the rubbish. He picks up a book whose elaborately laid out Arabic pages suggest a religious text, examines and discards it. A Hezbollah flag meets the same fate. I can't make out the little shiny objects that he does seem to be keeping, clutching in his hand, but they gleam in the sun. Further around the crater's rim, a woman in a black manteau and sunglasses is staring into its depths, holding a little girl's hand. 'Your house isn't there, I hope,' she says pleasantly as I pass. We both laugh at the joke: *ajnabiyas* don't have their houses bombed. 'My sister's apartment was there, she lost all her furniture, everything,' she volunteers. We stare down into the sea of broken stone, trying to visualize how an entire home, with its solid walls and domestic clutter could suddenly metamorphose into this. 'But she is safe, *hamdillah*,' she adds, before moving on.

Back at the plastic chairs inside the marquee, a middle-aged man has a point to make. 'How many ground zeros do you see here?' he asks. 'We have twenty to thirty here in Lebanon.' His name is Kamal

Wassim and he was in New York on September 11th, he tells me, so he knows what he's talking about. He lived in the States for sixteen years, teaching business and international affairs, before returning to Lebanon three years ago. 'I'm one of those people who wants democracy, but I doubt this will happen when I see my city get destroyed by the hand of those people who proclaim freedom and democracy,' he explains. 'So it's a paradox for us.'

He gives way to Dr. Bilal, a diffident man apologizing for his English. 'It is not as good as his,' he says with a nod at Kamal. The interview underway, Dr. Bilal methodically outlines the four stages of reconstruction: cash donations to those whose homes were destroyed in Dahiyeh, a period of rebuilding those apartments which are retrievable, followed by the demolition of those which are not. Then the work will move onto the south and the Bekaa valley. 'The reconstruction will take nine to twelve months in the south and Bekaa, and eighteen to twenty-four months in the suburbs,' he concludes, adding that in the south, the work will create more than six thousand jobs.

I'm impressed at this degree of precision so soon after the war. 'How did you manage to plan all this?'

'During the war, day by day we followed the bombs and we made a map of the destruction and a plan so we could start the reconstruction quickly,' he replies patiently, as if this were the most obvious thing in the world for a militia in the heat of conflict to do. 'Some people worked in the resistance, and some on the reconstruction. There were two sides.'

'How much will it cost?'

'We don't know,' he says. 'More than a billion dollars. Nobody in Lebanon expected this volume of destruction.' He enumerates the millions of dollars pledged by Arab countries: $250 from Saudi

257

Arabia, $200 from Kuwait, $165 from Qatar, $100 from Bahrain, $25 from Syria.

'Iran?' I prompt.

'No, not for the reconstruction of villages,' he replies. 'They have pledged $100 million to the Lebanese government for the reconstruction of the infrastructure: bridges, roads. The United Arab Emirates have promised to pay for the rebuilding of all the schools in the south.'

I decide to brave the question of the day. 'You must be talking to a lot of people, hearing how they feel about the destruction of their homes. Are they reproaching you?'

'No,' he replies calmly. 'They are sad, but the awareness of victory covers the feeling of sadness. I don't think they will hold it against Hezbollah. Maybe there will be a reaction against the government, because they think the reconstruction is the responsibility of the government.'

'Are you co-ordinating with the government?' The question of exactly who was responsible for what was emerging as one of the great mysteries of the post-war period.

'Yes, there is a committee between Hezbollah and the government to deal with the reconstruction in the suburbs,' he replies, his demeanour having gradually acquired just the faintest hint of patient suffering. 'We agree about making some places better after the war, by creating parks and green spaces and reducing the overcrowding and the traffic. And we want some changes for our security square in Haret Hreik.'

'Will the leadership return there when it's rebuilt?' I wonder aloud: so much for Israel's dream of destroying Hezbollah's base.

'Yes, yes,' he replies immediately. After a pause, he adds: 'Most of them are here now, but we can't show them.'

'It's too dangerous?'

'Yes.'

※

In the grounds of AUB, everything was as before. Watching the bombing from London, I experienced a sharp stab of pain as it suddenly occurred to me that this oasis on the eastern Mediterranean and my favourite haunt in Lebanon, could, at a stroke, be shattered from above. But here it all was again: the scented trees, the shaded paths and benches, all encircled by a wide-angled view of the sparkling blue sea. Yet I was beginning to realize that this apparent continuity was another defining characteristic of Lebanon: while on a certain level life went on as before, below the surface there was another, constantly changing story. It was even true of the city's cats that were so much a part of the AUB scene: families who had fled the country during the war had left so many abandoned pets that the Lebanese animal protection society, BETA, had teamed up with a US charity to have three hundred cats and dogs flown to adoptive families in the States. Many more were left to survive alone though, and I imagined that my particular feline friend, a well-groomed ginger cat, might be one of those who had recently lost her family. While many of the AUB cats started in feral alarm if you so much as looked at them, Orange Cat seemed particularly attuned to humans, climbing onto my lap at every opportunity and staring up at me with wondering, topaz eyes. Once, while we were spending an idle hour together, she sat bolt up right, ears pricked, listening anxiously to a child crying.

Beirut's skies had also acquired a new, double-edged significance. Now the low-flying jets that swept over the Corniche from the sea were a source of relief and reassurance, meaning *peace, the airport's open, tourism and business*. On the other hand, despite the ceasefire and UN Resolution 1701, Israel was still regularly flying into Lebanese airspace.

At the hotel the air of normality that reigned covered some lightly-buried sorrows. They suddenly surfaced as one of the young family members who ran it sat, trying to recover from a vodka hangover acquired the previous night. 'I can't talk about this war. Something broke inside me,' said Mazen, holding his head, and then his stomach. 'One month's war,' he mused on. 'It will take us fifteen years to get to the same point.' The hotel had been looking forward to a prosperous summer, and was booked up for three months ahead. 'Three hours, and there was no one. Three hours!' he repeated, recalling the abrupt exodus of customers. In the weeks that followed, he and the manager were in despair. 'Wissam and I, we sat, we smoked *shisha*, and we cried.'

One night he had just taken some customers to the airport when the Israelis started bombing it. The customers rang, begging to be rescued; suddenly the place was deserted and no one would get them out. The taxis he called refused to go: 'Leave it to the army,' they counselled. But in the end he borrowed his cousin's car and went to the airport. Just as they got back, the Israelis bombed it again.

Hadn't he backed Hezbollah like so many others under Israeli fire?

'It's not my war,' he replied, and went on to talk vaguely about 'They' who didn't like peace.

I wondered who he meant by 'They'. Israel? Syria? Hezbollah?

'We can't know who they are', he shrugged indifferently, and for the first time I saw that, from one perspective, it perhaps didn't matter exactly who it was who disrupted Lebanon's peace: the point was that they did. Now he was thinking of emigrating to Canada. 'I didn't think about it, until this war.'

The night following my meeting with Hezbollah, at around midnight, the last of the Israeli forces finally left south Lebanon. But

with Hezbollah's victory now established in the national consciousness, the development attracted little attention. Instead, the debate
that was now raging across Lebanese society concerned the future
direction of the country, and whether it should be determined by
the 14 March alliance or the supporters of Hezbollah. But while the
lineaments of this new polarization were becoming increasingly clear
to me, I was less sure about what this struggle for the soul of Lebanon was really about. I didn't want to start interviewing politicians:
their positions, expressed daily in the Lebanese press in the form
of statements and mutual insults, were predictable, their squabbling
scorned by most ordinary Lebanese. Instead, I decided to seek out
those who stood on the political sidelines, players who were making a contribution in a different way and seasoned observers of the
Lebanese scene.

So one Monday morning I perch at one of the perilous breakfast
bar tables outside Café Younis waiting for Nicole Fayad. As one of
the founders of 05amam, the new NGO that grew out of the pro-
democracy, anti-Syrian movement which had sprung up in the wake
of Hariri's assassination, Nicole represents, in a sense, the civil wing
of the 14 March Coalition, a key figure in the group of ordinary
Lebanese seeking a new way forward for their country. As I sit nursing a *café au lait* and a copy of *The Daily Star*, I wonder vaguely if she
will turn out to be one of the dynamic, slightly brash characters you
find among the movers and shakers of Beirut. But the quietly-spoken
woman with greying hair who turns up is the epitome of what the
French call *discrète*, the kind of thoughtful, good listener who makes
a good friend.

'I've never been in politics before, but after Hariri's assassination,
we went on the street as a group of friends asking the government
to resign. It was completely spontaneous, and we didn't think what

261

would happen.' The excitement of the movement's early days following Hariri's murder on 14 February is apparent as she talks. They had
set up a mass camp to support the large numbers of young people on
the streets, a financial and organizational feat for a group of inexperienced volunteers. Then came the founding of an NGO with its own
vision and projects, like setting up a mock municipal council in an
area lacking any sense of local democracy. The war ushered in a new
phase of work. 'I don't know how it happened,' she recalls. 'The war
started on the 12th and by the 17th we were already organized.' At one
point they stretched a giant Lebanese flag across the breach between
two ends of a bridge bombed by the Israelis. 'It was symbolic,' she
explains with a gentle smile. 'It was like the will of life against the
will of death.'

'What do you want now?' I ask.

'I think we need a whole new bunch of politicians in this country,'
she replies, her gaze fixed ahead where Hamra's mid-morning traffic
is crawling down the street. 'I want the institutions to work inde-
pendently. I want civil society to have its own leaders. I want a state
of law with freedom of speech, thought and belief. We are very far
from that at the moment.'

Her thoughts turn spontaneously to the Opposition, and her own,
complicated relationship with it. 'During the war, I said to myself,
"I am politically against Hezbollah." But I took risks with my life to
help feed their wives and children. I am not a traitor to the country.'
But the sentiments expressed in Nasrallah's recent 'divine victory'
speech worry her. 'In his last speech, it's like if you're not with him,
you're against him. We don't want to be forced to choose. We don't
want the, the'—she searches for the word before falling back on her
French—'l'existent—what is. We want something else. This is the
position of a lot of people.' She adds, with increasing passion: 'The

south is devastated. How can they talk about victory? It's a relative victory.'

'They are so organized,' I remark, recalling my encounter with Hezbollah a couple of days before.

'They are very organized,' she agrees, 'The problem is just their *objectif finale*. They are amazing people—organized, free of corruption. I wish they would run the state, but not with their ideology. The US was wrong. You cannot talk about Lebanon without talking about Hezbollah.'

'But where is their plan for Lebanon? Where is their plan for the economy? For society?' she continues. 'They don't want to work with others. They want to keep the danger or the war state, because it's here where they have their strength. They won't be strong in peace.'

Her thoughts turn to Lebanon's internal turbulence, to the possibility of another spate of assassinations. 'I think Jumblatt will be killed; it's just a matter of time. I'm afraid for Nasrallah. How long can he stay underground? Nothing has been solved on the security front. Everything is possible.'

'Would you leave?'

'*Non*,' she says decisively. She had spent a decade in Europe and the US but was one of the small number of returning émigrés who decided to commit themselves to Lebanon. 'I asked myself this during the war. No. During the war, many of my friends couldn't understand what I was doing, putting myself in danger. They said, "Why don't you go to the mountains?" But I have to do something on the ground. I can't just live here and try not to have a little impact.'

'So how do you see the future?'

'I am optimistic. I think the Lebanese have grown to be very solid—there is glue between people,' she replies, her tone firm. 'I'm not afraid of civil war. I'm afraid of foreign countries playing with us as they have always done. There is this will to live together. It's

263

very strong; it's not just a cliché. What is lacking is an alternative, an alternative to traditional political leaders and parties.'

Her organization will shortly launch a subversive advertising campaign, she goes on, a wry comment on the Lebanese tendency to categorize people in terms of their religion. To my Western ears it sounds innocent enough. 'Will people be shocked?' I ask.

She looks at me in amazement. 'Yes, it will be very shocking.' The campaign will challenge the Lebanese' deeply held attachments to clan and religious identity. It is only after we part that I realize that I don't know her sect.

Only a few hours later, I have a meeting with someone whose views are diametrically opposed to Nicole's. Abdo Saad runs the Beirut Center for Research and Information, a polling organization which charts the changing currents of Lebanese public opinion—broken down into the various sects, naturally—on key national issues such as the role of Syria in Lebanese affairs. Two weeks after the war, the centre had conducted some influential research which found that 86.9 per cent of the population supported Hezbollah's attacks on Israel. But it was Abdo Saad's personal views which interested me more than his work as an objective statistician; I knew that as a member of an educated Shia family sympathetic to Hezbollah he would have some decided views on the country's shifting political landscape.

I find him sitting behind a computer at one end of his wood laminate office, a smiling, slightly-built man who arranges his limbs in the manner of someone who spends too long hunched over a screen crunching numbers. Waving me into a chair, he comes out from behind his desk and re-composes his body into the armchair opposite. I'm working up to a question by way of a remark about Lebanon's increased profile in Britain when he leaps in with enthusiasm.

'Lebanon will be important for years to come,' he agrees. 'Like Sayyid Nasrallah says, Lebanon is bigger than its size. People in the West haven't grasped the importance of Hezbollah,' he smiles, waving his hands in illustration. 'This war has ended the myth of supremacy and scarcity. It has shaken the foundations of Israel. It has endangered the existence of Israel. We can never have peace in this area with Israel as it is today—it should be a secular state where Jews, Muslims and Christians live together in a democratic state.' He leans forward, animated by his subject. 'The main problem is the treatment of the Palestinians, the fact that Israel practises state terrorism.'

'What does this mean internally for Lebanon?'

'Hah,' he responds, as if I'm really onto something. 'Lebanon cannot distance itself from the Arab conflict. If you are living in a block of flats and there is a fire in one flat, you cannot say, "I don't want to be affected." The Shia were historically the most marginalized group in Lebanon, and the main component of the identity of the Shia is the Palestinian situation.'

'Why?' I ask, puzzled. The Palestinians' natural allies would surely be their co-religionists. 'The Palestinians are Sunnis.'

Abdo Saad re-crosses his legs and explains. 'With the Shia, oppression is forbidden in Islam. You have to fight oppression. If you can give your life for the sake of justice, you have to do that. So the enemy of the Shia is oppression. Israel embodies oppression to the Shia.'

In contrast, the Sunnis who control Lebanon's political establishment want to fudge the issue, creating an emasculated Arab nation, he goes on. 'Jordan is a satellite of Israel. They want Lebanon to become another Jordan, because part of the Lebanese do not want to fight Israel. They use the word "peace". But you can never have peace with Israel. You can have a truce. Peace is something different.'

265

'But internally,' I persist, wanting to get to some of the concerns expressed by Nicole that morning, 'aren't there other issues about the future of Lebanon?'

'No, no,' he rejoins swiftly. 'You can't distance that from the question of Israel, take it from me. We can't have a state—a state is something that defends itself. We need to build a state, but I cannot foresee it happening in the near future, with this very strong polarization. I fear that we may go to war now. The majority of Christians and Shia are now in one group, and a very large minority of Sunnis, with about 25 per cent of Druze as well. The other alliance—the 14 March—is mainly Sunnis and a minority of the Christians, a very few Shia and the majority of the Druze. This isn't a conflict across sectarian lines—you have the axis of America and France, and you have the axis of Iran, Syria and Hezbollah. There are deep divisions.'

His latest survey, he goes on, shows that seventy per cent of Lebanese support the calls for a national unity government now coming from the Opposition. 'One group is pushing hard, but the others are rejecting it, because they want to prevent Hezbollah and their allies from having the power to veto.' The proportional representation that such a government would involve would, he goes on, introduce some of the fairness into the system that the Shia felt was their due. We are deep into the minutiae of Lebanese politics now, but I feel that something else must underlie the preoccupation about voting mechanisms and the decision-making process. 'We're still not at the heart of the matter,' I say. 'Are they just fighting about power?'

Abdo Saad smiles irenically. 'Hezbollah will never accept to turn Lebanon into an American satellite.'

Almost imperceptibly, we slide into an impassioned debate, Abdo Saad insisting on the overriding importance of defence and pan-Arab alliances, while I try to get the bottom of what the battle for the heart and soul of Lebanon is really about. But I struggle to move the

266

discussion away from the nuts-and-bolts of power-sharing, and my attempt to point out some common ground between the two sides, like their agreement on the need to purge government of corruption, founders too. Like an estranged couple, each party was accusing the other of neglecting the family. 'They don't have any plan. They don't have any political plan for Lebanon,' says Abdo Saad in exasperation, echoing what Nicole had said about Hezbollah that morning. 'At least Hezbollah has a political programme.' After a while, the discussion dissolves into a kind of amiable inconclusiveness and Abdo Saad prepares to go and meet his daughter. Amal Saad-Ghorayeb, a lecturer at the Lebanese University, had been forging a reputation as an expert on Hezbollah and had just been made a fellow of the prestigious Carnegie Endowment think-tank. 'You should meet her,' he tells me, his face alight with paternal pride.

I can't resist asking him a final question about an issue that has recurred since my first steps into the Lebanese scene, the one that goes to the heart of the country's special character. 'If the Shia had more power, would it mean that Lebanon would become a more Muslim society?'

'No, no, that will never happen,' he replies. 'Muslims believe that the Christians have contributed a lot to this country. If we were Muslim, we would be like Jordan, like Egypt—backward. We are a liberal society. And we wouldn't have succeeded in creating a resistance.'

The two sides of Lebanon's latest domestic dispute ringing in my ears, I consult someone recommended for his neutrality. Former Druze minister Adel Hamiyeh has twice been in government, but always as an independent, never a member of a political party. A civil engineer by profession, he regards himself as a public servant rather than a politician, a refreshing position in Lebanon's partisan political scene. He's all Lebanese graciousness when I call him, immediately issuing an invitation for later that afternoon. A couple of hours later, I find myself in a white-walled office with bizarrely curvy walls at one end in the north of Hamra. Hamiyeh, a large man in late middle-age with an air of calm solidity, furnishes me with a 7Up and a straw, and devotes himself to the significance of Lebanon's re-aligned sects.

'It's more about Syria, it's more about the political level than something else,' he says, rejecting the idea that giving the Shia more power would irremediably change Lebanon's special character. 'I personally don't think they would Islamicize Lebanon—or that they could.'

'So when the Christians talk about the danger of this, it's really just their fears speaking?'

'Yes, yes,' he agrees emphatically. 'And they are worried by 12 July. They can't accept that someone else took the decision—Hezbollah took the decision to have the war and won the war. If only the Shia had paid the price, they would say, "okay". But everybody paid the price. They had invested for the summer, and all of a sudden they lost not only their summer's income, but also their investment. With this war, they felt that we are losing our economy through this unilateral decision.'

I try to sum up what I have understood so far. 'So really the disagreement is about where you focus – internally or externally. While one side focuses on defence, foreign affairs and relationships in the region, the 14 March group wants to concentrate on Lebanon, its nature and economy.'

'Exactly,' Hamiyeh nods encouragingly.

'Then the opposition say that, by taking this approach, they are being a puppet of America,' I continue.

'Exactly,' he responds again.

'So where do the Druze fit in?'

'Funnily enough, they have changed completely and shifted their position,' he replies, explaining how Jumblatt's battle against the Christians during the civil war had involved alliances with the Syrians and the Palestinians, whereas now he has thrown his lot in with the 14 March. 'Nowadays they share the same alliances as the Christians. The Druze are the people who fear most for the future of the country, because they don't have alliances outside. Almost all the Druze live in mixed Christian-Druze villages, and in the Chouf they are very keen to see the Christians back.'

'So what will the post-war politics mean for the future?'

'Being an optimist, I would like to see things settle, and by settling I mean we have to see that the foreign problems between Iran and Syria on one side and the US on the other cool down,' he replies. 'If it cools down, that would reflect on us. Then everybody would think about Lebanon, and see that nobody can live alone and that we have to make compromises for each other. The problem with the Shia is that they think they are the ones who made the sacrifices. With this war, they feel they should lead everybody.' The clash of views, he concludes, is likely to foment in the long, tense wait for the final report on Hariri's killing from the UN-backed investigation which might directly name the Syrian culprits.

I thank him and take my leave, well pleased with this new light shed on Lebanon's sectarian puzzle, my vanity flattered by my interviewee's readiness to corroborate my insights, a conversational style I recognize from previous meetings with Druze elders. But there was still a key element of the post-war scene that needed clarifying: the relations between the Sunnis and the Shia. I knew the man for the job, a leading Sunni theologian based at the Lebanese University who had written extensively on the need for reform within Islam. I had wanted to talk to Professor Ridwan Al-Sayyid about the rise of moderate Islam on a previous trip, but had run out of time. He, too, is receptive to my request for a meeting and invites me to his apartment in the Sanayeh district of Beirut one Sunday morning.

Sanayeh Park had taken on a new role during the war, briefly becoming home to around five hundred refugees who couldn't find room in the overflowing school buildings where most people sheltered. It was the site of some of the less savoury war stories: the well-to-do residents who overlooked the park, it was said, had complained about the noise and rubbish created by their fellow countrymen. Meanwhile, two English journalists were briefly detained there after children told the police they were Israeli spies. But now, as I walk past on a sunny, breezy Sunday, it is once more a tranquil haven for Muslim families to spend their leisure hours. A few moments later, I find myself in Professor Sayyid's spacious, elegantly furnished apartment, discussing the absurdly inflated property prices of London and Beirut.

The professor is a compact man with a compressed, rounded face reminiscent of Anthony Hopkins and a self-contained manner. Although fasting, he has his maid bring me coffee and begins to speak in the measured way of one accustomed to giving lectures to students. Like a bad student myself, I am slightly the worse for wear after a night of clubbing and, as I sit there with my notebook, appreciate his slow, ordered approach.

The changes of the past eighteen months—Hariri's death, the departure of the Syrians and their victory against Israel—have created a new situation in which the Shia are trying to get more power, begins the professor. 'We are of the opinion that the Shia are playing a bad role for the country. They are making wars with Israel and putting the whole country at risk. The Shia say the Sunnis are working with the US and France, even in some cases with Israel, against Islamic goals. They are not willing to permit changing the direction of the country,' he pauses, as I scribble dutifully away. 'Both views are exaggerated. The Shia in Lebanon are genuine Lebanese and they are about a third of the population. No one can have a suspicion about their integrity. On the other side, the Sunnis were in modern history the people who allied themselves to the Palestinian resistance against Israel. And they are also a third of the population of the country.'

'So I don't think it will come to a civil war—a bloody Sunni-Shia conflict,' he opens his hands evocatively. 'But the situation will not be solved because of outside forces.' He details the issues and alliances—the links between Hezbollah and Iran and Syria, US concerns about those countries, the impact of the forthcoming UN tribunal on Hariri's death, Sunni alliances with Arab nations such as Egypt and Saudi Arabia. 'So there are intervention problems in Lebanon about power-sharing. There is this conflict in the region, and the sides have different allies.'

'What will this mean for Lebanon internally?'

'I think there will be problems for the next two to three years,' he replies. 'There could be military engagement again in the south with Israel and some internal clashes between the Sunnis and the Shia. After that, perhaps in 2010, it will come to a new power-sharing so that the Shia have more weight in deciding the direction of the state. But the Sunnis will stay as the main party in alliance with the Christians. It means good relations with the Arabs, with America, with the EU.'

Much as I like his optimistic prognosis, I can't help asking: 'But supposing these problems are not resolved?'

'We will not have a future in Lebanon,' he says simply. 'If the problems between the US and Iran and the Palestinian issue are not solved, we will have the title used by the Bush administration of failed state.'

I'm conscious of my heart sinking at the sound of a term usually applied to countries like Somalia or Afghanistan. To me, Lebanon is

271

no longer a distant trouble spot, but a familiar place full of sunlight, honey-coloured Ottoman buildings and bougainvillea. Its descent into permanent chaos would be unimaginable. 'So what the West does now is important?'

'Yeah, yeah,' he replies. 'I think now they are changing. After what they saw in Lebanon and Iraq, they are now willing to make peace. I think there is a genuine intention now.'

'Does the disagreement between the Sunni and Shia extend to theological matters?'

'Until now, no,' he replies. 'If the project becomes sharper, extremists in both camps will start talking about theological matters. So far, it is political and social.'

'Is there any reason to fear an Islamic state in Lebanon?'

'Both Sunni and Shia have fundamentalists, but the Shia are controlled by their imam. Iran can decide to control them, or not. Sunni fundamentalism doesn't have a leadership, so you can't negotiate with it. But until now eighty per cent of the Sunnis are moderate and all the extremists come from Syria.'

I have heard about this movement of moderate Islam, I say, recalling the claims from Hani Fahes about its flourishing in Iran.

'There is a big awakening, a big enlightenment among the Iranian hierarchy,' agrees the professor. 'They are making a *ijtihad*—a new thinking. They are very energetic—they translate everything, and they have money. But the political leadership is still authoritarian and traditional, and there is conflict between them. We have a movement of enlightenment in Sunni Islam, but it is weak and the representatives are scattered. In the Shia, I think the new thinking will win. With the Sunnis, it is not yet clear.'

'In Britain now we are struggling how to have that debate,' I observe. On my TV screen in the hotel, I have watched the rise of new,

272

exotic debate in Britain—the question of whether Muslim women should wear the face veil—with some bemusement.

Dr. Sayyid nods thoughtfully. 'If we have a big enlightenment tradition, it will be a real answer to the Islamic fundamentalists. I am expecting it, in the next few years, to become a big strong movement.'

11
DEATH AND LIFE

BUT alongside all the problems, Beirut's joyous side was re-asserting itself with a vengeance. On my first Saturday night in the city, I could hardly sleep for the pounding music that flowed out of the nearby nightclubs, something that had never happened before. When I joined the revellers myself a week later in Fusion, a smart club in fashionable Monot, it was hard to believe that the country had been at war only weeks before. Except that, as usual, there was a distinctively Lebanese twist: the dancers made little triangles in the air with their hands, symbolizing the cedars of Lebanon.

One evening, I go out with a Radio France Internationale reporter to chew the journalistic fat, and we hit gold. Walimat Wardeh bar in Hamra had been converted from an old Beiruti apartment with a simplicity that gave it the atmosphere of an older Levant, with its tiled floor, dark wood furniture and embroidered cushions. Young Lebanese were drinking in corners of honeyed light. In the heart of the bar, five twenty-something men were making contemporary classical oriental music with an attitude of deep seriousness; one played an oud, another a guitar, while a third made judicious use of a tambourine. But it was an unknown instrument that drew our attention the most: a huge board that rested on the player's lap. He plucked at its strings with a plectrum, his hands constantly fluttering to the tuning keys as he played.

The music rose and fell in arabesque waves, a sound so rich that it seemed to absorb the air around it. But it was the pony-tailed vocalist who provided the main melody line, his lips hardly moving as he issued the low, sweeping tones. 'Folk singers look the same everywhere,' observed my companion acutely, and we both giggled. I preferred the uninhibited emoting of the guest singer who came next, a young man whose pretty features belied the power of the voice to which he gave free rein, stretching out the notes for what seemed like minutes on end. A second guest singer looked for all the world like a young Martin Amis with a Chris de Burgh haircut. This, too, turned out to be deceptive: out of his torso, encased smartly in a striped shirt, came a rich Eastern current that reached deep inside you, grabbed hold of some old, old feeling you hardly knew you had, and carried you on it for as long as he chose to maintain the sound.

As they played, the elfin-faced bar girl darted back and forth between serving drinks and brief turns on what was becoming a dance floor. The mystery instrument was an qanoon, she told me in her crystalline French. *C'est très difficile. Il faut quinze ans pour l'apprendre.*

The musicians—Ziad Sahab and his band Shehadine, the poster said—played for hours, a little crowd of dancers gradually gathering in the space in front of them. When they stopped, the audience clamoured for more. *Plee-eease!* called a girl, almost hysterically. The band obliged and someone seized my hand. 'Come and learn the *dabke*, our national dance.'

Five minutes later, I had mastered the simple but brain-teasing step. Five minutes after that, it all but had vanished from my mind. Outside, feeling the effects of several beers, I took a wrong turn, ending up almost in Ramlet el Baida. Half an hour's fast walking brought the hotel into view. The lunatic of Ain el Mreisse was sitting

275

on the kerb, bushy-haired and half-naked, proclaiming to the night-time traffic. The hotel had closed for the night over two hours ago, but the youngest, adolescent member of staff, his hair sticking up in an asymmetrical quiff and blinking sleepily, opened the door with the sweetest of smiles.

So far the press trip was going almost comically badly. It had taken a series of calls, emails and a trip to the Lebanese Red Cross office to arrange and, even then, it only came about by accident, when a young blond woman introduced herself as I was having a beer in the hotel one night. A TV journalist from Iceland, she laughed when she heard my name. 'Oh, the Red Cross are trying to get in touch with you, but they didn't have the right number. They wanted to ask you to join me to see their work in the south tomorrow.'

We set off at first light the next day, and make the long journey to Tyre, where we spend the next hour waiting in Red Cross centre number 702. 'What do you want to see?' we are asked. '*Les soins,*' we say firmly and finally we are off, with promises of mobile clinics serving the local people too impoverished by war to get regular health-care. I imagine fine young men in orange overalls dashing about in a brave yet caring manner, as they had done during the war. It had been a huge operation, involving over two thousand volunteers and six thousand rescue operations over the thirty-three days. But the healthcare centre we visit has just one patient talking to a doctor about changing her contraceptive pill. 'There will be more people at the next one,' we are promised and, after a fifteen minute drive, we enter the white-walled clinic in the village of Bouchrieh. There is not a patient in sight. 'They came at nine o'clock,' says the nurse who is clearing up, surprised. 'Everyone has gone.'

276

Now we are in the middle of the countryside, negotiating our passage with Hassan, a relentlessly cheerful Red Cross volunteer from Tyre. It turns out that, having offered to drive us to the control centre at Tibnine for some petrol money, he wants the top whack for a private taxi. Slightly taken aback, we agree to pay most of what he asks and the car moves off over the dry, undulating hills.

At the roadside, there are signs of destruction and construction in equal measure. A stretch of recently created wasteland is followed by an orchard with a bombed-out bald patch; a man is carrying pots of saplings to replant the gap. Then, on the rise of a hill, we enter a village full of flags flapping in the mountain breeze. 'Here, Hezbollah,' Hassan informs us.

'Are you Hezbollah?' I ask.

'No, I'm not Hezbollah,' he replies easily. 'I'm Lebanese.' He reflects for a moment, and then adds: 'Hezbollah, they're okay. But me, I'm not Hezbollah.'

Our early start meant that there was no food available in Beirut and I have been on the lookout for several hours. The tension from our negotiations having dissipated, I confide my heart's desire to Hassan. *Nam, mannoush nos zatar, nos jibneh!* he repeats enthusiastically and sets about looking in earnest, slowing down at likely spots and asking locals where we might find some. But, apart from some rumours of bakeries on distant hilltops, there is nothing cooking.

We drive on through the parched, stone-laden landscape. 'Here, it's not like Britain,' he says cheerfully, waving at the view. 'I know, because my brother lives there.'

'Where?' I ask, with interest.

He thinks for a moment. 'Big Ben.'

There's a pause, while both of us consider whether this can be right. Then he says uncertainly. 'London, Britain, right?'

277

The Red Cross centre in Tibnine was the co-ordination centre for the relief effort in the south. So far my own experience of the organization might have been a little chaotic, but I knew that the war story was different: the Lebanese Red Cross, with its local knowledge and contacts, had been quicker and more effective than the larger international NGOs brought in by the conflict. We pull up in front of a modest three-storey construction of unplastered breeze blocks, a fleet of ambulances resting in an open garage on the ground floor. An ambulance which had been hit by Israeli fire was parked outside, the rocket still piercing the centre of the cross on the roof. While Herdis films this iconic image, I hang about on the balcony. I am falling on some little cakes that someone has deposited on a table in front of me when Ali Saad, the Red Cross' head of information in the south, arrives from his day job as a bank manager, immaculate with his smart black suit and neatly trimmed moustache. I stop eating and apologize, explaining that it hadn't been possible to find anything to eat since leaving Beirut early that morning. Ali Saad smiles serenely. 'Yes, most of the people are fasting in this area.'

'I don't look like a Red Cross volunteer, do I?' he says, as Herdis readies her camera to film him. 'No, you look like a bank manager,' I agree. He pins a Red Cross badge the size of a saucer to his lapel, and begins broadcasting to the world. 'This has been one of the biggest operations that Lebanon has ever done,' he announces, in a voice that is exceptionally mellifluous and well-modulated. 'We were in great danger. Every time we went out to evacuate someone, we thought we would not come back.'

With eight ambulances bombed and one Red Cross volunteer killed in the course of duty, he has a particular message to get across. 'This is a violation of the Geneva Convention and international law. The Red Cross should be protected. We were targets, quite simply. A mistake could happen once; it wouldn't happen more.'

278

'Was Israel's approach very different from the last time it occupied south Lebanon?' I ask.

'Of course, of course,' he replies, losing his formal tone. 'They threw a million cluster bombs the day after the ceasefire. Why? To kill people for the next ten years.' He shakes his head sadly. 'I don't know, this is my opinion.'

He resumes his upbeat broadcasting manner. 'I never thought we would have Red Cross personnel killed,' he declares to the camera. 'But this is God's will, and God will protect us, not the international community.' He raises his eyebrows ironically, and smiles. As he and Herdis go to get some shots by the bombed ambulance, he hands me a digital camera. 'Will you take photos of me being interviewed?'

Then we set off in his smart car for a tour of the area. Tibnine had been heavily bombed and was desolate for some days, he tells us, its roads scattered with cluster bombs. But they were quickly cleared by the Mines Advisory Group, and local people got on with the rest. I am amazed at how quickly normal life has been restored. Ali Saad waves to the secondary school, an unremarkable building set back from its gates. 'It was completely damaged, but it has been repaired,' he says, with a flourish. 'It will open next week.' But the nearby hospital still bears the scars of war: blackened pine cones cling to a scalded tree outside. Next to it is a pile of burnt-out cars.

On the road out of Tibnine we pull into a driveway. A rumbling sound is coming from the valley below and a troop of UNIFIL vehicles, dazzling with their pristine white paint, come sailing up the road, their long snout-like guns cleaving the space ahead of them. Only one is a compact, armoured personnel carrier.

'Why do they need to use artillery vehicles?' I ask once they have passed, puzzled. 'I thought they were a peace-keeping force.'

Ali Saad's silence radiates agreement. 'I'm Red Cross. I could say something else,' he says carefully. Then he lets himself go a little,

279

adding with some irritation: 'Why do they use artillery tanks for patrol? Why not use smaller ones just to go around?'

Further south, passing through the village of Beit Jahoun, he points to a piece of wasteland at the side of the road. Just six stranded pillars and a plastic chair break up the empty space. 'There were three houses here; that's all that was left of them.'

'Where have the people whose homes were destroyed gone?'

'Some of them still live in their homes,' he replies. 'They fixed up a room or two. Some live in their neighbour's house. Some left the area, but very few.'

A few yards further on, an eager householder is in the middle of his own personal reconstruction effort, his half-built house surrounded by ladders, cement mixers and a bulldozer.

'This was one of the most dangerous areas during the bombardment,' he tells us. 'No one could drive here; they were completely isolated. They were bodies lying here.'

'Were the press here?'

'Nowhere; the press were in Tyre and did not cover the isolated villages. They came only when there was a ceasefire for two days.'

We drive on, higher into the hills across a more desolate landscape. Along the way Ali Saad points out the post-war sights: here a half-filled crater at the side of the road, there a tangled mass of car wreckage. In between times, he flips through the many photos in his digital camera, looking for more pertinent images to show us. 'You like taking photos,' I remark. 'Yes,' he smiles. 'I took twelve hundred during the war.'

We arrive in Bint Jbeil, the main town in the south and the scene of the fiercest fighting between Israeli and Hezbollah forces. The Israelis had been forced to retreat, having lost nine of their soldiers, but they still managed to shell the town to rubble. Before we go to see the damage, we stop off at Ali Saad's bank, a branch of Byblos.

He sweeps us into his air-conditioned office and sits down, checking the bank of CCTVs at the side of his desk. The cool air and polished wood furniture is a shock after the heat and dust outside. 'It's a different world, eh?' he says, with evident pleasure. On the shelf behind him several brass plaques testify to his good management of the branch. There's a 'Best Branch 2004' and a 'Best Customer Service 2003'. Ali Saad whips a letter out of his breast pocket and shows it to me. It is from the Irish foreign minister, thanking the Lebanese Red Cross for rescuing three Irish nationals. 'This is nice,' he says. 'I didn't get anything like this from my own government; it's an appreciation for me.'

We spend ages in the bank. Ali Saad opens the safe and pulls out a bundle of blood-stained dollars, taken from a dead man's pocket and on their way to be changed for more useable notes. 'No use to lose them,' he says. 'They are needed for the family.' After he has assured himself that everything is running smoothly with his team, he and Herdis do another TV interview, this time in his capacity as bank manager. He is proud of how quickly the bank managed to re-open after the war. 'Six days after the ceasefire, I had the banking system working. I was online, real time, with the whole world,' he tells the camera. 'It meant a lot to people that the bank opened that fast. It brings life back to the place and the economy.' I take more photos of the proceedings and then the three of us pose to provide him with a record of his latest encounter with the press. I think we are finally done, but Ali Saad hands me his camera again. 'With my staff!' he says enthusiastically, and the entire branch team lines up for a few more shots.

Back outside on the main streets, there are other signs that the town is bouncing back. We go into a little shop next to a large, burnt-out building. The shelves are two-thirds full of a motley selection of clothes and sports gear, all its owner, Hassan Mohsen, has

281

managed to buy to replace his lost stock. 'I had another, bigger shop, a few metres from here. That was destroyed completely,' he says. 'I didn't give up. I came here and opened a new shop.' He puts a pair of trousers into a black plastic bag for a customer. 'Little by little, it's getting better. All my customers are coming to my shop again.'

But it is a different story in the town's main market place a few hundred yards away. It is like a natural disaster area, an apocalyptic film set in a big budget movie. Building after building, street after street, has been reduced to piles of broken stones. The guts of the buildings spill out, pipes and steel girders exposed to the air. The few trees poking out from between the piles of concrete are thickly coated in dust. Herdis and I clamber over the rubble in silence, filming and looking. Ali Saad's voices his memories of the war. 'There was no way, after the ceasefire, we could drive through here. We used to walk through, shouting, "Is anybody there?"' There has clearly been no attempt at rebuilding here; it's hard to imagine where one would begin. 'It's bigger than a private effort,' explains Ali Saad.

In the back streets of this strange ghost town I glimpse a couple of figures amid the ruins. A washing line and a bed behind a doorway suggest a makeshift home. 'Are there people living here?' I ask, surprised. 'They're Syrian workers,' Ali Saad replies. 'They don't have anywhere else to go.' Further along the street, someone has stretched a large banner across a devastated doorway. 'That was a halal chicken and fish shop,' he explains. 'It says that they have moved to another street, near the Red Cross. 'Come on,' he adds. 'We will be late for the family.' He has arranged for us to visit people who lost nine relatives to an Israeli bomb. I'm worried about how I will deal with this, knowing that my resources have almost gone. Nearly twenty-four hours with almost no food, I feel vague and empty.

The destruction seems more arbitrary in the village of Aitaroun where the Awada family live. Most houses are intact, but every so often there are strange gaps in the street as if a house has unexpectedly been whisked off somewhere. Ali Saad leads us up a garden path and into a solid-looking building. Inside, half a dozen adults are sitting around a high-ceiled, tiled room lined with sofas. There is an elderly woman swathed in black and her two grown-up children, a daughter and a son who lives in Australia, plus an elderly couple who are cousins. The old women clutch Herdis and me as if we are long-lost relatives, smacking kisses on our cheeks, while the bearded brother announces: 'I welcome any press to show the facts. Without the press, no one could see us.'

The daughter Kamila is sitting silently on a chair in blue tracksuit bottoms and a black sweatshirt, a patterned headscarf woven tightly round a face with huge, sparkling hazel eyes. I smile tentatively at her, but get a blank. Then I realize why: her eyes carry that indefinable expression of someone so immersed in grief that they are not fully present. But when asked, she begins to quietly recount the family's story.

'It was Monday 17 July, about midnight,' she begins, with Ali Saad translating. 'The family were sitting down having a chat at home'—she points up the road. 'At 12.20, we felt the house collapse on top of us. There were twenty-two people in the house. When I went to go out, I couldn't, because another bomb hit. We heard little voices calling out from the ground. We managed to clear some stones from the house, and we saw hands and legs. We got the first girl out—Jana, who is seven years old. When we got Jana from the ground we saw her sister Katryn, who is fourteen. She was still alive, but she was hurt in her back and her shoulders. The neighbours gathered round the house. One of them got my brother Hussan out, but we realized he was dead.'

283

A few questions establish who died—Kamila's brother and nephew, her sister, brother-in-law and their five children. She, her mother, sister in law and two nieces were only hurt.

I'm wondering, hazily, how to elicit some sort of emotional response, but Herdis does it for me. 'It may be a difficult question to answer, but how do you feel?'

'I'm still shocked,' replies Kamila simply. 'I can't believe it happened.'

'Do you see this as a victory for Hezbollah?' asks Herdis.

This time, it is Kamila's brother who replies. 'Even though this happened, it is still a victory for Lebanon and for the resistance,' he says firmly. 'We blame Israel and we blame the international community, because the international community did not do anything to stop it for thirty-three days.'

I look to see his sister's reaction, but can't fathom anything from the hazel eyes. Then another, less direct way to see what is going on for her occurs to me. 'Now, during the holy month of Ramadan, what is your main prayer?'

Again, it is the brother who answers in her place. 'In this holy month, we hope and we pray that we will always win against our enemy, who destroys our families, houses and villages.'

I'm still wondering about the effects on the person behind the hazel eyes, the emotional life behind the slogans, once all the fuss has died down. Her brother, presumably, will have a partial escape to his life as an émigré halfway across the world. 'Are you going back to Australia?' I ask him.

'Yes, I will stay here for six weeks, and then I will go back,' he replies.

'And you will stay here?' I address Kamila directly.

'Yes.'

284

As we start to take our leave, Herdis is crying. It is her first time in the Middle East. But I, now in the grip of a full-blown blood sugar crash, feel empty. The older women of the house kiss us fervently again and we troop out. As we make a final tour of the destruction, visiting the pile of rubble that had been the family's former home up the road, I realize there's another reason for my lack of emotion: it's also because this glimpse into this latest misery of Lebanon's Shia is almost wearyingly familiar, despite the fact it represents a new chapter in their history. I cast around in my mind for the provenance of these now-familiar elements: the sudden deaths of civilians, families sitting around in mourning, rubble dotted with the debris of domestic life, the sense of an ever-present enemy, all under a blazing Eastern sun. Where had I seen all this before?

Ah yes, that's it: Palestine.

It was by a circuitous route—everyone knows everyone in Lebanon— that I hooked up with the relief wing of Nicole Fayad's organization, Aid Lebanon: the Civil Campaign for Relief. The link was Maya, a young woman who had spent most of her life in the West but had come back to live in Lebanon. In the weeks following the war she was spending her spare time identifying projects that needed funding for charities in the West. Like Nicole, she was typical of the group I was coming to think of as the 'new Lebanese': dynamic individuals prepared to invest their time and energy in building a new future for their country. Meeting people like her made a refreshing change from the endless stream of aspiring émigrés whom I usually encountered. She was planning an informal trip to the south to assess fundraising needs, and invited me to join her. Among other people, we would meet the head of Aid Lebanon, a larger-than-life character called Walid Fakherddine, recommended to me by several people.

She sounds horrified when I warn her of the difficulty of getting food in the south during Ramadan. 'Really? I have to eat. I'll take loads of sandwiches.'

It is a friendly, female party that sets off in a four-by-four the following Saturday. As well as Maya, there is Aline, a lifestyle journalist and Wendy, a British woman married to a Lebanese. To make sure we don't get lost in the winding roads of the south, Maya has begged the services of Mohammed, the family chauffeur.

'Are there any new post-war jokes?' I enquire. Maya twists round from the front seat with a grin. 'Why do the *tantes* of Achrafieh all carry pictures of Mr. N?' She nods in Mohammed's direction to indicate that she doesn't want to upset any Shia sensibilities, and we all understand that she means Nasrallah. Then, pulling the skin above her ears to suggest the effects of a face lift, she delivers the punch line: 'Because he took them back thirty years!'

Someone else has another little gem, a reference to the destruction of Beirut's suburbs. 'Why have the prices of flats in Dahiyeh suddenly risen?' We think, and fail to come up with anything. 'Because now they have a sea view!'

On the road out of Beirut we meet up with Walid, a big-bellied man with a mane-like ponytail and bundles of energy. Wendy and I jump into his car, so that we can ply him with questions about what he's trying to do in the south. He talks practically non-stop, driving so fast over the potholes that increasingly fill the road that every now and then I, sitting in the back, am thrown up so that my skull hits the roof. Sometimes, as he makes a point, his hands leave the steering wheel entirely, floating a few inches above it.

A snapped-off flyover and two damaged bridges fly past the window, one after the other. 'There was no reason to bomb both of them; it had no strategic value whatsoever,' comments Walid. 'They bombed here and there because they wanted us to remember the volume of war.'

Soon, the damaged highway becomes impassable, and we cross onto the old coastal road. 'You know, in '96, this was the only road,' observes Walid. 'It was very dangerous from here on; the Israelis bombed it often.' He recalls with amusement how he used to take it regularly, to the amazement of his friends. 'The point was, you put high music in the car, and you close the windows so you don't hear anything. *Yalla!*'

The car speeds on, and I gasp as the top of my head meets the roof again. 'Sorry, I'm forgetting the potholes,' he apologizes.

The discussion turns to the effects of the war on the south. 'In an area which is historically underdeveloped, we have a catastrophe with all these cluster bombs,' he says. 'People couldn't harvest their crops in 2006, they can't plant them for 2007, and we're not sure what they're going to do in 2008. These people have nothing. And there's a social thing,' he goes on. 'When people get a bit of money, or get educated, they leave the south. They don't go back or, if they do, they build a villa and go and stay in it for ten days. They don't invest anything.'

Aid Lebanon had started new projects a few weeks ago, making the most of the way the war had opened up the south to new influences. The sudden influx of NGOs were effectively loosening Hezbollah's grip on the population. 'The needs are so huge now, that Hezbollah cannot resist,' he says. 'They would be faced with the people if they tried to resist.'

'So what's your philosophy?' I ask.

'We operate with two concepts,' he replies. 'First, we promote a culture of life—a culture of democracy, peace and justice. Fighting poverty can't work without that. And we think that relief can't work on its own—there's a danger that it creates dependency. What is needed is social development.'

'You must be starting from a very low base,' I remark.

'Yeah,' he replies. 'You're talking basic issues like sex education. Now there are thousands of UNIFIL around here, but people have little knowledge of sexually transmitted diseases. You cannot simply do advocacy because, in a conservative society, it would sound like suggesting that the girls of the south should sleep with UNIFIL. You cannot do that. You need to place it in a wider scope of health issues.'

Our progress is slowed as the road gives out completely and the car follows several others slowly negotiating a narrow muddy strip over a river. We drive through Tyre, past large, unrepaired craters and finally pull up in front of a large building in the village of Deir Qanoun. Inside about forty small children are seated on the hall floor, listening to a traditional Arab storyteller. They are captivated by this eccentric yet recognizable character, with his cap, stick and splayed-leg walk, demanding their full attention as he exhorts them to sing. Upstairs, past an exercise class and a bank of papier-mâché masks, the fruit of a previous week's work, several visibly keen young adults, all volunteers, are sitting in the staff room.

The Saturday project started almost immediately after the war to give local children an alternative to their limited, traditional school-ing, Walid explains. 'It's nothing to do with pushing the capacity of the kids. They are just told to do things. The culture of dialogue is not present, even in families. Many of the kids haven't gone outside the region. There's one image they see of Lebanon, which is of the south—conservative, gloomy. So we thought, what about discover-ing other parts of Lebanon?'

288

'How easy has it been to get parents on board?' I ask, wondering how the local Shia were reacting to this sudden influx of do-gooders from Beirut.

Walid smiles knowingly. 'Not that easy,' he replies. 'This is why we buy the snacks from the locals. When you buy a hundred bottles of juice from the local shop, it's everything they've got in the shop. Then you're contributing on an economic level, and they know you. They say, "oh, they're our customers, they're good people."'

'You've got to respect their values,' he goes on. Then he adds, his smile deepening: 'Although we've got some social changes going on. Leila?' He looks at an alert-looking young woman in a pair of stylish spectacles across the room for confirmation.

'She took off her *hijab*!' confesses the volunteer, Hala, and guilty laughter ripples round the room. 'We didn't do anything! We never talked about it.'

One of the project's early triumphs has been persuading the parents to let the children take part in an overnight camp in Khiam, Walid goes on. 'Ever since, they changed,' he says and slides seamlessly into his more general point. 'People are not conservative or closed because it's their own way. They don't have a choice.' A way of illustrating his point occurring to him, he points to two glasses of brightly coloured juice sitting on a tray in front of him. 'You have pineapple and you have guava. It's impossible to choose if you haven't tasted them both—if all you have is pineapple, you get to like it. What we want to do is give them the choice.'

As the meeting breaks into little conversations, I slip over and talk to Hala, the volunteer of the *hijab* story. 'There are very few traumatized kids, which is normal,' she tells me. 'The normal average is three to five per cent in every war. Nevertheless, we have kids who come from families who were displaced during the war or who lost

289

people. We are trying to be very careful not to confuse mourning with trauma.'

'We have traumatised kids, but not because of the war—it's because of the environment they live in is sexist and violent. We have kids who are nine, ten, eleven years old who are working in the fields or in construction; we have kids who don't know how to write. The first weeks the parents were afraid, because they didn't know us. They used to come to the classes. Some used to come three times a day.'

I'm intrigued by how she and the others are prepared to devote so much of their free time to the project. 'What's your motivation?' Hala shrugs and smiles as if her involvement is so obvious as to be beyond explanation. 'I started in the relief effort during the war. This is just an extension of that.'

We say our goodbyes and set off again, across the rolling hills to Qana. The village—reputedly the site of Jesus' first miracle of turning water into wine at a wedding—has acquired a special, dark place in the Lebanese consciousness since the Israelis bombed it in 1996. Over a hundred civilians were killed as they sheltered in the UN base, and Hezbollah preserved the site as a memorial museum. Then, almost unbelievably, the bombing in July brought a repeat experience. Twenty-nine people, mostly children, died as the house they took refuge in collapsed under Israeli fire. Now the place has a double symbolic significance, with two cemeteries marking what is widely considered a double massacre.

We pull up by a bombed-out house and mosque. There, on a plateau on the edge of hillside, is the new cemetery, a marble enclave of elegant grey and black tombs neatly laid in rows beneath fluttering yellow and black Hezbollah flags. 'It's just like the first one!' exclaims Maya involuntarily. Mohammed goes round the twenty-nine gravestones, quietly reading out the Arabic inscriptions—the occupant of this one was two years old, that one six. A display of photos of the dead has been mounted along one side wall with, somewhat surreally, a large banner from a Korean NGO expressing condolences.

We wander among the tombs, taking in the atmosphere. It's a peaceful spot in the afternoon sun, overlooking the mountains. 'I'm surprised there's no one from Hezbollah to take us round,' remarks Maya.

'Yes, you get to expect a certain standard of service,' I reply, only half-joking. Their absence is strange: in the back of our minds is the question of whether, as some people suggested, their influence is declining.

The atmosphere at the cemetery at the other end of the village, is less reposeful. With its off-colour walls, the place has a tatty, abandoned feel. 'The least they could do is give it a facelift', says Maureen. The white tombs are strangely elongated, housing the unidentifiable remains rather than bodies. On a large banner behind, stylized lettering drips with blood, mingling with pictures of the victims and the Shia speaker Nabih Berri. We walk through the cemetery, to the UN building behind. It has been left as it was after the bombing a decade ago: a rusty frame, containing debris and fragments of glass. I peer in tentatively through one of the window frames and see a shoe. And here, at last, is our guide, a little man bearing a photo album of the massacre. The pictures of charred remains are horrific and, already nauseous from the winding roads, I find myself stepping back. Undeterred, he carries on until the last photo, pointing out this or that seared limb with a well-rehearsed commentary. But no one in our party is looking any more, and we return to the car.

As we drive further south, the signs of destruction multiply. There are open areas of wasteland where all traces of buildings have been effaced. 'Everything gone,' says Mohammed, waving at the empty space. One roadside plot has been turned into an impromptu dump, where locals are bringing the rubble that they need to clear in order to rebuild their houses. A couple of men are disentangling steel rods from their concrete casing and loading them into a truck; in the wake of the war a new trade of collecting and re-selling scrap metal has developed among entrepreneurial southerners, the local press has reported. Many of the houses we pass are in a strange halfway state, and it's hard to tell whether they have been recently bombed or are just part of the long, slow development of the south. 'The trouble with Lebanon is that you don't know what's coming up and what's coming down,' comments Wendy.

We enter a lush valley on a road which winds between verdant hills and terraced plots. Slender saplings wave at its edges. For a few moments everyone gives voice to a fantasy that we could be in Italy or southern France, where the preoccupations are peaceable ones of cultivating and eating. But soon the realities of south Lebanon return: turning to examine a particularly impressive burnt-out house, we find two boys in a back lane, wielding rifles. Then a car with blacked-out rear windows shoots past, the unmistakeable set expression and smart attire of a security guard in the front seat.

In the village of Beit Lif, Mohammed knows everyone and is constantly leaning out the window for handshakes and kisses. I stare incredulously at a house whose entire roof has curled round, as if it were a piece of melted toffee: one end is in the sky where it should be, but the other rests on the ground. 'That's his cousin's,' says Maya. 'He grew up here.' Nearby is a row of white tents for people whose homes have been completely destroyed, each with its own plastic front door. We stroll along a dusty lane, passing a three-storey house whose roof is balanced against its walls almost at a right angle to the ground. It looks as if it might collapse at any moment 'The three people who were sleeping here are dead,' Mohammed says matter-of-factly.

There has been no rebuilding here so far. But despite the destruction, the village, late on a Saturday, is full of bustling sociability, with people walking up and down and standing chatting in front of their houses. Then, with everyone wanting to be back in Beirut for the evening, Mohammed declines invitations to stop for coffee and we make our way out. At the village edge, he slows to greet another relative walking on her vegetable patch, a young woman in a bright floral headscarf. Despite protests from the passengers, she insists on loading cucumbers in through the car window.

We head towards the coast road, approaching the Israeli border near the village of Marouahine. It is peaceful and deserted. The chalk-white border road is just a walk away, curling round the hillside, and the shiny wire of the border fence gleams in the afternoon sun. Behind it, the orange roofs of the Israeli chalet-style houses are clearly visible. It is hard to believe that just weeks before this had been a battlefield; the only sign of the recent conflict is a strip of blackened earth.

The car turns north towards Beirut and *iftar* for Mohammed, who has been fasting all day. At one intersection, we pass six UNIFIL soldiers standing in a line, legs astride, proudly ensuring the security of Lebanon. 'Oh, *les Italiens!*' exclaims Aline with enthusiasm. '*Ciao, bambini!*'

The carload of women scrutinizes them carefully as the four by four makes its way slowly onto the next section of the road. 'They're not very tall,' remarks Carole, voicing my thoughts. 'Look at their sunglasses!' says Maya. 'I bet they're all Prada. That's quite a statement.' Indeed, every single soldier is sporting a stylish pair of shades beneath his blue beret. It's as if they're really models on a photo shoot, albeit rather short ones, who have been kitted out in military chic and made to pose in a post-conflict zone.

A little further on, the most difficult roads and an enforced detour behind us, we head north up the dual carriageway. As the sun lowers itself into the sea, it could almost be the end of any other day out,

293

the car journey back to the city. Except that, every now and then, a vehicle hurtles alarmingly towards us on our side of the road, the driver frustrated by the time it takes to get to the new points of entry created by the bombing. The Lebanese, I think as we dodge the oncoming traffic, are dealing with their damaged infrastructure in their own, inimitable, pragmatic fashion.

'You are welcome,' Hanadi tells me over the phone. 'We don't have anything to do tomorrow.'

Hanadi was a cousin of the Charaff Deen family I had met in Essex, one of the family who had stayed in Tyre while her aunt and cousins fled to Britain. Before I left Lebanon, I wanted to talk in more depth to some ordinary Shia about how they now saw things. So I make a final trip to Tyre, this time making sure I eat before I go, even having a coffee in a café round the corner from their flat.

Coming down the stairs of her apartment block to meet me, Hanadi is a smiling young woman with a bush of dark, shoulder length hair. Her mother Mariam has an even bigger smile which flashes regularly her face as she wanders around the flat in a blue and gold kaftan, bringing me trays of food and drink. Then, with no English, she sits and watches as her daughter and I sit on the sofa and talk.

The family had fled after six days of bombing to the village of Darayah near the Chouf, she recalls, and had been taken in by a Sunna family. 'The people were so nice. They gave us a house without any price,' she smiles. 'They treated us like family. We feel we are in a second house of us, *yanni*. Other people who went to the Chouf were not treated like this. The Druze took money for rent—about $1,000 a month, without any furniture.'

'Are you still in touch with them?'

294

'Oh yes,' she smiles. 'After the war, they came to us, and we felt we had new friends. We always talk on the telephone.'

An hour after the ceasefire was declared, the roads were blocked with thousands of refugees unable to resist the pull home. But two days later, once the roads had cleared, the family returned to Tyre. They found their flat intact, but the body of their great-aunt was lying on the eleventh floor of a bombed-out high rise block. It took a Red Cross volunteer, swinging on ropes from a neighbouring building, to extract the month-old corpse, which was in several pieces.

There's a knock at the door, and Mariam admits a highly made-up woman staggering under the weight of two enormous bags. She sits down, evidently complaining about the hardships of Ramadan, and accepts a coke. Then she opens the bags to reveal boxes of perfume and make-up, and I realize she is a travelling saleswoman, a kind of Lebanese Avon lady. As product after product is enthusiastically presented and feeling under pressure to contribute to the Lebanese economy, I purchase a Lancôme mascara, a gimmicky double-action affair with two wands. The saleswoman departed, Hanadi and I resume our conversation.

'In Lebanon the whole thing could happen again,' she explains. 'We don't feel so safe, because Israel is not far. Every day, we feel the airplanes. Every ten years, it can happen again, and Israel can bomb us.' Lebanon's internal situation is little better, she goes on. 'Kidnapping, bombing—we don't like these things to happen,' she goes on. 'I feel so sorry about the killing of Hariri. He was a nice guy, a good leader. So, in Lebanon the inside politics and the outside politics is not good for us.'

'Where do you sit in terms of the internal politics?'

Her eyes gleam as she answers, clutching one of the sofa cushions to her stomach. 'Hezbollah is good for us; we are so proud of what they do. If we didn't have any resistance, Israel could kill us or get

295

to Beirut. We so appreciate them. Without Hezbollah, and without Nasrallah we would be killed by Israel in a very terrible way.'

'There is a lot of disagreement between the politicians now,' I remark.

Hanadi nods. 'I decided not to watch the news. They always fight about silly things, about opposite views. Everyone of them loves Lebanon, but in his way. They could meet and decide what is best for Lebanon, not to say "Hezbollah is not good," or "the 14 March is not good." We all love Lebanon.'

Mariam, perhaps frustrated at being excluded from the conversation by her lack of English, interjects excitedly: 'Hezbollah—Good, Good, Good!'

'And everyone in Lebanon is good,' adds Hanadi, pacifically.

'What's your view of the West now?' I wonder if attitudes have shifted as a result of Britain's position on the conflict.

'We love the American people and the British people so much,' she replies. 'But we don't agree with their leaders. They say that people in the south are terrorists. We don't think that we are terrorists. We are nice people. We are all human, and we all have the right to live.'

'The idea that the West takes of us is wrong,' she continues. 'Islamic people—we don't live in a closed circle. We love to meet other people. We have our own traditions, and we want our traditions to be respected. British people resisted Hitler for many years, and Hezbollah resisted Israel for many years. Like you, when you fought Hitler, we are fighting Israel. Britain is a good example of resistance.'

There's a moaning sound from the chair opposite, and we both look over at her mother who is holding her head in her hands and rocking slightly. Instantly the flashing smile returns. 'Coffee! Cigarettes!' she explains, clutching her forehead. 'Ramadan!' But shortly after, she slips into another room and returns, her head and upper body

296

encased in snowy white fabric. Then she sits in her prayer clothes, telling her rosary beads and mouthing the words of prayers. 'Can you pray with us here?' I ask doubtfully. 'Oh yes,' she smiles.

'Do you like Ramadan?' I ask Hanadi.

'Yes,' she smiles. 'We love fasting. It makes us feel that eating and drinking is important.'

The door swings open and her sister Farah comes in, school bag over her shoulder and sinks into a chair. At sixteen, she looks older, and her aquiline face has a look of keen intelligence. Hanadi starts singing her sister's praises, recounting how she always gets top marks at school and her teachers don't know what to do with her. Farah smiles faintly and says little, recovering from a day at school without food or drink. But she soon recovers and joins in the political discussion, which has now turned to the position of the 14 March camp.

'Some of them want to stop the war in a very easy way, like making peace with Israel. We can't do that,' she says. 'The 14 March say that we don't want Syria to go away. We do. We're not saying, "Come, Syria, and interfere in our business again." We're saying, "stay where you are, but we will have a relationship with you."'

'We can live with Syria in a peaceful way, but not have her interfere in our politics,' adds Hanadi.

'She defended us,' Farah goes on. 'We cannot forget this. She's our neighbour, one of the Arab countries. They want to end the relations, but that's not good for Lebanon. Instead of one enemy, we would have a lot of enemies.'

Her mother, clearly following her own train of thought while we gabble on in English, suddenly puts out her hand and grabs her daughter's right breast. I look startled, and Farah laughs at my consternation. 'It's normal here,' she reassures. 'She wants to check how they're growing.'

'I can hardly believe that you're both so young,' I tell them. 'You're so well versed in politics. People of your age at home don't talk like this.'

Farah smiles. 'Here, we bring up children to talk about politics. The little child is going to be the president, a politician from the day he is born.'

Their mother is pressing lunch on me, but I don't want to eat a meal while they are fasting. Why don't I stay for *iftar* then, and go back to Beirut the next day? Repeated invitations and refusals pass back and forth. But before I go, I would very much to see Tyre's Christian quarter. 'Will you come with me?' I ask, with a mixture of hope and doubt. It would be unusual for locals to walk about in the afternoon sun, especially during Ramadan.

They will, but it's almost two hours until we finally leave. 'First, I need to pray,' says Hanadi and disappears to wash and change into her prayer clothes. About twenty minutes later she's back. 'Now I need to pray,' smiles Farah, and slips away into another room. I go to the bathroom and try my new mascara, also a time-consuming operation because the lash-lengthening gel takes so long to dry that I keep blinking it onto my face. 'I've got that one. It's not very good,' says Hanadi. We sit around some more, waiting for a neighbour to give us a lift. Time passes, a cousin turns up, but the neighbour doesn't and it's decided we will take a *servis* instead. Hanadi, now pale and rather less smiling, excuses herself. 'She can't come, her head is turning because of Ramadan,' explains her sister.

Just as we are on our way out, one final thought occurs to Mariam. 'Can you take something to England? Just two kilos?'

In the other Charraff Deen family's apartment across the road, several rooms of sofas sit redundantly in the gloom, and the blinds drawn tightly down over the windows. In the kitchen, Mariam wraps up a large bag of *zatar*, the crucial ingredient of *mannoush*. They ask for it every day, when we call them,' says Farah. Then, with a glance to gauge my consent, her mother slips in a packet of bulgar wheat. Now a special bag is needed, so she heads back to her flat to find just the right thing. Ten minutes later, she returns with a weighty, tightly wrapped package in a carrier bag. 'And there are some prayer clothes in there too,' says Farah. 'They are very light. Now they can pray.'

'You won't forget this on the bus to Beirut, will you?' worries her mother.

A short *servis* ride takes us to the port. Pretty stone buildings cluster round the harbour in the late afternoon sun. Everything is on a tiny scale. 'That's the prison,' says Farah, pointing to an elegant honey-coloured façade that looks more like a hotel or a monastery. A few people sit in the dockside café while on the waterfront, fisherman are cleaning their nets. Brightly painted boats bob in the water. We could be in a scruffy fishing village in southern Europe.

'Are you Maronite?' asks Mariam as we approach the quayside church. 'No, there are no Maronites in England, it's a Lebanese thing!' I laugh. Inside, walls of pale stone are set off by dark wood pews and doors. Light shines through the square cross of stain glass in the pretty mullioned windows. By way of homage to its seaside setting, the marble altar stone bears an anchor. Suddenly, we're all tourists: no one can work out the church's denomination, and my hosts seem even more at sea about Lebanon's various Christian sects than I am. But a man, having come in to do some ecclesiastical housekeeping, confirms that it is the Maronite church. 'What's that?' Mariam gestures to the confession box in the corner. I explain about the confessing of sins in Catholicism, and the role of the priest as intermediary.

She's intrigued. 'And for Protestants, what's your relation with God?'

'Direct,' I reply.

'Good, good', says Mariam approvingly.

We go back outside and admire the sparkling clear water. Fisherman stand on solitary rocks, holding their rods high, and two small boys are playing on the shore. 'I love churches,' muses Farah, as we stroll along the esplanade.

'Do you go to the mosque?'

She shakes her head, smiling faintly. 'I would like to, but there are no mosques for women; I don't know why. At least, not near here.'

On the near horizon, the spire of the Greek Catholic church St. Thomas beckons. But when we get there, the gates are chained shut. So we walk through the souk to the square where I can pick up a bus to Beirut, which is bustling with people making their last purchases before *iftar*. 'Mama says she is sad that you didn't eat at our house,' Farah tells me. I promise to eat a huge amount on my next visit, privately thinking that I will never get this Ramadan thing right.

Outside the bus we all kiss. 'Take care of the foreigner,' Farah instructs the driver.

The journey to Saida is full of diversions. The driver's assistant, a boy of about eleven, is so officious that a consensus of amusement quickly spreads among the passengers. Every time he bosses someone into a seat or hustles a passenger off, people roll their eyes or smile complicitly. I, the foreigner, get star treatment: he collects my fare with hushed tones and a gleam of reverence in his eye. At one rural stop, three gypsy-like women jump on, strong-limbed creatures with black hair and flashing eyes. I observe them, fascinated: I have never seen such flamboyant, earthy women in Lebanon before. They banter furiously with the driver, emitting loud raucous laughs. At their stop, one of them hitches up her shirts and jumps out of the window into the oncoming traffic with a delighted scream. The bus from Saida to Beirut is less amusing, as the driver screeches round corners and leaps over potholes, throwing his cargo against the sides.

As the sun drops into a coral horizon, two sporty looking men in shorts get on, their hair still damp from swimming in the sea. One is big-shouldered with a spiky haircut and Italianate features; the other diminutive and dark. 'We are footballers, in the first team,' he tells me. He has a stream of questions, many a little intrusive: What is my work? Am I married? Where am I staying and am I alone? But I soon realize his concerns come from a position of religious conservatism rather than any roguish intentions. 'When I first saw you, I thought you were Lebanese,' he adds as an after-thought.

'Really? Really?'

Wallah.

I am inexpressibly delighted by this enormous compliment.

On my last evening, I retreat to AUB for a final time. It's the hour of sunset, and an autumnal mist hangs over the trees; the sea ahead is grey and uninviting. It's mid-October and Lebanon's long summer is finally drawing to a close. Two mornings ago, I awoke to find the streets gleaming under a cloud-laden sky: it had actually rained. Now, on this equinoctial evening, there are few people strolling along the long, snaking campus pathways and for once the benches are lover-free. The cats, on the other hand, emboldened by the onset of night, are everywhere, confidently anticipating the moment when they will have the run of the place. Beneath every tree and litter bin, tabbies, black and white and calico cats are lolling, washing and prowling. I walk on, looking for Orange Cat: I have a tin of tuna in my bag just in case.

The calm is broken as a helicopter flies nosily overhead. A young man on one of the paths breaks his stride and looks up anxiously into the skies.

SELECT BIBLIOGRAPHY

Abu-Izzeddin, N. M., *The Druzes: A new study of their history, faith and society.* Leiden, 1984

Armstrong, K, *Islam: A short history.* London, 2001

Bill, J. A., and Williams, J. A., *Roman Catholics and Shi'i Muslims: Prayer, Passion and Politics.* North Carolina and London, 2002

Dana, N., *The Druze in the Middle East: Their faith, leadership, identity and status.* Brighton, 2003

Dalrymple, W., *From the Holy Mountain.* London, 1998

Davis, S. C., *The Road from Damascus: A Journey through Syria.* Seattle, 2002

Eliade, M., *Patterns in Comparative Religion.* London, 1958 (seventh impression. 1997)

Fisk, R., *Pity the Nation: Lebanon at War.* Oxford and New York, 1990

Glass, C., *Tribes with Flags.* New York, 2000

Hourani, A., *A History of the Arab Peoples.* London, 1991

Jaber, H., *Hezbollah: Born with a Vengeance.* London, 1997

Johnson, M., *All Honourable Men: The Social Origins of War in Lebanon.* London, 2001

Joris, L., *The Gates of Damascus.* Melbourne, Oakland, London and Paris, 1996

Lewis, B., *The Middle East: 2000 Years of History from the Rise of Christianity to the Present Day.* London, 1996

Makarem, S., *The Druze Faith*. New York, 1974

McDowall, D., *Lebanon: A conflict of minorities*. London, 1986

McDowall, D., *Lebanon*. London, 1996

Nerval de, G., *Journey to the Orient*. London, 1984

Saad-Ghorayeb, A., *Hezbollah: Politics. Religion*. London, 2002

Salibi, K., *A House of Many Mansions: The History of Lebanon Reconsidered*. London, 1992

Seale, P., *Asad: The struggle for the Middle East*. London, 1989

Sennott, C. M., *The Body and the Blood: The Middle East's Vanishing Christians and the possibility for peace*. New York, 2001

Thubron, C., *Mirror to Damascus*. London, 1967

Thubron, C., *The Hills of Adonis: A Journey in Lebanon*. London, 1968

Wedeen, L., *Ambiguities of Domination: Politics, Rhetoric and Symbols in Contemporary Syria*. Chicago and London, 1999

INDEX